BEYOND REDEMPTION

The Truth Behind the Raid on
Her Majesty's Prison Blantyre House

Eoin McLennan Murray

Copyright ©2023 *Eoin McLennan-Murray*
All Rights Reserved

This book is dedicated in loving memory to my late wife Dorit, and our three children; Natalie, Alastair and Edward.

About the Author

Eoin McLennan-Murray began his career in the prison service in 1978 and served for 37 years in 10 different prisons, including three as the governor. He led the Prison Governors' Association for five years, chaired the Trustees for the Howard League for Penal Reform, and served as a patron for Beating Time, a charity promoting prison choirs. Eoin has judged the Robin Corbett Award for prisoner rehabilitation for 11 years and advised the Justice Select Committee. He now resides in Spain.

Foreword

Nick Hardwick

This is a jaw dropping book. An extraordinary tale of plots, skulduggery, reformed gangsters, parliamentary intrigue and fight backs that rocked the prison system back in 2000 following a controversial Prison Service raid on Blantyre House, a small resettlement prison in Kent holding about a hundred men nearing the end of long sentences for serious offences, and the sudden removal of its Governor earlier the same day. That Governor was Eoin McLennan-Murray and this book is his account of the events that led up to his removal and 'The Raid', and the events that followed. I should start by declaring an interest in that I count Eoin as a friend but I am also friendly with some of the other protagonists in the book with whom Eoin clashed.

The book presents a powerful case for the defence (or, in view of the criticisms it contains, perhaps that should be the prosecution,) and before hearing directly from the other side of the dispute, those not involved should perhaps withhold final judgement. I note here however, that a thorough inquiry into the raid by the House of Commons Home Affairs Select Committee (HASC) later that year was highly critical of what took place and completely exonerated Eoin. The work that Eoin was engaged in at Blantyre House was always going to arouse strong feelings and it was played out in the peculiar world of the Prison Service. In my experience, the culture of the Prison Service often reflects the culture of the institutions it is responsible for.

The culture can be inward looking and mistrustful. It creates strong friendships and toxic rivalries. Management processes are highly regulated and overly bureaucratic - yet a Governor's career will depend much more on who they know than what they do. Senior managers seem curiously remote from what is happening on the ground (I, like other Chief Inspectors, was constantly infuriated when the obvious failings we found in some prisons seemed to come as a complete surprise to Prison Service senior managers). This was not a culture that was likely to reach a calm resolution of the disagreements about where the right balance between security and rehabilitation should be struck at Blantyre House.

Overall, now I have finished the book and put it down, I believe 'Beyond Redemption' has great merit simply as a journey seen through the eyes of one prison Governor of the trials and joys of running a prison and what it's like for one individual to be caught up in, and to fight, a reputation destroying public scandal that is not of their making. There will be other perspectives to be heard about these events and I for one would welcome the accounts and explanations of others involved but as it stands, this is a persuasive and disturbing story.

Chapter 1

The click of the electric motor on the garage door was a familiar sound to me as the May sunshine began to fill my rearview mirror. I reversed out and soon I was meandering down the quiet Country lanes of west Kent, through the picturesque village of Goudhurst on my way to HMP Blantyre House, which I governed. Blantyre House had a functionally chequered existence. Originally a Fegan home for destitute and troubled boys who were trained in farming skills before being sent to new lives in Canada, (the home was established by philanthropist James Fegan in 1911 as a 'Canada Training Farm') - the buildings were taken over by the Prisons Commission in 1954 serving as a detention centre for young males. In 1987 it was reclassified as an adult male Category C prison when a visionary Governor, Jim Semple, took charge and initiated a bold and innovative experiment, taking long-term prisoners nearing sentence completion and instead of coercion and control, subjecting them to an enlightened, humane and dignified regime. I was thrilled at this stage in my career to be Governing such an innovative penal setup.

Semple's methods, which were geared to successfully resettling men with serious criminal histories back into crime-free lives in the community, were so successful that in 1992 the then Chief Inspector of Prisons Judge, Steven Tumin, described the prison as, "An example of all that is best about the Prison Service." A year later, Judge Tumin's successor Sir David Ramsbotham, said after an inspection: "The whole ethos of Blantyre House and the excellence that it represents is that of a resettlement prison, and I strongly recommend that it should be so treated and regarded." A couple of years after I took over the then Director General of the Prison Service, Sir Richard Tilt remarked following a visit to the prison, "I was delighted to see such a constructive atmosphere… The Governor and staff are to be congratulated…" It was hard to imagine a better prison to be in charge of.

Most of my working days began with this pleasant journey. It was such a welcome change from commuting into London on a packed train which I had endured for four years before securing this post. I arrived at my office and began my day's work with hardly even an inkling of what was to befall me and my prison just a few hours later.

A week or so earlier, my area manager, Tom Murtagh, had called and told me that he wanted to speak with me and my senior management team when he next visited the prison. This was a bit strange and I instinctively thought that something was afoot. Within a few days of that conversation, while I was up in Cambridge, I had a chance meeting with Peter Leonard who I had worked with when he was appointed to govern HMP Morton Hall open prison. Peter had subsequently been promoted and was now working at headquarters. During our conversation, he asked if I was ready for the change. "Are you looking forward to your new posting?" he said. I shot him a quizzical look. "Where is that then?" I said. There was an embarrassing pause, and then he said, "I'm sorry. I thought you knew." This was obviously the news that Tom Murtagh intended to share with me on his planned visit. "Don't worry Peter," I said, "I won't say a word."

I arrived at the prison and the day began with the usual cup of tea made by my hard-working secretary, Dorothy. "Don't forget that you have the two healthcare visitors arriving this morning and then Tom Murtagh at 12.30 pm," she said. I thought about my earlier conversation with Peter Leonard. I expected to find out that I would be moving to another posting soon, but no idea where.

The two visitors had been shown around the prison by one of the prisoners and were now in the Board room next door to my office, waiting for me to join them for a discussion. I entered and introduced myself and within a few minutes, we were engrossed in conversation. Like all visitors to the prison, they expressed a really positive and enthusiastic interest in what they had seen and been told.

There was a knock on the door and Margaret Andrews, my Head of Management Services, came in. "Sorry to interrupt, governor but can I have a quick word?" She sounded concerned. I stepped outside of the Boardroom and went to go into my office so we could speak privately, but Margaret grabbed my arm and said quietly, "Tom's in there Eoin, he arrived early and seems agitated." I said that was fine and asked her to give our visitors my apologies. "I'll see Tom now," I said.

Tom Murtagh was normally a very confident man, but when I entered my office, he was standing up and looked apprehensive. I moved to greet him with a handshake which he awkwardly ignored. I invited him to sit down. But he seemed nervous and unsure of what to do or say. Then he stepped quickly towards me and thrust a letter into my hand before stepping back. "You should read that," he said.

Because of what Peter had said, I was expecting to be told about a move, but Tom's manner disconcerted me. I opened the envelope and read the short note that had been written by Ivor Ward, a prison governor also working at HQ and in charge of career development for other governors. The note said that with immediate effect I was to leave Blantyre House and take up a post as Deputy Governor at HMP Swaleside, a closed Category B prison on the Isle of Sheppey. This was not "career development" at all. It was such an unusual way to receive a new posting that I could barely take it in. Such an instant removal from the post only ever happened when a governor was in trouble and there were serious concerns relating to the safety or security of his or her prison.

As my mind scrambled to make some sense of it, I could hear Tom mumbling in the background. I stared at him, but he wouldn't look me in the eye. "Don't blame me," he said eventually, "I'm just the messenger. Martin has made the decision." Martin Narey, now Sir Martin, was then the Director General of the Prison Service, but I was certain that Tom was the instigator of the move. Normally when he visited, I would offer him tea but on this occasion there was to be no such nicety. I felt my blood pumping. I was so hurt by this letter my hands were trembling. I wanted to shout, "You liar!" Somehow I managed to hold my composure. "Well, I hope you are proud of yourself now," I said at last.

There was a history behind this moment. For the previous two years, Tom had been on my case, with various investigations giving me a hard time about the way I was running the prison. I got the impression that he hated the ethos of trust and responsibility we championed for people who on paper were supposedly hardened criminals. But we had evidence that what my team and I were doing was working, changing lives and making society safer. What he was doing to me now was just so wrong. Tom was renowned for his intimidating management style, but as I glared at him he seemed to visibly shrink and backed away towards the office door.

I took a couple of deep breaths and managed to compose myself as we stood opposite each other in silence. "Fine," I said eventually. "I'll call a full staff meeting. My team needs to know I'm leaving. And just as a matter of interest, who have you got to replace me?" Sheepishly he replied, "Chris Bartlett."

Chris was the deputy governor at Swaleside. So Chris was coming to govern my prison and I was going to deputy govern his. The whole thing seemed ridiculous. A few minutes later, Tom left the prison with the expectation that I would be following shortly after him.

Chapter 2

When Tom left, I called my Senior Management Team (SMT) together in the boardroom to tell them what had happened. Our admin block was housed in a big timber-framed traditional Kent cottage and even though the walls were thick, our offices were close enough for loud conversations to be overheard. My confrontation with Tom had been heated. As the team made their way into the boardroom, it was obvious by the looks on their faces and their body language that they already knew what I was going to tell them. "I guess you heard my, er, conversation with Tom," I said, trying hard to make light of it. Nobody smiled. "I'm so sorry it has come to this," I said. Before I could say anymore, there was a chorus of voices, it was "out of order," somebody said. "It's outrageous," said someone else.

My head was down as I left them to go and address a full staff meeting in the visits hall. I was angry, hurt and confused. But word had spread quickly. Blantyre was such a small prison with a real community spirit. The staff were really proud of the positive work they did with the prisoners. The respect the prisoners had for them and for the philosophy of the prison was a reflection of the fact that we all wanted the same end result – to get people out, working and living well. Blantyre had a proven track record of low reoffending rates for released prisoners, some of whom had at one time or another been considered among the most dangerous in the system. We had lifers at the end of long, long sentences. We had career-armed robbers and others whose criminal activities had caused a lot of pain for society. Here they were given trust and respect as people as a matter of course and almost to a man responded positively. We all felt we were achieving something special together.

As I walked along, thinking about what I was going to tell the staff, individual prisoners approached me and spontaneously offered words of consolation. Others were angry. One man walked right up to me and shook my hand. "Thank you for what you and your staff have done for me here," he said. I lifted my head and thanked each one. It was all I could do to hold back the tears. The whole mood of the prison had changed in an instant.

As I walked into the visits hall, a hush descended. Sad faces stared back at me as I tried to think of something reassuring to say. I hadn't really planned a speech, so my words just came from the heart and I said it as it was, repeating much of what I had told my senior team. "I'm so sorry it has come to this," I said. I explained that Chris Bartlett was to be the new governor. "I'll be handing over when he arrives. Please give him your full backing - and thank you all so much for your support and for working so hard with me to make this prison the success it is," I said. Every now and then, I had to stop to catch my breath and stop the welling in my eyes. My emotional state was obvious, the anger and hurt I felt was just overwhelming. The reaction of those present matched how I was feeling, and there was a mixture of wanting to console and comfort me and anger at what was perceived to be a blatant injustice. "I'm so very, very sorry," I repeated before leaving the visits hall with the heaviest of hearts.

Back in my office, I was gathering my personal effects when a call came from the gatehouse to say that Chris Bartlett had arrived and they wanted to know what to do with him. I asked them to bring him round to my office and within a minute he arrived. I could tell he was embarrassed.

"Hi Chris," I said. "Hi," he said back. It was awkward. I'd known him for 14 years. He'd been a junior assistant governor at HMP and YOI Bullwood Hall in 1996 when I transferred there as the third in charge. We had worked well together and became friends as well as good colleagues. Chris had been a police officer with the Hong Kong force prior to joining the Prison Service as an assistant governor. He normally had a great sense of humour. But the Chris in my office that day was not the Chris I thought I knew. He was uneasy, much more so than the situation called for. It was like our friendship over the years had evaporated in a few seconds and been replaced by something politely sterile. The conversation was difficult. I said that I wanted to sort through some papers and take my personal stuff. "Eoin, take what you want," he said. He stood silently for some moments and said, "Look, I'll leave you alone. Take your time. I'll come back later."

By the time he returned after an hour or so, I'd packed all my bits and pieces into two plastic boxes and was getting ready to leave. Before either of us could say anything, his mobile phone rang. He answered it quickly and I immediately heard Tom's voice barking instructions out. Chris looked even more embarrassed as he realised I could hear what Tom was telling him. He looked at me, raising his eyebrows and then turned and went outside to finish the conversation. When he returned, there was more embarrassing silence until I broke it. "Well," I said, "he's told you to keep an eye on me and watch what I am taking before you get me out of the prison. Do you want to search me?" He looked away and said again quietly, "Just take what you like, Eoin."

For a few fleeting seconds, I thought he might be defying Tom for the sake of our friendship and was cutting me some slack. I wanted to talk to him and ask him why he thought this was all happening, but I felt he'd probably feel too compromised to say anything. In the end I thought it best not to make the situation any more uncomfortable than it already was for the both of us. I'd filled the plastic boxes with my personal effects and several papers which I thought I might need to deal with what I suspected was to come. As it happens, at that time I had no idea of what was to come. Had I, then I would have taken other papers, including my Governor's journal which subsequently went missing.

I carried the two boxes out of my office and as I was making my way to the gate, a couple of prisoners were waiting there to see me. They insisted on carrying the boxes to my car and loaded them into the boot. Driving away, I felt so sad, almost empty of hope for the future and wondering what would happen next.

As I retraced my journey back home, my mind was churning over and over. I dreaded telling my wife, Dorit, what had happened. I arrived home, kissed Dorit quickly and went upstairs to change. I was unusually quiet but Dorit didn't say anything. I began to make some small talk, not knowing how I was going to tell her what had happened. In some way I felt ashamed, I felt I had let her and everyone down and now I had to try and find the words to explain something that I still did not fully understand myself. Before I could start to get the words out Dorit said that Molly Tipples, the chair of our Board of Visitors, had phoned to see how I was. The BOV was the precursor to the current Independent Monitoring Board, the independent watchdog whose members are appointed by the Home Secretary to check prison conditions. Dorit paused and then said, "When were you going to tell me?" I just froze, shaking my head and broke down in floods of tears.

Chapter 3

That Friday night in bed was awful. I could not sleep. My mind was so full of the day's events. No matter how much I tried to rationalise what had happened, there was just no sense to it. Why move me out in such a humiliating way and then, to add insult to injury, post me as a deputy governor to another prison? Why? I couldn't stop asking that simple question. After long hours of tossing and turning, morning arrived and the chaos in my mind was interrupted by Dorit's voice. "Eoin, come down, breakfast is on the table."

I went downstairs and Dorit put her arms round me and hugged me tightly. "Darling, I know it's absolutely awful what has happened, but we will get through it. We have had difficult things to deal with before. Now, let's eat. We have to be at the school in an hour for the fete."

With everything that had happened, the school fete had completely gone out of my mind. There was no choice. We had to go as the school depended on me and the group of Blantyre prisoners who had volunteered to help out, as they had in previous years, organising a range of fundraising activities.

As we made our way to the school, I had very mixed emotions. What would I say to the headmaster about my situation? How would it be with the prisoners? We arrived early and there were only a couple of teachers and the head, Nigel Blackburn, there. Nigel was a tall man with a kind face. He had a natural authority about him and even the most disruptive pupils would succumb to his authority. I felt nervous as I approached him, fearful of his judgement but I felt I had to let him know that I had been removed as governor, although uncertain as to why. "Hello, Eoin," he said, "so pleased to see you and Dorit here and nice and early as well. When will the lads from the prison be here? he said.

I told him their licences ran from 9 am so they should be arriving soon. I then tried to explain to him what had happened to me the day before. My voice was shaky, and I could tell by the look on his face that he was shocked. "I don't understand Eoin. Why would that happen and so suddenly?"

"In all honesty, I don't know," I said. I explained that there had been tensions between me and my line manager for some time, "but I can't believe that he would do this to me." I could feel my emotions rising again. Before I could say any more, Nigel reached out and hugged me. "It's outrageous," he said, "and if I can do anything to help you in any way, you must let me know."

I thanked him and said I would let him know what was going on once I knew myself. I felt better having told him about my situation and I was relieved at his reaction. His offer of help was genuine and before I could think too much more about it, we were distracted by the group of prisoners noisily bustling through the school gate. They were making a beeline straight for me and I sensed something wasn't right.

Terry George, a swarthy East End man serving eight years for robbery was the first to reach us. "Hello Gov," he said, "Did you know the raid was going to happen?" I didn't know what he was talking about. "Raid?" I said, "What raid?" He smiled a grimacing smile and swore. "You really don't know. That's why they got you out of the place so quick."

By this time, the other prisoners had gathered around Nigel and I and were telling us the story of what had happened the night before. It sounded horrendous. The prisoners were animated in their descriptions of what had happened. One told me that John Podmore, the Governor of Swaleside prison, had led the raid, but it sounded like disorganised chaos. "They piss-tested everyone and turned the whole place over," said another man, adding, "One guy got shipped out for giving a dilute sample but it's only the test lab that can know if a sample is dilute so that was a lie." Before I could say anything, a third man was speaking over the first. "The drug test governor was going mad because after hours of testing, they still had no positive tests. That's when they started to smash the place up, and they were smashing down doors. They did the hospital, the chapel – just crashing and smashing all over the place."

Smash the place up? Why would they do that? I could barely believe what I was hearing. It was no surprise to me that the drug tests were all negative but why would prison officers cause such wanton damage? Why would they break down doors when all the keys to all the departments were available?

"They shipped five cons out including Jack," said a third man. This was a huge clue as to what the raid was all about. Getting Jack Wells out of the jail had been a central part of Tom Murtagh's campaign against me and the prison over the past couple of years. The third prisoner added that the raid officers had taken away "loads" of their personal property. "It's like they wanted trouble and were deliberately winding us up," he said. All the prisoners had something to say. They were clearly hurt and upset. It all just sounded so unbelievable and irrational to me but we had to get on with preparing for the fete and so I told the prisoners that I would talk with them later.

I was shocked, but then the shock gradually gave way to an odd sense of relief. At least I now had some understanding of why I had been summarily moved out. It was still very confusing however, as I'd never heard of anything like it ever happening in any other UK prison in the over twenty years I'd been a manager in the Service.

Nigel just looked at me, and I could tell by his expression that he could scarcely understand what had happened. "Is this what they normally do when they search a prison?" he said. "No," I said, "this just sounds crazy." Nigel asked me if I minded if he told his staff about the raid and my move from the prison. I couldn't object, it was hardly going to be a secret with all the prisoners talking about it. I wandered off to find Dorit but my mind was working overtime. What the hell were they after? It had to be about more than just moving out a handful of prisoners. And it seemed incredible to me that after such an unprecedented operation any prisoners would be allowed out in the morning to help out at a school fete.

My mind flitted back to my meeting with Murtagh the day before. In the shock of everything, I had said that I would report to HMP Swaleside as Deputy Governor on Monday despite being offered a few day's leave.

But the information that the raid had apparently been led by John Podmore, and the fact his prison was the home of the Chaucer team stopped me in my tracks.

The so-called Chaucer Team came about around four years before the raid when Tom Murtagh and the Governors of the other Kent prisons, of which I was one, met at the Chaucer Hotel in Canterbury to discuss how investigations into serious alleged staff wrongdoing should be managed. It was decided that a central investigating team should be established within Kent and this team would be headed by Podmore. Members of the Chaucer team were junior governor grades or uniformed staff. The more permanent core members of the team, with the exception of Podmore, were temporarily promoted to a higher grade on the personal authorisation of Murtagh. I have no doubt that most of the Kent governors initially thought the creation of this Chaucer team was a sensible way forward. Few of us ever imagined, however that it would become a servant to Murtagh's distrust and it would exist to provide him, on occasions, with what he wanted to hear. It was hard not to conclude that the raid had been masterminded by this long-discredited outfit.

The madness of my decision to accept the move to Swaleside suddenly hit me. I think it was the shock of my sudden removal and my struggle to maintain some sense of professionalism that made me agree in the first place. In reality, I could not really refuse. My terms and conditions of service stated that I was a mobile grade and could be posted to any prison within England and Wales. But my acceptance could be construed as a signal that I was culpable in some way - and of course, I made the decision to accept the move without knowing what was going to happen that same night.

I began to see and feel that my move to Swaleside was a very bad idea. How could I be the deputy governor of Swaleside when the evidence strongly suggested that Podmore was one of the main architects of the raid on my prison? That I should have to move to a position directly under him to effectively serve the very people who may have crushed my career would just add more weight to my public humiliation. My instant removal from the prison was obviously not enough. But I quickly learned that when you feel that you have lost everything, there is no more fear in you, and within that context a courage emerged within me that made me strong enough to want to fight.

I began to think through how my fight back would start but for the time being my mind was fixated on the fact that the prisoners had still been able to leave the prison and attend the fete. This told me that whatever was being looked for hadn't been found. Despite all the drama in the background, the fete was enjoyable and successful in raising much-needed funds for a new school mini-bus. But it proved to be the calm before the storm - a storm that would overshadow my life for the remainder of that year.

Chapter 4

Saturday night was another sleepless night, but for different reasons. Now, I was planning my fight back. First thing on Sunday morning, I phoned Lynne Bowles, a member of the National Executive Committee (NEC) of the Prison Governors' Association (PGA). I had known Lynne for 19 years, and we worked together as junior assistant governors at HMP Holloway in the early 80s. As I was telling Lynne what had happened, she kept interrupting me and saying that I should stop winding her up with this crazy story and what was the real purpose of my call to her. I persisted and it was probably more the tremble in my voice and the disjointed account I gave her that convinced Lynne that this was no hoax call but a real cry for help.

Lynne was brilliant, and she immediately gave me unquestioning support. She told me that what had been done was outrageous and that we should insist on having a meeting with the Director General, Martin Narey, as soon as possible. She agreed with me that the move to Swaleside was madness and our call finished with a plan that I would write a letter declining a move to Swaleside and she would arrange a meeting for both of us with Narey.

During the late afternoon of Tuesday, 9 May, Lynne and I were ushered into Narey's office in Cleland House in London, where we hoped to get some answers. Lynne took the lead and combatively questioned Narey about the reasons and the need to both remove me as Governor and authorise the unprecedented raid on Blantyre. Narey objected to Lynne's questions and said he did not see it was any business of the PGA. He appeared to be angry and blurted out that I had been "disloyal" and "had betrayed" him but he found it hard to believe that I could, "be corrupt." He did not expand on either of those points but instead went on to describe all the "contraband" that had been found on the search. He spoke about one prisoner having "escape equipment in his room," and another having two driving licences with different names and a passport. There were also bank debit cards found as well as cameras and hard-core pornography he said.

By then, I'd heard all about the so-called contraband. The day before supportive colleagues had briefed me on almost every detail of what had taken place during the whole of that Friday, so I probably knew even more than Martin. I knew that the briefing for the raid had taken place in the afternoon in the Swaleside prison gym. The plan had been to attack Blantyre in the evening when prisoners who had been working out in the community would have returned.

The convoy of vans and private cars full of prison officers must have been quite a sight snaking along the Kent Countryside on such a sunny evening. After parking up on the leafy lane leading up to the prison just after 9 pm the raid officers gathered for another mini-briefing in a barn just outside the prison fence. John Podmore then gave more details about what the officers were looking for. "Ammunition, drugs, explosives" were referred to - and soon the raid was on.

Only four staff were on duty when the raid officers arrived at the gate. The night crew consisted of one Senior officer, who was the Orderly officer, one regular officer and two Operational Support Group staff known as OSGs. As the officers were streaming in, the Orderly officer was in the prison hospital collecting medication for a prisoner suffering from asthma. When she heard the commotion and saw the mass of officers in riot gear spreading around the place, she locked the hospital and made her way back to the gate, noticing on the way more and more prisoners' faces at windows. Once at the gate, she recognised some managers from HMP Swaleside who told her they were now in control of the prison and that she and her three colleagues should go into the main building and "keep out of the way." Alarmed, she explained that the prisoners were becoming concerned and agitated at the arrival of the riot squad and suggested in order to avoid an escalation of the situation, she should go around the prison rooms and explain to the prisoners what was happening: that they were to be searched and drug tested and that they should keep calm and co-operate. The raid leaders agreed.

But then something happened which led me to believe even more in the sinister intentions behind the raid. Before heading over to the main building, the Orderly officer confirmed that all the keys to all the departments and offices were in the gatehouse and available. Some years earlier, the Head of the Works department had constructed a key box incorporating individual boxes for every office key which had two access points. On the outside of the gate lodge, access to the keys was via a locked cupboard door. Staff could open the cupboard as they walked past on their way to their various departments. In case of an emergency on the inside of the gate lodge, the key boxes were covered by a glass panel which could be broken, and the keys retrieved.

Coincidentally, one of the senior raid officers had worked at Blantyre House for a number of years before being transferred and knew precisely how to access the office keys. For reasons known only to himself he apparently chose not to share this information with colleagues. Also, every Orderly officer in every prison in the Country holds a master key which will give access to every office in the prison and the Blantyre Orderly officer that night was no exception. All the managers in charge of the raid knew this. Yet nobody sought to ask her for help.

And so the raid began in earnest. Squads of officers dispersed around the prison. One squad summoned all prisoners out of their rooms and told them to prepare for the testing of their urine for drugs. Normal practice is that a prisoner taking an MDT (Mandatory Drug Test) will attend a room in the Hospital or Healthcare Centre and in a private booth, give a sample of urine in a plastic container, which is then sealed and signed in his or her presence and sent off to a laboratory for testing. Instead, that night, the prisoners were lined up outside the communal toilet area dressed only in their underpants. One by one, they were tested through the night. Tellingly, as the prisoners told me at the school, not a single sample proved positive.

Meanwhile, other squads of raid officers, still ignoring the availability of keys, were smashing their way into various departments and offices around the prison. One squad forced their way into the Health Care Centre before breaking into the Dentist's office and the Dispensary leaving a trail of shattered glass and broken doors and doorframes. Another squad attacked the Print workshop, breaking the doors and door frames to the entrance, the office and the rear store. The main gym office and the mini gym were broken into, again causing irreparable damage to doors and door frames. A squad broke into the education department and smashed open a cupboard containing exam papers completed by prisoners awaiting assessment. The papers were scattered over the floor and stamped on. A raid officer chalked on the blackboard: "Mark Taylor Woz Ere". Even the chapel was not exempt from the attention of the raiders. The offices of both the CofE chaplain and the RC chaplain were broken into and their desk draws were forced open and rifled.

The raid continued until dwindling in intensity into the early hours. By 4 am on the Saturday morning, I was told, many of the raid officers had left the prison – leaving just a small team who retired to the staff mess to rest and sleep – at which time command of the prison was handed back to the four shocked Blantyre staff.

I was also told that the most significant finds during the search of the prison were a few unidentified tablets, some top-shelf adult magazines, several debit cards, a small quantity of Cannabis discovered in a roof space and three non-working mobile phones. A set of tools, including a lump hammer, a trowel and a spirit level were confiscated and later listed as 'escape equipment' (despite the prisoner in question protesting that he was working outside the prison as a Bricklayer and these were the tools of his trade,) which was obviously what Martin was referring to.

Five prisoners were transferred out that night. One man was moved because he was unable to provide a urine sample (due to the fact he had just used the toilet prior to the test. In Elmley prison the next day he did provide a sample which proved negative.) Another because he allegedly "gave a dilute sample". Two others, one of whom was Jack Wells, who's situation I will explain more fully in due course, were shipped out based on unspecified "intelligence" – the fifth man was shipped out after financial papers were found in his possession which the raid officers suspected might be part of a 'criminal conspiracy'. In fact, the papers were legitimately in his possession and he was later allowed to return to Blantyre.

The next day, most of the items seized from the prisoners during the search were returned. Men with jobs outside the prison were allowed to leave and go about their business – and as I saw at the school, those who were due to help at the charity fundraising event were permitted to attend. A more subdued anti-climax to such a high intensity Prison Service operation would be hard to imagine.

Martin probably had no idea that I'd have known as much as him by then about the scale and result of the raid. I could hardly contain myself when he brought up the so-called escape equipment. "For God's sake," I said, "You must know by now that that was a set of bricklayer's tools – and the chap was due to leave the prison in the morning to go to work." The two driving licences he mentioned belonged to a prisoner who had changed his name by deed poll and his passport had been needed to verify his identity. As for the cameras, these were prison property and belonged to the photography class in Education and the bank cards had been authorised by me, I said, as I insisted that all prisoners who were in outside paid employment had a bank account and a debit card.

In reality, the most serious finds from the search were three broken mobile phones. These phones should have been left in a locker at the gate and not brought into the prison. Once prisoners became aware that they would be searched, the phones had been broken and placed in a communal rubbish bin. However, routine searches undertaken in other prisons, far more secure than Blantyre, have yielded much greater quantities of mobile phones and other more serious contraband so the outcome of the search on the unprecedented scale of the raid should have been seen in that context.

Whatever Tom Murtagh and his Chaucer team had expected to find or uncover did not exist and rather than face that truth, Murtagh instructed his staff officer, Steve O'Connell and another junior governor grade, Guy Baulf to produce a report which would create the impression that the raid had been successful. It was Guy who told me this and he said that they worked over the weekend and really struggled to come up with anything. Confronted with my outburst, Narey became more conciliatory and said that there would be an investigation and then all the facts would be available.

Both Lynne and I were of the opinion that Narey had been briefed that the outcome of the search was much more disturbing than it really was.

Chapter 5

My work had brought me into contact with Tom Murtagh long before I took up my post as Governor of Blantyre House. Previous to taking over at Blantyre, I worked at Prison Service HQ working with psychologists in the Programme Development Section (PDS). This was a fascinating experience and gave me an excellent grounding into the range of interventions and treatment programmes that had been developed from the 'What Works' research.

Research into why people offend hit a low spot in the 1970s. The general research view was that nothing works, but in the 80s there was a revival and using a technique called 'meta-analysis', the 'Nothing Works' philosophy was successfully challenged by the 'What Works' research. PDS were naturally very interested in this research and I was dispatched to Canada for three weeks to visit prisons where offending behaviour programmes based on the What Works' research were being run. What followed was the development of national offending programs that would benefit large swathes of the prison population, including sex offenders. The research indicated that if these programs were run correctly then offenders who participated with them would likely have a 10% less chance of reoffending on release.

The Prison Service of England and Wales then decided to run a cognitive skills programme that had also been developed in Canada. This program was designed to challenge the 'cognitive deficits' or faulty thinking that research had shown was a common trait within offending populations. This was an expensive program and PDS developed a British variant named 'Enhanced Thinking Skills' which superseded its Canadian forerunner.

PDS also developed an offending behaviour programme specifically for sex offences. This was known as the Sex Offender Treatment Program (SOTP). To date, thousands of prisoners have participated in these offending behaviour programmes. However, further research undertaken between 2010-2018 concluded that the SOTP programme was more likely to increase the risk of reoffending as opposed to reducing it. Consequently, the SOTP programme was withdrawn from prisons in the UK in 2018 and has now been replaced with two new programmes, Horizon and Kaizen.

Prior to working in PDS, I was a staff officer to the then Director General (DG) of the Prison Service, Derek Lewis. Lewis was a private sector industrialist who was appointed by the then Home Secretary, Ken Clarke in 1993. He was subsequently sacked by Clarke's successor, Michael Howard in 1995 following two high profile escapes from HMP Whitemoor near Cambridge and HMP Parkhurst on the Isle of Wight.

My time with Lewis as his staff officer and minute taker at Prison Board meetings was fascinating. Lewis transformed many aspects of the Prison Service. He introduced privatisation and Key Performance Targets and initiated the end of "slopping out," the practice where prisoners used plastic buckets in their cells for toilets. Emptying the buckets in big sinks in communal wing areas was called "Slop out." Lewis also radically altered the processes for funding new prison builds and much of his work is still deeply embedded in the Prison Service today.

As part of my role, I would have to brief and liaise with the senior civil servants at the Home Office. The service had recently undergone a major restructure from having four geographical regions, each overseen by a Regional Director, to thirteen smaller regions, each managed by an Area Manager. As part of my duties, I would have regular contact with these area managers, one of whom was Tom Murtagh when he was promoted from Governing Dover prison to Area Manager for the Eastern Region.

At that time, I was Head of Inmate Activities and Services at HMP Highpoint - but had just been promoted to Governor 3 and was awaiting a posting to HQ. I remember meeting him at Highpoint on a few occasions but my interactions with him were seldom since he mainly dealt with the Number 1 Governor, Ron Curtis. At that time, the only thing I knew about him was that he had come over from Northern Ireland where he had worked as a governor grade.

After I left HMP Highpoint to become the staff officer to the Director General, I had more dealings with Murtagh. I found him to be quite jovial and bullish as a manager but I was never close enough to him to have any real opinion of him as a man.

My first experience of Blantyre House was while I was working for the DG. As the DG's staff officer, I accompanied him on prison visits and we visited the prisons in Kent, including Blantyre. At that time, Jim Semple was still the Governor. Jim was a thoughtful Irishman who spoke incredibly eloquently about his little Goudhurst prison. His vision was to develop a regime that would be unique to the Prison Service. Subsequently, it became the first resettlement prison in the Country.

I guess that I must have made some kind of impression on Jim because a few months after our first meeting, he asked me if I would look after the place for a couple of days while he and his senior management team went away for a strategic planning event. Naturally, I accepted and really I was only there to provide a senior manager presence. The staff and prisoners continued with the daily regime and I could see that it was a different type of prison to what I had experienced before, but I wasn't really there long enough to engage with it or really understand its ethos.

Nevertheless, I made a mental note to have it high up on my career radar as it was close to home. It also was of a manageable size and seemed a very peaceful place. I remember Jim telling me that other governors would joke with him that his biggest problem was "preventing rabbits burrowing under the security fence." I thought that that was a problem I could live with and that I would have the opportunity to develop my governor skills in a relatively safe environment. Yes, it would certainly be a great prison to have as a first posting to Governing Governor.

Coincidentally, while I was working in London, my wife Dorit successfully applied for a teaching position at Blantyre House and due to her previous IT experience found herself in charge of the IT department in the education block. Dorit would often tell me about things that happened at work and about some of the prisoners who were in her classes. She continued to teach maths as well as leading on IT and it was while teaching IT that she employed a very able prisoner to be her IT orderly. His name was Michael Raft.

Raft had arrived at Blantyre directly from maximum security HMP Whitemoor. At the time, I thought this was odd, since usually most of the prisoners that go to Blantyre are transferred from the medium secure Category C estate. She also mentioned another prisoner by the name of Ron Todd. She said he was very different from most of the other prisoners and didn't seem to fit into the Blantyre culture. It was clear to me that Ron Todd's behaviour towards my wife was problematic and I suggested that she placed him on report so that the Governor could deal with him at an adjudication.

I don't think she mentioned Todd to me again, but she often spoke of Michael Raft. He gained her trust and he was clearly an asset in the IT department. He had been a BT engineer and this was where he apparently learnt many of his skills.

Some weeks later, on returning from work, Dorit told me that the police had come to the prison and arrested a number of prisoners, including Michael Raft and a senior member of the discipline staff, Principal Officer Gary Catton. Dorit was quite upset and angry as she felt she had been totally duped by Raft. I did my best to console her and said that it was not her fault and also it should not stop her from trusting other prisoners. In all the previous prisons I had worked in, I came across many staff, of all grades who were quite cynical about prisoners. Their cynicism was either born out of previous experiences they had when prisoners had conned them or let them down in some way or that was just their general attitude towards some aspects of life. I never wanted to become like that, always convincing myself that when a prisoner asked me for something there was not some sinister ulterior motive behind it. I had trusted prisoners before and, on occasions, been let down - but most times, I was not. I found that generally where a good trusting relationship existed, it was genuine and seldom abused.

On another occasion, I remember Dorit coming home and being quite upset about another of her students. Part of the resettlement experience at Blantyre was that a number of men were allowed to have cars for work purposes. Dorit had taught a prisoner, Mr Begum, in her Maths class and she said that he had been severely injured in a car crash. She said he'd been a passenger in a car being driven by another prisoner, Mr Busby, who had been returning to the prison from his work placement. The driver came out of the accident unscathed but Mr Begum suffered serious brain damage and the driver of the other vehicle involved was killed and her young granddaughter severely injured. I later learnt from Dorit that as a result of the accident, all prisoners at Blantyre had been stopped from driving. Although these two incidents were serious, it did seem that on the whole life at Blantyre was calm and relaxed and Dorit certainly enjoyed her work and liked the people she was working with.

The possibility of me being appointed Governor of Blantyre came about several months later. I was on the M3 motorway returning home after giving a presentation on a cognitive skills intervention programme to the Governor and management team at HMP The Verne when my mobile phone rang. I stopped to take the call and it was Brian Pollett, who had been Governor of Blantyre for two years. He told me that he was leaving Blantyre to undertake a six-month project at HQ before taking command of Dover prison. He asked me if I was still interested in Governing Blantyre. "Absolutely," I said. Within the course of a few minutes, we had checked our diaries and pencilled in a start date for me to take up my new post. We both agreed to contact Tom Murtagh and put this fait accompli to him.

The Prison Service will often advertise Governor vacancies and existing governors or other Governor grades who are eligible for promotion to Governor can apply in open competition with one another for the post. However, the Prison Service also sometimes just appoints a Governor without advertising the post. This is known as 'a managed move'. Both Brian and I were attempting to manipulate a managed move for me since this would be quick and allow Brian to move on without delay. It suited both of us and we would do our best to sell the idea to Tom Murtagh.

I left it a couple of days, since I knew Brian would make contact with Murtagh, before sending a meeting request to him. Murtagh's secretary then contacted me, and we agreed on a date and time for me to meet with him in his office at Cleland House.

The day came for my meeting with Murtagh and his secretary ushered me into his office.

"Is this a dry shift or what?" he said in his heavy northern Irish accent. His secretary immediately asked me if I would like a drink. "Oh, tea please, white with no sugar thanks"

I sat down and smiled at Murtagh. "So, you and Brian have been plotting, have you?" he said smiling.

"Well, you know us Tom," I said, "We like to try and help you out when we can."

He grinned.

"Well, I had you in mind for the post anyway and I spoke with the DG about it."

"Did he agree?" I said.

He grinned again.

"I had to twist his arm a bit but eventually he did."

The office door swung open and our tea arrived.

"I know Brian wants to get away as soon as possible but I have some commitments with PDS. I was thinking of a start date in early June, Monday the 10th. Does that work for you?" I said.

He looked up and nodded and in a very serious voice said, "There is one issue that I need to discuss with you, it's about your wife who works in the Education department at Blantyre."

"Is that a problem?" I asked cautiously.

He shook his head and said, "It's not a problem as long as you are not directly involved in agreeing to any expenditure in Education that could be construed as a benefit to your wife or the IT department she heads up. Is that understood?"

I told him it wouldn't be a problem at all as I'd see that the Deputy Governor would deal with those issues.

"You need to have a handover with Brian before you start," he said. "You'll need three days." He said as it was my first command, it would be a good way to get an understanding of the place before I took over. I told him I'd work something out with Brian and confirm with him.

Murtagh sipped his tea and nodded. I asked him if there were any priorities at the prison, anything particular he wanted me to do. He leaned forward and said, "Just don't fuck up."

Chapter 6

June 5th was another bright sunny day as I prepared myself for my handover with Brian. I played through my mind how I would be as Governing Governor. It was like a new start, an opportunity to reinvent myself. Apart from the few days I'd been there for Jim Semple I had no real history with the prison or its staff. It was like a blank canvas.

I parked up in the car park and walked the short distance to the front gate, my new briefcase, which was a present from Dorit, tightly clutched in my hand. I pushed the bell and heard the ring from the gatehouse. Almost immediately, an athletic looking officer strode out from the gatehouse and opened the gate. He introduced himself as Jonno. "You must be the new governor, sir," he said. "Yes, I am," I said, "Would you like to see my ID?"

"Only if you want to show it to me sir," he said, smiling. "Mr Pollett's expecting you so if you would like to follow me now, please." As we made our way to the Admin block, I thought how homely it looked, not stark and soulless like so many other prison administration blocks. My experience to date had been with mostly very secure prisons holding what were officially on paper at least some very dangerous and manipulative men. I just assumed that my role as Governor would be to maintain an orderly routine which, hopefully would be constructive and ensure that proper security measures were in place to prevent escape and maintain safety and good order and discipline, both for prisoners and staff.

As Jonno showed me in, I noticed various titles on office doors, cashier to my right and deputy governor to my left. Directly ahead through a set of glazed double doors was the board room. Just before this, on the right, was the Governor's office and Jonno gave a firm knock on the door.

"Come in," said a voice that I instantly recognised as Brian's. He had prepared some paperwork for me, Performance Management information and budget spreadsheets and the like and suggested that after our tea, we walk round the prison and he could introduce me to staff. But first, he wanted me to meet members of the senior management team who were on duty that day. He told me that the chair of the Board of Visitors wanted to meet me the next day, as did the chair of the local Prison Officers Association (POA).

The POA are a trade union and there was an elected committee from the Blantyre staff. They met formally with the Governor every month but, in reality, had regular contact with prison managers on a daily basis. It was important to establish a good and constructive rapport with both the BOV and POA. Brian gave me a good briefing on both of these committees as well as a general assessment of the management team. Although mindful of his assessments I always held the view that it is best to keep a totally open mind and speak as you find.

After my three-day handover from Brian, I could see that Blantyre really was unlike any other prison I had worked in. In all honesty, now I was fully in charge I did not know what to make of it. It felt like my previous experience would not equip me to deal with the sort of issues that I imagined might arise here. A good example of this was the Release on Temporary Licence (ROTL). Probably about two thirds of the prisoners at Blantyre left the prison each day to either perform community work locally or go to full-time paid employment. It is the responsibility of the governor to be satisfied that all prisoners out on ROTL are not a danger to the public and present a very low risk of breaching the terms of their licence. I knew that it would not be long before I would have to make decisions on this release programme but how was I to do this when I did not know the prisoners? Should I just trust the judgement of other staff and have to carry the responsibility of that if the prisoner failed in some way? Or should I refuse applications for ROTL until I felt I knew the prisoners better? The former action would be a matter of blind trust and the latter would be totally disruptive to the prisoners and regime. This was something for me to mull over in my mind over the weekend before starting on Monday.

Chapter 7

I woke early on Monday, and I was excited and apprehensive about my first day in full charge of a prison. I felt that I had to make a good impression and over the weekend, I had played countless scenarios in my mind of how it would be. The drive to the prison was a relaxing tonic, beautiful Kent Countryside, uncongested roads. What a perfect start to the day.

Jonno, the gate officer I'd seen the week before, welcomed me and gave me the roll of the prison. The prison roll is the number of prisoners that were unlocked that morning and on this day, the prison was at its full capacity of 120. "The security PO (Principal Officer) Pete Collard, is on his way down from the house block to see you and issue your keys, Sir," he said.

A couple of minutes later Pete Collard arrived and I recognised him from the week before during my handover with Brian. He looked like a security PO, with a face that gave nothing away. I took my keys from him and thanked him for his efficiency and said that it would be good to catch up after I had got my feet under the table. He nodded and as quickly as he had arrived, he was gone.

With my keys in hand, I made my way to the office. The admin building was very quiet as most of the staff who worked there were not in yet but my secretary, Dorothy was and so was Dave Newport, Head of Inmate Activities and Services. They both greeted me and after Dorothy had offered me tea, which I readily accepted, Dave said he'd leave me for the time being to settle in and we could have a good catch-up later.

My office must have been a spacious lounge when the building was a family home. It had French doors which opened up onto a small, but beautifully kept private garden. There was a good-sized desk, a couple of easy chairs and a bookcase full of various Prison Service manuals neatly stacked together as well as other books. Compared to some of the offices I had in my early career, this was like a paradise.

Other governors I had spoken with said that it was a good thing to call the staff together and introduce yourself on your first day so that everyone knew who you were. I liked the idea of that but thought it would be better to do it later in the week after I had met all my senior managers and had some briefing from them on their areas of responsibility.

When I visited Blantyre with Derek Lewis, Jim Semple had given me a fairly comprehensive overview of the philosophy of the prison. As I sat there, I drifted back to that time and reflected on what he had said. His 'vision' had been to create a prison that ran on trust rather than control and coercion. He wanted long-term prisoners who had known a life of crime and were well-versed in the prison subculture to confront their past and take responsibility for their future lives. He wanted them to abandon their antisocial values and behaviours and adopt more pro-social values before returning to society. He firmly believed that conventional prison regimes tended to reinforce negative attitudes and values and this significantly contributed to the high rates of recidivism.

The regime had certain guidelines. Prisoners had to be fully occupied in some regime activity from nine in the morning to four in the afternoon. At least ten percent of the time had to be in education or something educational such as art, pottery, music or sculpture. The rest of their time was spent in work including gardening/horticulture, building repair and maintenance, domestic cleaning, food preparation, woodworking and looking after the chickens and being responsible for egg production. There were also opportunities to use the gym and participate in other sporting activities. All meals were eaten communally in a dining Hall.

This approach contrasted significantly to that in other prisons where the daily regime was prescribed by the staff and prisoners had little or no say in what they did. The Blantyre approach achieved a number of goals. Firstly, it began to challenge the ingrained institutionalisation that most long-term prisoners had succumbed to. Secondly, it began to build their self-confidence and self-esteem. Surprisingly, many prisoners lack real self-confidence when they are required to act in a pro-social manner and participate in a lawful and law-abiding society. Thirdly, and perhaps quite subtly, it successfully challenged the stereotypical view prisoners have of prison officers. In secure prisons, there is a real 'us and them' culture. Many prisoners would avoid interacting meaningfully with prison officers. To do otherwise would put them at odds with the prison subculture and the consequences for them could be quite drastic. At Blantyre prison, officers were not ordering prisoners about or driving the regime. By contrast, they discussed options with prisoners, and they were there as a support to help and assist rather than direct and coerce.

So, apart from making the prisoners take responsibility for their own daily regime, there was a structured journey through a well-defined and staged pathway. The first six months were spent on participating in the daily regime and planning future employment and accommodation arrangements post-release. After that there was a review. If sufficient progress had been made and the prisoner had clear ideas about his future plans for employment, then the second stage of his pathway would begin. This involved spending time out of the prison working in a voluntary capacity on some projects that benefited the local community. Such projects could be working in charity shops or assisting a groundsman in the local school. Some men who had a trade behind them could be involved in building/repair work. One prisoner was engaged in making alterations to a house so that it could be accessed easily by a wheelchair user.

The third and final stage was to obtain paid employment or full-time education at a local college. The prison had established a good reputation within the local area and a number of local businesses and charities offered a variety of employment opportunities. Some prisoners would commute into London while others had the use of a company car/van. The plan was for the prisoner to be in full-time paid employment by the 18-month stage. He should have at least six months wages and money in the bank by the time he was up for release.

Prisoners were encouraged to maintain relationships or rekindle old ones which may have faded with time. The visiting arrangements for prisoners at Blantyre were more generous than those in most other prisons and the facilities for visitors were good with the ability to be able to sit outside in a garden during good weather.

Once prisoners were leaving the prison on ROTL during the second and third stages of their journey through Blantyre, they could apply for 'town visits' which in essence meant that they could meet up with family or friends for up to six hours in one of the nearby towns or villages within a 20 mile radius of the prison. This privilege was highly valued by the prisoners and their families.

A knock on my office door brought me sharply back to the moment.

"Come in," I called.

The door opened and my deputy governor, Tom Wright, bounded in. Tom was a stocky, expressive man. I had also met him during my handover the week before but we had very little time together and I was looking forward to getting to know him.

Tom and I chatted for the next hour and I told him that I needed time to settle into the prison and get to understand the place. I was not going to be one of those governors who came into a new prison and begins to change things right away. If I was going to make any changes, then it would only be when I felt I knew and understood how the place functioned. A good long chat gave me a sense of how I was going to proceed.

He left the office and I suddenly remembered that I had not asked him about the police arrests that Dorit had told me about several months earlier. In fact, it had totally slipped my mind and Brian Pollett had not mentioned it on the handover either. Thinking more about it nor had Tom Murtagh when I saw him in his office last month. All he'd said to me was, "Don't fuck up." I made a mental note then to ask my colleagues about it when I had my one-to-one meetings with them.

The next two weeks flashed by as I was learning a lot about the reality of this unusual prison and the attitude of the staff. Speaking to prisoners, the driving ban came up a lot following the fatal car crash. They wanted to know if I would reinstate driving as for many of them, it meant they had lost their employment and were restricted now in what they could do. All I could say was that once I had settled in, I would look to see what the options were and they would just have to be patient. But over those two weeks, I suspected that below the relaxed and cordial atmosphere there was something quite mysterious that had happened.

Chapter 8

During one to one conversations with my senior managers, small snippets of information came out about the arrests Dorit had told me about. But when I pressed them, I was surprised to learn that they were not all that well informed about what had actually taken place. The picture I was left with was confused and disjointed. References had been made to a notorious organised crime boss, who I'll call Mr Zane, who'd been there - and there was talk of staff corruption and prisoners being able to buy their way into Blantyre House. During my conversations with them, reference was often made to the prison chaplain, John Bourne. John had been a police officer with the Met police prior to taking up a career in the church.

I arranged to meet up with John to see what else he could tell me. What he told me was incredible, almost unbelievable. Apparently, Michael Raft, the prisoner Dorit had told me about, had not been arrested with the other prisoners and members of staff but had been taken into protective police custody. John explained that Michael had confessed to him after a Sunday church service and revealed he was being coerced by other prisoners to work on a criminal credit card fraud and if he refused to cooperate his elderly mother would bear the consequences. Michael wanted John to help him and said that he believed the Governor must be corrupt because he could not understand how all these things could be happening without the Governor's knowledge. John didn't believe that Brian Pollett was corrupt and told Michael that he would speak with him and if nothing happened, then he would escalate the matter to Prison Service headquarters.

John did speak with Brian Pollet who, although surprised about Raft's information, said that he had recently been invited over to the neighbours, who lived in a converted barn opposite to the prison, for drinks. While chatting with them, he was told that a police officer had been staying upstairs during the day observing prisoners coming and going from the prison. Brian apparently was surprised at this. When he got back to the prison he contacted Maidstone police. But even more surprisingly, the Maidstone police said that they knew nothing about it and would make further enquiries. Brian was later told that it was the Met police who had been keeping the prison under observation, since they had some vague intelligence that some criminal activity involving some major criminals in the community could be happening.

It was a combination of these two bits of information that led to the Prison Service and the Met police running Michael Raft as a kind of double agent. He was asked to continue to work on this criminal activity and every evening, on returning from work, he would call in to the vicarage at the nearby village of Marden where police officers would debrief him. This undercover activity ran for three months and culminated in a dawn raid on a farmhouse in Kent, where arrests were made of some prominent criminal figures. The same day the police made arrests at the prison.

When I got home that night, I couldn't wait to tell Dorit that her trust in Michael Raft was not misplaced as he had been taken into protective custody and he was helping the police. Dorit looked relieved, but still a little shocked. "I was sure Michael wanted to tell me something but he never got the chance as we always got interrupted." I felt really pleased for her as I knew the Michael Raft issue had played on her mind.

Although I was pleased for Dorit, I realised that there must have been some serious corruption going on in the prison at the time this Michael Raft episode was going on. Certainly, John Bourne felt that was the case but he had been a bit guarded with me. I could understand that as we did not really know each other yet. I knew that I would have to find out more about what had happened. I had to be sure that there was no corruption still in the prison and it seemed to me that the best way of finding out about this would be to meet with Michael Raft.

John had told me that Michael was in a police safe house so seeing him might not be so easy, but agreed to see what he could do. Now, I felt uneasy. Why hadn't Pollett or Murtagh said anything to me about this? After giving this matter some thought, I decided not to speak with Murtagh about it until I had spoken with Michael Raft.

John Bourne was away for a few days and on his return made the necessary arrangements for me to meet with Raft. I organised a time, date and discreet location for it. I had no idea of what to expect from this meeting but I just knew that the outcome would be vitally important to me and influence how I would govern the prison.

We met in a central London government building. The room had been booked for two hours. After four hours with him, however I emerged in a state of almost disbelief. Michael had come to Blantyre directly from HMP Whitemoor, a maximum-security prison that holds some of the most dangerous prisoners in the Country. He did not know why he was moved out, but on arriving at Blantyre he was soon to find out. It was explained to him by certain prisoners that he was there to build various items of IT hardware and write software to run what he had built. He said he didn't want to do this but was coerced into it, the threat being that they knew where his elderly mother lived and she would get hurt if he did not cooperate. He then told me that he was involved in discussions relating to three major crimes that this criminal gang were planning.

One plan was to hold up a bullion van and Michael's job would be to design, build and programme an electrical device that would block all radio signals from the van so that there would be time to cut it open and steal the contents before help could arrive. The second plan was to build a device that could be installed inside a container that was packed with drugs. If the container was opened and checked by Customs, then the device would activate and the criminals would know not to try and collect it. The last plan, and the one they actioned, was to get Michael to develop some hardware that could be wired into a BT telephone exchange. This hardware would intercept information coming from ATM machines, and store it in memory so that it could then be downloaded and used to create thousands of American Express (AMEX) credit cards. The information captured would be the account and PIN details which could then be encoded onto blank credit cards which were to be produced by a company in the North of England.

Apparently, AMEX cards were selected since they had a £500 limit on cash withdrawals. Once the cards had been produced they would be distributed to groups of criminals who would then target as many ATM machines as possible to withdraw cash. Such was the audacity of this scam that one or more individuals who worked in the banking industry were bribed to monitor the level of fraud and feedback information so that the criminals could keep the scam going for as long as possible. It was estimated that this scam could yield hundreds of millions of pounds and at the time would have been the biggest credit card fraud ever in the UK.

For Michael to be able to build the hardware required and do all the programming, he would need equipment that was not in the prison and also he would have to work full time on it. Clearly this was not possible for him to do while in Blantyre so Gary Catton arranged his work placement at a front car and van hire company, where Raft was supposed to be computerising their car hire processes. In fact he was working for this criminal gang and it was there that he met Mr Zane who delivered various items that Michael needed for his work.

As time went on, Michael was getting more and more stressed and eventually he reached his breaking point and shared this terrible secret with the prison chaplain, John Bourne. Some of what Michael told me I already knew from my conversations with John but what I didn't know was whether there were corrupt staff still at Blantyre. Michael was adamant that PO Gary Catton was corrupt and he named three other staff who he thought were involved. One in particular he believed to be Gary Catton's right-hand man.

Michael explained how Gary Catton would task him to do small electrical jobs for various members of staff. These jobs could be installing a burglar alarm or fitting a car radio. Michael also said that other prisoners would do various favours for staff like mechanical work on their cars. It was not that the prisoners received any payment for this work, they wanted to do it because they believed that the staff were really helping them and they wanted to show their appreciation. I could understand that sentiment, but it is an extremely thin line between that and corrupt practice.

He also told me that the other prisoners who were arrested at the same time as Catton had been transferred into the prison by Catton and then allocated to particular outside work placements by him. Ron Todd, the name rang a bell with me from what Dorit had told me months ago, was Michael's minder. His job was to keep Michael on task and monitor him closely. Apparently, this small group of prisoners who had been transferred into the prison by Catton were given pagers so that they could be warned when staff from the prison were dispatched to check on them in their work placements. There can be no doubt that this was a well organised team and they may well have been successful in their endeavours if it were not for Michael confessing to the Chaplain.

After my secret meeting with Michael, I thought it would be worthwhile getting some history on the prison during the time Zane was there. My deputy, Tom Wright, had been at Blantyre during the latter stages of Jim Semple's time as governor so I thought it would be worth picking his brains. Tom confirmed that this man had been at Blantyre house during the latter stages of Jim's tenure as governor. Tom said that Jim wasn't keen on him coming to Blantyre but was persuaded to accept him by principal officer Gary Catton. By all accounts, the man was a very able individual and he applied himself completely to organising and improving the cottage industry of egg production from the free-range hens that were part of the farms and gardens enterprise at the prison.

I quizzed Tom about Gary Catton. What sort of man was he and what roles did he perform at the prison? Tom told me that Jim Semple trusted Gary Catton totally. He said Gary was a strong leader and was responsible for selecting prisoners to transfer to Blantyre from other prisons. Tom said that Gary had requested a change of role. He stopped being responsible for the transfer of prisoners into Blantyre and took on the role of allocating Blantyre men to community work projects. All of this confirmed what Michael Raft had told me and I felt I could now put the jigsaw pieces together to form a picture of what had happened.

It is my belief that during the time Zane was at Blantyre, he was able to turn one or more members of the uniformed staff and this was the first stage in him planning with outside associates criminal activity. The man's time at Blantyre was successful in that he progressed while there and then transferred to another resettlement prison, HMP, Latchmere House prior to being released from prison. I believe he saw an opportunity to organise criminal activity using serving prisoners at Blantyre. I assume he figured that the police would not consider looking at a serving population of prisoners as being responsible for the crimes that he was planning with others to commit.

As I sat in my office, my mind wandered back some years and I remembered, having visited Blantyre with Derek Lewis, how I thought this lovely little prison would be a great first posting as governor and my only worry would be how to stop the rabbits burrowing under the security fence. How different the reality was now. I was governing a prison which played host to a criminal conspiracy, the likes of which had never been seen before in a prison, and I potentially had some staff who could be corrupt. I certainly needed a plan of action, a plan that would prevent staff from being corrupt, but I did not want to jeopardise the trust that existed between prisoners and staff. After thinking about this problem for a few days. I decided to do three specific things.

Firstly, I had one-to-one meetings with the three members of staff that Michael had indicated had been involved with possible corruption. I told them that I knew what had happened but I could not prove it, and this is why they would not at that moment be subject to the discipline code. Two of the three staff admitted the prisoners had done favours for them, but they said this had been arranged by Gary Catton. I made it very clear to these two staff that they would have to earn my trust and I would be keeping a very close eye on their activities. The third member of staff said very little, and this confirmed for me that he was very close to Gary Catton. It was not too long before he volunteered to transfer to another establishment.

Secondly, I published a Governor's order that required staff to submit a written application to me if they wanted a prisoner to do something for them or if a prisoner offered to do something for them. I would then decide if it was acceptable or not, and there would be a written record of whatever was agreed. From memory, I think I only ever had two requests to deal with.

Finally, I changed the process by which prisoners were selected to come to Blantyre and also the process which governed the allocation of community and work placements. None of these processes would be at the discretion of a single person but would be made by a committee. No one, with the exception of the governor, would have the sole power to decide who came into the prison and where they were allocated for their community and work placements. I believed these three measures, although not a perfect solution, would preserve the trust and ethos of Blantyre whilst guarding against future corruption.

Chapter 9

My first few weeks at Blantyre had not exactly gone as I had planned, I had completely been caught off guard by the revelations of John Bourne and this had distracted me from focusing on the regime of the prison and getting to understand it. Whenever I walked around the prison, which was most days I was on duty, many prisoners would ask me the same question. Governor, when will you reinstate driving for us?

It was clear to me that I could not continue to stall on this answer as for many prisoners it had a direct bearing on their ability to gain employment. The difficulty I had was that there had been, and rightly so, a lot of concern and publicity following the fatal accident that had been caused by Mr Busby. Many commentators questioned whether serving prisoners should be allowed to drive while on ROTL.

Dorit had mentioned Busby's incident to me because one of her students, Mr Begum was in the car. She'd explained that he had progressed well and was moving to that stage in the Blantyre pathway where he would be starting a work experience placement. This placement was at a car dealership in the Medway area of Kent and he was being shown the ropes by Mr Busby who had just completed his work experience at the same place. Both men were returning to the prison in the late afternoon in a powerful 4X4 that had been provided by the work placement and was being driven by Busby.

A patrol police car spotted their car speeding and followed them before attempting to stop them. Mr Busby became aware of the police vehicle and increased his speed to try and outrun it. Over the next few minutes, there followed a very high-speed car chase which culminated in the 4X4 colliding head on with another vehicle driven by a grandmother with her young granddaughter in the rear seat. The impact was so severe that the grandmother was killed instantly, the grandchild seriously injured and Mr Begum, the passenger in the 4X4 sustained serious life changing head injuries. Mr Busby escaped with relatively minor injuries and was subsequently convicted of causing death by dangerous driving and imprisoned for a further six years.

The incident attracted a lot of local publicity which was to re-emerge again when Busby was dealt with at Maidstone Crown Court. Brian Pollett had been the governor of Blantyre during the time when the crash happened as well as when the Michael Raft episode unfolded. However, I was now the man in charge when the consequences of these events manifested themselves and I would have to deal with the fallout. Again this Busby incident did not form part of my handover when I took up post and, in true fashion the circumstances around the fatal crash were investigated by Adrian Smith, Governor of HMP Elmley.

The Prison Service investigation into the car crash was lowkey, and it apparently did not warrant a disciplinary investigation despite the fact that a member of the public was killed and a young child severely injured at the hands of a prisoner who had been temporarily released from the prison by Governor Pollett. I can understand why Brian Pollett, facing such media attention, stopped all prisoners at Blantyre from driving. One of the difficulties I had was that the inquest into the death of the grandmother was due to start soon. I knew this would attract a lot of media attention and timing wise I would have been very foolish and insensitive to reinstate driving at Blantyre.

Adrian Smith's investigation report made a number of recommendations, the most memorable being that prisoners undergo some cycling proficiency training as prisoners would now be reliant on bikes or public transport to get to their places of employment.

I could certainly see the need to reinstate driving but felt that I could not do this until after the publicity surrounding the inquest had passed. This was the message I gave out to prisoners and although they did not like further delay, they fully understood my reasoning.

During the process of settling into my new office and going through all the files and reports that were there, I came across a laptop computer. It was not password protected and on it I saw a completed application form that Brian had written out requesting to be considered for a voluntary severance scheme that was on offer to prison staff at that time. This struck me as being quite unusual since Brian was relatively junior in his career and had every chance of progressing to a much higher position in the service.

I did not understand why Brian made such an unusual application and it was a mystery to me until some months later when I was discussing some security issues with Pete Collard, my security PO. He related to me that he had seen Brian Pollett a few days before the fatal car crash to discuss what actions should be taken about a number of prisoners who were causing concern.

Pete Collard was asked by Brian to draw up a list of ten prisoners who were of most concern and arrange their names in priority order so that the most risky were at the top. Busby, who caused the fatal car crash was second on that list and Brian decided that the top three would be transferred out to another higher security prison where they would not be eligible for ROTL. For some inexplicable reason, Brian then decided that Busby should not be transferred out of the prison – a decision that would cost a human life. Pete Collard told me that he was incandescent with rage and accused Brian of virtually murdering the grandmother himself.

I can only speculate that Brian thought that this would come to light in a disciplinary investigation and would have serious repercussions for him. This would then explain the reason behind his application for voluntary severance, but he never submitted his completed application because the investigation was a low-key one and not disciplinary in nature.

As I expected, there was a wave of publicity surrounding the inquest and I was asked to give an interview on the local TV news. I decided to do the interview because I wanted to let the family of the grandmother know how sorry I was. So, it fell to me to take the decision to lift the driving ban for prisoners which I did some weeks after the inquest.

Although there was no evidence to suggest that Busby had been drinking, I decided to tighten up the criteria used to decide whether prisoners could drive or not. I decided to introduce breathalyser testing for all prisoners who were allowed to drive. Unlike the law of the land, there would be no acceptable level of alcohol for prisoners, it would be zero tolerance and if anyone failed then they would be transferred out of Blantyre and returned to a mainstream prison. I also had all the prisoner's previous driving history checked and if there were indications of regular speeding offences or careless driving/drunk driving then they would not be permitted to drive. Legally, I had no authority to breathalyse prisoners, but I overcame this obstacle by prisoners voluntarily taking the breathalyser test. Obviously, if they refused then they would be transferred out of the prison.

During all of my time at Blantyre, only one prisoner who was driving failed the breathalyser test. His reading was the lowest that the breathalyser could register and his defence was that he had drunk two cans of alcohol free lager while out at his work placement. However, so-called alcohol-free lager does contain a small amount of alcohol and this was just enough to register on the breathalyser.

The more time I spent in Blantyre, the closer I got to understanding how the regime and pathway through Blantyre worked. Not only did I get to know the staff very well, I also got to know the prisoners. I made a point of meeting each new prisoner who arrived, and I would surprise them by joining them for lunch in the communal dining hall. From their point of view, this was a very unusual thing and initially most of them were incredibly suspicious of my motives and felt awkward when I engaged them in conversation. This simple act gave me a very high profile amongst prisoners, and it helped me get to know prisoners as they were transferred into the prison.

There had been a tradition at Blantyre to hold what was called 'Mencap Day' on the August bank holiday weekend. This event, which involved the whole prison was essentially a fun day for a range of individuals who had various levels of learning difficulties. These individuals would be accompanied by carers and/or family members and enjoy the catering and entertainment that prisoners and staff had organised. When you consider that Blantyre has 120 prisoners and that on Mencap day, there were about 1000 visitors then you can begin to see the scale of this event.

Planning for Mencap Day preceded my appointment, but as the August bank holiday approached the level of activity increased exponentially. The prisoners and staff had developed a good range of contacts over the years and one of the main attractions for this year was a range of funfair rides. As with previous years, the event was hugely successful and over the next two weeks, I received countless letters of thanks from many of the visitors who had attended the event.

As autumn approached, I felt that I had really been accepted into the prison by the staff and prisoners. I understood how the regime worked and I could see the impact it had on the prisoners. Their attitudes and behaviour changed in front of my eyes and they transitioned from institutionalised beings to pro-social individuals who actively participated with the regime and embraced the opportunities it gave them. My relationship with the POA and BOV was really good since they recognised that I had become a champion for Blantyre, I actively engaged with the prisoners and staff and they welcomed my ideas to expand the regime and develop further opportunities not only for the prisoners but also the staff.

As a new Governor, I was required to participate with the senior command course which was designed to help newly promoted governors. I also had the opportunity to participate in a course run by the Tavistock Institute. This simply was an opportunity for a small group of governors to come together and discuss, in complete confidence, aspects of their work that might be problematic for them. I remember that I was listening to some governors speaking about incredibly difficult and complex issues which they were trying to resolve. Some of these governors were running the biggest and most complex prisons in the service and when it came to my turn to speak about something which was troubling me, I felt a little bit inadequate and even embarrassed. After all my prison was so much smaller and simpler than theirs and what kind of problem could I have that would compare with theirs?

So, I decided to talk about the credit card scam and corrupt staff and the fact that none of this had been mentioned to me in my handover, either by the outgoing Governor, or my area manager, Tom Murtagh. My colleagues were amazed at hearing my account and strongly advised me to speak with my area manager about it. They were concerned that perhaps I was appointed as Governor of Blantyre simply to be a scapegoat when the story eventually broke in the media. Such was the intensity of the discussion and level of concern about my welfare. The facilitators of the course broke confidentiality and spoke to Bill Abbott, who was head of security for the Prison Service.

I took the advice of my colleagues and arranged a meeting with Murtagh where I was going to tell him everything I had found out. However, before the meeting could take place events on the ground were moving forward and Pete Collard came to see me to say that there were TV crews filming outside the prison. Somehow the media had found out about the arrests that were made at the prison the previous year. They had also been attempting to film and interview the chaplain, John Bourne at his vicarage in Marden. I had by then been told that the trial of those criminals who were arrested following the undercover operation with Michael Raft were due to attend a pre-trial hearing at Southwark Crown Court.

When I met with Murtagh, I was staggered by his response. He claimed not to know anything about the credit card scam, and he told me that I should write a submission which could go to the then prisons minister, Ann Widdecombe and Home Secretary, Michael Howard. I left that meeting, not knowing whether Murtagh had been honest with me, although I knew he was not the area manager when this under-cover operation took place, his predecessor, John Hunter was the man who brokered that arrangement between the Prison Service and Metropolitan police force.

On 15 October, Richard Tilt, the then director general of the Prison Service (now Sir Richard) wrote a submission to Ann Widdecombe and Michael Howard outlining the issues I had raised. Attached to this submission, and reproduced below, is the annex I provided which gave a detailed synopsis of the undercover operation.

Prison Service/Metropolitan police cooperation at Blantyre House from 9 June to 25 July 1995

1 During March 1995, it was discovered that Blantyre House was under police surveillance. This was traced to the Metropolitan police, but no information was gained as to its purpose.

2 On 11 May 1995, Michael Raft who had been on a work placement at Meopham van/car hire, informed the Rev John Bourne that he had been approached at his place of work to provide technical information to assist in the planning of bank fraud and security van robberies. On the same day the Rev Bourne reported this information to the then Governor, Brian Pollett, with the full agreement and consent of Raft. Raft was immediately withdrawn from the placement and Kent police were informed. Approaches to Raft, who is an electronics engineer, continued in the prison with fellow prisoner David Coxon taking a major role in this. (Coxon is one of the defendants in the forthcoming trial.) It transpired that Coxon had visited the workplace, while Raft was there and had been involved in the original approach to him. Again, this information had been passed on to Kent police. Raft indicated that the robbery and fraud offences were still in the planning stage with their execution still some time away. It was decided to allow Coxon to continue with community work in order not to jeopardise police investigations.

3 A meeting with the flying squad at Kent police headquarters on 8 June 1995 confirmed Raft's information and the flying squad's involvement in the surveillance of Coxon at Blantyre House. The police requested that Coxon be allowed to continue with his normal activities at Blantyre until Tuesday, 13 June 1995 in order to allow observation of a planned theft of radio equipment on 11/12 June 1995.

4 With the agreements of the area manager (John Hunter) and operational director, Coxon was permitted to remain at Blantyre House and continue to be released on temporary release for community work. This situation was reviewed regularly and extensions were agreed by the operational line.

5 Michael Raft continued to collect information about the bank fraud and armed robberies and also stated principal officer Catton, who is responsible for community projects at Blantyre house, was connected with men planning the robbery and fraud offences and could be persuaded to arrange placements as necessary.

6 The Flying Squad stated that they had information that principal officer Catton will arrange for the transfer of specific prisoners to Blantyre House when requested to do so.

7 It was agreed that Michael Raft would meet the police secretly at the vicarage so that he could be properly debriefed. During the course of this prison/police cooperation, it was necessary to retain an outward air of normality, bearing in mind that the senior manager (PO Catton) was in the prison and appeared to be working for members of the criminal fraternity. Regular meetings between Michael Raft and the governor would undoubtedly have caused PO Catton to become suspicious and thus jeopardise the whole surveillance operation.

8 The vicarage offered a safe environment in which Michael Raft could be debriefed by the police without arousing any undue suspicion. It was this factor, combined with the trust that Michael Raft had placed in John Bourne that necessitated the chaplain's involvement and presence when the police were debriefing Raft. The chaplain's role was clearly one of supporting Raft and not one of directing or planning any elements of the police/prison operation.

9 The planned offences were due to take place on 25 July 1995. The criminals in the London area involved in the fraud were arrested in the early morning of 25 July. Coxon was arrested at his home address in London later the same morning (having been temporarily released at only 08.15 hours on a facility licence for local community work).

10 Principal Officer Catton was arrested by Kent police at Blantyre House at 11:00 hours on the same day. PO Catton has also been suspended from duty in view of the police action against him.

An internal enquiry into his actions has been formally commenced but will not get underway until the completion of the criminal trial.

11 Michael Raft - one of the other six prisoners involved - was taken into police custody under section 29 of the Criminal Justice Act to assist with enquiries. He has since been released from prison on parole.

12 Following PO Catton's arrest at 11:00 hours, staff from HMP Swaleside were deployed to remove three of the remaining prisoners from Blantyre House to Swaleside. car park Staff then picked up prisoner Ron Todd from an outside community placement and again transferred him to Swaleside. Unfortunately, another prisoner who was also on an outside community placement evaded the staff who went to collect him and after a short period of being unlawfully at large was recaptured. It was not possible to cancel the facility licences for these two men for the day, as this would have raised the suspicions of PO Catton

There were five defendants who had been charged for the credit card fraud and they were all pleading not guilty. The Judge at Southwark Crown Court directed that there should be a pre-trial hearing to be heard in camera. In camera hearings are closed to the public and press so there can be no media coverage. At this pre-trial hearing a decision would be taken on the admissibility of evidence from the two prosecution witnesses, Michael Raft and John Bourne. The Judge accepted their evidence as admissible and purely on the strength of it the five defendants over the course of the five-day pre-trial hearing changed their pleas from not guilty to guilty.

Since the pre-trial was in camera, there was no media reporting and due to the guilty pleas there would be no trial, only sentencing. However, the media did pick up on the story and it made all the popular tabloids and the broadsheets. The media coined the phrase 'the hole in the wall gang' and said that had the fraud gone ahead then it would have been the biggest ever.

I remembered that Michael Raft had told me that the gang had produced 100,000 fraudulent AMEX cards and I believe 80,000 were recovered by the police. Whether the unaccounted 20000 were ever used is still a mystery to me.

Christmas at Blantyre was relaxed and I was pleased to have put the credit card scam and fatal car crash behind me. My first six months as governor had been a steep learning curve and I was looking forward to some degree of normality in the New Year but those past events would still impact on my Governorship in ways I would never have imagined.

Chapter 10

Tom Murtagh would visit the prison most months to review our performance indicators and check if the prison was operating in accordance with Prison Service policies and instructions. In addition to these monthly visits, he held a monthly area meeting for all the governors from the Kent prisons. The quality of catering at Blantyre was outstanding and much of this was to do with our head of catering. The prison kitchen and dining area were accommodated in one purpose-built building and the food was served fresh from being cooked. In many prisons, this is not the case. Food is cooked in a central kitchen and then placed into heated food trolleys which are transported to the various prison wings. This is a similar arrangement in many hospitals and it is widely accepted that the quality of food suffers from this arrangement.

The cafe style arrangement at Blantyre meant that the food was very good and the head of catering created an imaginative menu. The majority of the food was prepared and cooked by prisoners under the supervision of the two catering staff. Tom Murtagh's monthly meetings were held in a different Kent prison each month and lunch was provided by the prison. After the monthly meeting at Blantyre, Tom asked me if all the monthly meetings could be held at Blantyre because the catering was so exceptional. I readily agreed and the prison, especially the catering department, received some kudos from this.

Early in the New Year, I received some surprising news from the Kent police. The Crown Prosecution Service (CPS) had decided that no criminal charges would be brought against PO Gary Catton. He had been suspended on full pay since July 1995 and now there were going to be no criminal charges, it would become a matter for the Prison Service to investigate internally. It was not long before Tom Murtagh contacted me to say that I and John Podmore, Governor at HMP Swaleside, would investigate Gary Catton's involvement with the credit card scam.

Before commencing our investigation, John and I met with one of the Kent detectives to see what information he could share with us. It was an interesting meeting because the detective firmly believed, on the evidence available to him, that Gary Catton had a close liaison with the crime boss behind the scam. He also intimated that there were sums of money deposited in Gary Catton's bank account, which were not, in his opinion, explainable. He was at a loss as to why the CPS had not recommended prosecution.

None of the information shared with us by the detective could be used in our investigation and we would have to concentrate on how Gary Catton organised prisoner transfers into Blantyre and arranged work placements. We would have to check that the proper processes were followed. This would be tedious and time-consuming work.

The Kent governors were due to meet at the Chaucer hotel in Canterbury and discuss Tom's idea about forming a Kent investigation team. This team would investigate alleged wrongdoing in any of the Kent prisons. The team would be headed up by John Podmore and most team members would be based at John's prison, HMP Swaleside. As a group of governors, we endorsed this plan, and subsequently three members of staff, one was a Governor grade and the other two were uniformed ranks, all received temporary promotions on Tom's authority. It would be the newly formed Chaucer team who would undertake the disciplinary investigation into Gary Catton.

As springtime approached, I was asked by a few prisoners if they could increase the number of charity events they organised. The main driver for this was to raise money to fund the annual Mencap Day, which had grown in scale and complexity year on year. Additionally, the prisoners wanted to raise money for some other worthwhile causes and had ideas about how they could do this. Officer Pat Gerathy had been a leading light in coordinating the activities of prisoners who were engaged in raising money for charitable purposes. I spoke with Pat about the ideas that prisoners had put to me and he could see no difficulty in allowing it to happen.

Governors are not permitted to use public funds for charitable purposes and the accounting system for public money is very tightly regulated and governed by a large finance manual. Under the financial rules, there is a provision to set up subsidiary accounts for charitable purposes. These accounts do not have to be operated in the same way as the public money accounts, but of course it is still necessary to account for income and expenditure accurately. Nevertheless, permission has to be sought from the finance directorate before any subsidiary accounts could be set up. My head of Management services and finance, Margaret Andrews obtained permission to set up these subsidiary accounts which could then be used to facilitate the financial transactions associated with the various fundraising activities that prisoners undertook.

Over the coming months, thousands of pounds were raised by prisoners and this money went to a number of worthy causes. The prison attracted a lot of positive publicity from these activities and it is fair to say that Blantyre was an integral part of the local community and fully accepted by it.

I would brief Tom about these activities on his monthly visits and although he noted them he seldom said anything positive or encouraging about them. He seemed far more interested in a large pile of steel panels that were stacked up at the far end of the car park and had been there for over two years. He told me that these panels, which were 2m x 1m were to be fixed to the wire mesh security fence so as to improve the perimeter security of the prison and act as a greater preventative measure against escape.

The perimeter fence around Blantyre stretches for the best part of a mile so it would be a major works project to clad this amount of fencing. It would also cost a lot of money and change the character of the prison by restricting the open views over the Kent Countryside enjoyed by prisoners and staff. I questioned why the cladding was necessary when there had been no escapes from Blantyre and with budgets under pressure would this be a sensible way to use our limited financial resources? I could see that my questioning was irritating him and he simply said, "it will be done." There would be no further discussion about it.

At my next scheduled meeting with the local POA I had the cladding of the perimeter fence as an item on the agenda. The POA committee were surprised, but accepted that if this is what the area manager had decreed then it would happen and although they did not like the idea it was not an issue that the trade union would oppose. However, when I reported on this idea at the monthly BOV meeting there was a very different reaction. Every member of the BOV was opposed to the idea and they believed that the local community would be against it as well.

This issue would drag on for 18 months, and it became a real battle of wills between Tom Murtagh and the BOV. Tom was confident that he would win the day and he was fairly contemptuous of the BOV. He made it perfectly clear to me that I was to support his plan of cladding the perimeter fence and do nothing to undermine him. Although I thought the idea was mad I had been given a lawful instruction and I had to respect that.

In early June, I was contacted by the governor of HMP Downview. He explained that he had established links with the Norwegian Prison Service. He asked me if Blantyre would host a visit for staff from the Norwegian Prison Service. I readily accepted as I thought it would be really interesting to see what the Norwegians, who had the reputation of being quite forward thinking in Penology, would make of Blantyre.

Within a couple of weeks, a delegation of about 20 staff, mostly prison officers in their final year of training and a psychologist spent a day with us. The Norwegians invest heavily in training their prison officers. They have a three year training programme as opposed to the eight or so weeks we give our prison officer recruits and their attitude to what imprisonment should achieve for society was incredibly refreshing. The visit was very successful - the delegation had visited some other prisons in London and Surrey, they said, so they could appreciate just how different Blantyre was.

The psychologist, Per Vaage was fascinated by the regime at Blantyre, and he spent a good two hours picking my brain about the ethos of the prison and how it was set up. Little did I know then that this was to be the beginning of a close liaison between myself and Per which would lead on to me addressing all the Norwegian governors in a seminar held the following year in London. A number of Norwegian governors visited Blantyre and it was not long before Blantyre was a household name at Norwegian Prison Service HQ.

They say that imitation is the best form of flattery and the Norwegians decided to set up a resettlement prison in Norway based on the principles and methods used at Blantyre. This prison is on Bastoy Island in the gulf of Oslo. It became the first ecological prison in the world and it still flourishes today, boasting the lowest reconviction rates within Europe.

There was no disputing the success of Blantyre. All of our key performance targets were exceeded and we had the lowest rate of drug abuse of any prison in the UK. I was authorising in the region of 18,000 ROTLs/year and our failure rate was non-existent. There was no violence in the prison and the only attention we got from the media was all positive. The culture in the prison was so healthy and pro-social that prisoners helped to identify those of their number who were abusing, in some way, the trust that had been placed in them. In any one year, I would probably transfer out between 20 and 30 prisoners who had breached their trust or broken any of our three golden rules: no drugs; no alcohol; and no violence: physical or verbal.

Every month, a random sample of prisoners would be drug tested. This was part of the mandatory drug testing (MDT) program that every prison in the Country ran. Blantyre had always enjoyed exceptionally low positive results so it came as a great surprise to me when after testing one month we had six positive results. A positive result would lead to the immediate transfer of the prisoner back to a secure prison. Never before had I had to transfer out so many prisoners in one go. All the prisoners protested their innocence and so I asked for a confirmation test to be undertaken. One of the prisoners, who I knew very well, did not smoke so I was doubly surprised that he had proved positive for cannabis. I felt uneasy about these results. However, they were the result of an independent laboratory test but despite this, I still had my reservations.

After a few days, the confirmation test results came back and they were all negative. The laboratory said that there had been a problem with cross contamination and the original results could not be relied upon. This cross contamination affected a number of other samples taken from prisoners across the Kent prisons. However, Blantyre was the only prison that demanded confirmation tests as we were more inclined to believe our prisoners than the independent laboratory results. This illustrates the level of trust that existed between me, my staff and the prisoners.

The Chaucer investigation into Gary Catton was tediously slow but eventually culminated in several charges under the code of discipline being laid. Not surprisingly, the charges were heard and proven guilty. Gary Catton was dismissed from the service, but he decided to lodge an appeal against his dismissal and the findings of guilt. The appeal had to be heard by someone who was a rank above the governor who originally heard the case and so it went to a senior civil servant, Robin Masefield.

Robin was a career civil servant, very able and experienced. I had known him when I worked in headquarters as a staff officer to the DG and maybe because of that, he felt he could speak to me informally about the appeal. I gained the impression that he was not overly impressed with the quality of the Chaucer investigation and had serious misgivings about some of the findings of guilt. I was not able to comment on the quality of the investigation as I had not seen any of it but I did share with Robin my belief that Gary Catton was corrupt and should not be reinstated. Whether this had any impact on Robin, I will never know, but he did overturn a number of the guilty verdicts but confirmed that a number were safe. This was sufficient to confirm Gary Catton's dismissal from the service.

The prison was gearing up for the annual Mencap Day which the prisoners had decided to rename as 'Stir Crazy Day'. Fund raising had gone exceptionally well since the new subsidiary accounts had been set up and additional funfair rides had been booked for the day. The prison was expecting about 1000 visitors and the weather forecast for the day was good. Many of the prisoners knew that I flew a microlight aircraft and they asked me if I would put on a little flying display. I contacted a friend of mine who was also a pilot and between us we worked out a simple, but safe way of performing a display which could easily be seen from the ground.

The day was immensely successful and everything went exactly as planned. It was fantastic to see what were once seemingly hardened criminals helping mentally impaired people of all ages, genders and colour participate in the range of rides and other activities that had been organised by them. After such a huge event, it takes a few days for the prison to return to normal running but within a week everything was back to how it was.

Earlier in the year, a chap called Tony Giles, CEO of a small charity, Comeback had introduced me to Val Lowman. This lady worked for a large property development company called Lend Lease and she wanted me to provide prisoners to work on the construction of a huge new shopping centre being built at Bluewater. This would be a fabulous employment opportunity for many Blantyre prisoners and as the scheme developed it led to about 50 prisoners being ROTL'd each day to work at Bluewater. The great thing about the Bluewater employment was that prisoners could earn very good money and some of them were able to learn new skills which they got accreditation for.

As I've said many times, employment and accommodation are the two major cornerstones for successful resettlement and this is why so much effort went into developing good links with employers who were prepared to employ prisoners. The powers of the governor do not extend to securing accommodation for prisoners on release and this is why it is so important that the prisoners have a pot of savings to fund their accommodation needs on release.

Every few months, with the help of Tony Giles from Comeback, we would organise an employers' day at the prison. Basically, we would invite a number of CEOs and heads of personnel from a range of businesses to the prison where they could look around, meet with prisoners and enjoy a superb lunch. We found this a successful way of getting employers on board and we had men working for the railway industry, British Telecom, major supermarkets, as well as several other smaller enterprises.

Since prisoners were earning real wages and enjoyed free board and lodging their day-to-day expenses were minimal and so they could save the bulk of their earnings. It was a real problem for prisoners to have bank accounts, but I was able to negotiate with a local bank that they would allow Blantyre prisoners to have an account and a debit card. Prisoners were allowed to spend £30 per week and they could use their debit card to withdraw this amount of cash. My staff monitored the monthly bank statements to ensure that prisoners did not exceed their £30 limit. There was a provision for prisoners to apply to spend more money if needed and justified, and this would be agreed to if I believed it was necessary.

The Blantyre pathway guaranteed prisoners at least six months of paid employment and most men were able to save thousands of pounds during this time. About a third of the prisoners had accommodation to return to on release. The rest had to find accommodation on release and this is why their savings were so vital. A number of prisoners chose to stay with their current employer on release and relocate to the area where their employment was. As part of the visit, I would give a short presentation to the employers and I would use statistics on the retention rates of prisoners, which were extremely high. Perhaps this was not surprising since when most prisoners are given a chance they really appreciate it and become very loyal employees.

My career was progressing nicely at Blantyre. I had really got a feel for the place and had been pushing the boundaries. I allowed prisoners to use mobile phones when they were outside of the prison and in fact, with some employers, it was an absolute necessity. The Kent police liked the idea as well since it meant that prisoners could be tracked, if necessary, using their mobile phone history. I had a great team of staff who shared the same passion I had and this made coming to work so enjoyable.

One Monday morning, when I was engaged in a meeting with my senior managers in the Board Room Margaret Andrews, my head of management services, noticed some unusual movement in the car park. The Board Room overlooked the staff car park. "Who are those people grouped together by the blue car?" she said. We all looked, and then my

Dep, Tom Wright said, "It's the inspection team, looks like we're getting an unannounced inspection."

He was absolutely right and within 10 minutes, I was entertaining the deputy chief inspector, Colin Allen in my office. Unannounced inspections can be quite disruptive since you have to provide them with all sorts of information and make sure they have adequate office accommodation. They always want to see the BOV and POA and they have complete free movement around the prison. The last inspection report on Blantyre had been led by Judge Stephen Tumin and it was an excellent report. My hope was that the new Chief Inspector of Prisons (HMCIP), Sir David Ramsbotham, now Lord Ramsbotham would be as generous in his assessment of Blantyre as his predecessor was.

After spending the week with us it is customary to meet with the inspectors on a Friday morning for a debrief. If possible, the Chief Inspector attends as does the governor and area manager. We met in the Board Room at 10.30 am and listened to the feedback. It was excellent, there are always some things they find fault with but these were so minor in comparison to the praise we received for our regime and management of the prison. I was so proud to be the governor and I looked at Tom Murtagh, expecting to see him smiling, but that was not to be. His expression was emotionless, and he couldn't even find it in him to say anything encouraging to me. Nevertheless, it did not detract from my feelings of euphoria. It would be some weeks before the HMCIP published their report and on the day of publication, we held a press conference which Tom Murtagh chose not to attend.

As 1997 drew to a close, I felt that Blantyre had moved on from its controversial past and the future looked promising and bright. I had no inkling at what 1998 would bring but it was to be a very mixed bag that contained the seeds of my destruction.

Chapter 11

I started back at Blantyre on Friday, 2 January as that was the day Tom Murtagh had planned for his monthly visit. I did have a few days leave over the Christmas period but I came into the prison on Christmas day for a few hours to walk round and chat with staff and prisoners. I had high expectations for 1998 as we had a new Labour government that had won a landslide election the previous May. Tony Blair had famously said that we would be "Tough on crime and tough on the causes of crime." I was not sure what that meant exactly but there was talk of social inclusion and more funding for prisons so I knew we were in for interesting times. The Murtagh visit passed without incident. The prison was quiet and many prisoners who were on outside work were still enjoying a holiday and would return to work after the weekend.

Murtagh had left the prison by lunch time and since it was quiet, I decided to look at my forthcoming meetings and plan out my time for the next 3 months. I knew that I had several commitments in the first quarter of the year. I was still very much involved in promoting the roll out of cognitive skills programmes across the service and was required to give presentations to governors around the Country.

I had also become involved with an organization called Common Purpose. This was a scheme that brought together a variety of leaders from the public sector, the private sector and the third sector. We would meet for a day of team exercises and the idea was that a network would form which would enable more joined up working between the three sectors.

On the home front, Dorit was starting a new job with Capgemini, a large consultancy firm, and had to attend six weeks training in Torquay and this meant she would only be home at weekends. My daughter was soon to begin taking her GCSEs. The annual Prison Service conference was due in February and I also had two weeks away in March for the senior command course (SCC).

The SCC was for newly promoted governors and the Prison Service had decided to collaborate with the Institute of Criminology at Cambridge University and offer governors the opportunity to enrol into a 2 year Master's degree in Criminolgy and prison studies. I had discussed this course with one of the lecturers and decided to apply. My application was subsequently approved and signed off by Tom Murtagh later on in the year.

With all these commitments, it looked like I would be out of prison more than being in over the next three months.

January was good, in as much, as I was in the prison a lot and could spend time with staff and prisoners. At our February area meeting, I was told, in confidence that I would be transferring to HMP Canterbury in April as the governor there. The current Governor Gareth Davies was moving on to a new posting at HQ. I had very mixed emotions, the transfer would be a promotion but Canterbury was a local prison and therefore, totally different from Blantyre. I had worked in local prisons before so I knew what to expect but Blantyre was so special and I had only been there for 20 months. That night, I had my usual telephone call with Dorit and I told her about my new posting. "It's a much longer journey there from Tonbridge," she said.

She was right about that and the point of her remark was that it would impinge on our home life as my working days, with travel, would be much longer. When I got to work the following day, I spoke with Gareth and arranged to visit the prison in early March.

The journey to Canterbury from home took just over an hour, about three times longer than my journey to Blantyre. Canterbury was very much as I expected it to be and one of the nice things is that it is possible to walk into the town from the prison. By contrast, Blantyre was far more isolated. The news of my transfer was still confidential and so other than Dorit, I had told no one. Literally, a few days after my visit to Canterbury I was told that the transfer would not take place since the job that Gareth was supposed to be moving into at HQ was given to somebody else. I actually felt relieved, as in my heart I did not want to leave Blantyre so soon, if ever.

Sometime later that month, Kent governors were informed that Tom Murtagh was going into hospital for heart surgery and would be off for some months. In his absence, Adrian Smith would be acting up as area manager for Kent. Adrian was a very different kettle of fish to Tom. He had a much quieter personality and he was a stickler for detail. He certainly had the reputation of being a company man through and through and you could never imagine him stepping out of line or doing anything which could cause embarrassment to the Prison Service.

In May, I was contacted by the Secretariat at HQ to say that Richard Tilt, the director-general would be visiting my prison. I have known Richard since he was my governor when I worked in the high Security estate at HMP Gartree in Market Harborough. Richard, now Sir Richard, succeeded Derek Lewis and he was the first operational Governor ever to be appointed as director general. When Tom found out that Richard was visiting he reminded me not to say anything against his idea of cladding the perimeter fence.

Whenever I had visitors to the prison, I would always ask one of the prisoners to show the visitors around and explain how the regime operated. Richard Tilt would be no exception and I asked one of the lifer prisoners, Greg Peters, to show the DG round. All the prisoners knew about the plan to clad the perimeter fence and so I thought it was highly likely that Greg would mention this particularly when they reached the lower compound where the views over the Kent Countryside are most spectacular.

Having had a very comprehensive tour, Greg dropped Richard off at my office and it was there, over tea, that we spoke about the prison. It was clear that Richard was very impressed with what he's seen and he commented on the fantastic atmosphere and culture. He then said, "What's all this controversy over the cladding about Eoin?"

I knew I couldn't duck the issue. "Well, Tom has told me that the perimeter fence has to be cladded and so this will happen once we have secured a contractor to do the work," I said.

"Yes, but as governor what do you think about that?" he said.

I paused for a few moments, what should I say? Should I adopt the party line? Or give him my true opinion? Well, he was asking me what I thought so I decided to tell him honestly.

"I am required to obey the instruction that Tom has given me but in all honesty, Richard I think it is a stupid, costly idea. We have had no escapes and it seems madness to me to waste money on cladding the fence when I am having to make cuts to my education budget."

Richard just looked at me, there was no expression on his face and then he moved on to another topic of conversation. Tom was on a gradual return to work and I received a call from him informing me that the plan to clad the perimeter fence had been dropped and I should make arrangements for the disposal or the steel sheets that were stacked up in the car park. I was expecting him to quiz me about the DG's visit and whether or not the cladding issue was raised, but he didn't mention it.

It was at about this time that I had a phone call from Mike Conway who was deputy Governor at HMP Elmley. He explained that he had a fairly high-profile prisoner by the name of Jack Wells. Wells's wife had been diagnosed with terminal cancer and due to her state of health Elmley found it very difficult to accommodate her on visits to her husband.

Elmley is a large local prison that holds prisoners on remand and prisoners who are freshly sentenced. Due to this, it has a very transitory population and there is always great demand on visits. Visitors often have to queue for some time before getting into the prison and Mrs Wells was simply physically not up to this. Mike asked me if I would consider taking Jack Wells at Blantyre since he knew our visiting arrangements were very good and extremely family friendly. A further compassionate component to all of this was that there were two young children who would soon be motherless. I asked Mike if his governor, Adrian Smith who was also acting area manager was ok with this. Mike said he had talked it through with Adrian and he was content for the transfer to take place subject to my agreement.

Blantyre had an admission criteria and Jack Wells was outside of that, because of the length of his sentence and the time left still to serve.

However, for compassionate reasons Mike wanted me to put that to one side. I did not know anything about Jack Wells and I spoke with members of my management team about Mike's request. Some of my team knew of Jack Wells and thought he was quite a high-profile criminal. There was also some anxiety about accepting a prisoner outside of our criteria, bearing in mind the recent previous history with regard to Gary Catton and suspicious transfers into Blantyre.

Their collective view was not to accept him but that did not sit easily with me. Jack Wells was undoubtedly a serious criminal but humanity almost dictated to me that his wife and children deserved to spend time with him. They have not been convicted of anything, and certainly the children were innocents in all of this. I decided to go to Elmley and speak with Wells so that I could form an opinion of him. I also asked Mike to have all his documentation available so that I could go through this before actually meeting him.

True to his word, Mike had all of Wells' files ready for me and I read through everything. It was lucky I did this because apart from his 11 year sentence he also had an unpaid fine of £100,000 or a further 3 year consecutive sentence making his total sentence 14 years and not 11.

Wells presented as a reasonable man, he was well groomed and mild in his manner. I decided to be absolutely straight forward with him and I told him that if I thought he was being untruthful to me at all then I would not consider him for Blantyre. He told me about his criminal past and was very frank about the money he had made from crime. He spoke about his wife and two young children, and his concerns about what would happen when his wife died. There was sorrow in his voice and I had no doubt that he was being truthful and genuine with me.

I explained to him how my management team were against his transfer to Blantyre but at the end of the day, it would be my decision. With his recent 11 year sentence, he was outside the criteria for transfer mainly because he had served very little time and had not even been transferred to a category C prison yet. But, with the 3 year consecutive sentence as well he was absolutely ineligible for Blantyre unless he paid that fine off. When I told him this he didn't look surprised. There was a moment's pause and then he said he would speak to his lawyer and arrange the transfer of £100,000 to the court. The deal was done and when I had confirmation from the court that the fine had been paid I arranged his transfer which was likely to be in July when we would have a vacancy.

It had only been a few weeks after the visit from Richard Tilt that I was notified that Martin Narey intended to visit Blantyre. Martin had been a junior governor grade but transferred across to the main civil service on their FastTrack scheme and was now a senior civil servant. He had been appointed as director of regimes for the Prison Service and he was at the forefront of negotiating a large settlement for prison regimes. Martin lived in Tunbridge Wells and so Blantyre was quite local to him. The visit went very well and I really believed that Martin understood the ethos of Blantyre.

In July, I was due to go on a two-week course on criminology held at Cambridge University. During this two-week period I would be attending seminars given by some of the most eminent criminologists in the Country. The course was fascinating and it was quite easy to drift into the academic culture of university life. However, during my second week at Cambridge I received a pager message asking me to contact Tom Murtagh urgently. I phoned Tom and he said that he was sending in an investigation team to look into the various charitable activities that Blantyre prisoners were involved with. I was shocked at this news and said that I would return to the prison immediately. Tom said that wasn't necessary and that I should finish my course and we would meet during the following week. I could not really engage with the course for the last few days as I was preoccupied with the investigation at Blantyre. There had been no warning or build-up about this investigation and I had no idea what caused it to happen.

My management team had accepted my decision about the transfer of Jack Wells and he had arrived at the prison during my absence at Cambridge. We set about planning how we would deal with him during the coming weeks as his wife moved ever nearer to her death.

The visiting arrangements were very generous and flexible and it was easy for us to accommodate as many visits as Mrs Wells could manage. Within the first two weeks, she was able to visit regularly during the week but then the frequency reduced as her cancer progressed. It was only a matter of weeks after Wells' transfer that she was admitted into a local hospice.

Normally, prisoners had to be at Blantyre for six months before they could be assessed for any outside supervised activity. I decided that I would ROTL Wells so that he could spend time with his wife at the hospice but I arranged for him to be accompanied by our hospital officer, Skippy Harman. Skippy was originally from Australia, hence his nickname and he had a very good way with prisoners. He was a good choice and I wanted him to befriend the family as well as a supporter to Wells. Previous experience had taught me that bereavement can be a very difficult time for family members in terms of their relationship with the prison. Often they will have expectations about what will happen and they fail to understand the constraints that governors are under. It would be important for Skippy to get to know the extended family and forge a good relationship with them.

It was only a matter of days before Mrs Wells died on 27 August and Jack Wells dealt with it very well. I guess he knew it was coming and so had a lot of time to prepare himself. There were no issues with the family and I am sure this was in part due to the work Skippy had done.

Managing death in prison, whether it be a prisoner or a next of kin outside, can be problematic. When it is not a sudden death but a progressive illness it raises a range of issues and sometimes problems. I have dealt with cases of terminal illness which have run on for months when the initial medical assessment indicated death would occur within days. The prognosis for Mrs Wells was poor and her life expectancy was measured in weeks and not months. Had that prognosis been wrong then it would have impacted how I managed the situation. It would not have been possible, from a resourcing perspective, to have an open ended accompanied ROTL arrangement for Jack Wells.

Wells was now the primary carer for his two young children who were being looked after by his mother-in-law. She too had some medical issues and her sister had just died. It was difficult to know how long this arrangement of child-care could continue for and under Prison Service instructions, there are arrangements governors can put in place for prisoners who find themselves as primary carers. In most cases, the primary carer is the mother but now it would be the father.

Putting to one side the punishment aspect of the sentence on Wells and just looking at the humane consideration, I thought it would be worth submitting an application to the Home Office for a Compassionate Early Release for him. If granted this would safeguard the future care arrangements of his two young children in the event that his mother-in-law's health failed. Accordingly, a submission was drafted by Dave Newport and submitted to the Home Office.

On 10 September, I received a response to the request and, as I half expected, it was a flat refusal. The Home Office judged that Wells would be at high risk of re-offending over the period of his lengthy compassionate licence. I broke this news to him and although disappointed it was not unexpected, I had made sure that his expectations were structured prior to submitting the application.

After some discussion with the senior probation officer at Blantyre, Issy Richmond, I decided that for the next few weeks, I would ROTL Wells one day a week to spend time with his two children. Wells would be accompanied by a member of staff. I knew this could only be a temporary arrangement since the resource cost to the prison was too high. However, I hoped that the impact of the mother's death on the children would be eased if they had some contact with their father.

It was only a few weeks later that Izzy Richmond told me that Kent probation wanted to pilot a new system which could monitor the whereabouts of prisoners who were on licence. The system was called Voicetrack. Essentially, this system used voice verification technology and a BT landline. Predetermined or random telephone calls could be made to a specific phone number where the prisoner would be. Thus, in the case of Jack Wells, his home number would be used and using

Voicetrack it could be ascertained that he was there during the period of his ROTL.

On 17 November, I chaired a meeting with prison and probation colleagues to determine whether Wells would be suitable for this pilot and after some discussion, it was agreed to pilot Voicetrack alongside the accompanied ROTL that was currently in operation. I was content with this outcome as it satisfied my aim to enable him to maintain regular contact with his children whilst ensuring that the level of risk he posed to the community was minimised. My hope was that this arrangement would continue until Wells became eligible for ROTL following a risk assessment at the six-month stage of him being at Blantyre.

I sent Tom Murtagh a note about the Voicetrack project with the expectation that there would be no problem. However, on 21 December, he wrote to me to say that under no circumstances would Voicetrack be used in connection with Jack Wells. He also told me that I should not risk assess him for outside activities. Furthermore, he required me to attend a meeting at his office on 5 January 1999 at 10 am to discuss any proposals I had. I was surprised at this sudden intervention and concerned that there had been no discussion with me prior to the instruction to ditch the Voicetrack pilot.

I felt very uneasy about the situation and thought back to an incident which occurred at our Kent area conference which had taken place at the Flackley Ash hotel near Rye on 25/26 June. During this event, I had a fall out with John Podmore about the selection criteria for Blantyre. He believed that Blantyre were not taking long term prisoners from his prison but selecting short term prisoners from other Kent prisons. I told him that he was wrong but he persisted with this untruth so I contacted Blantyre and requested they fax me a breakdown of our population by sentence length. As I expected, the information on the fax showed quite clearly that our prisoners were all long termers. In fact, the average sentence length was just over 8 years. Faced with this information, Podmore was forced to back down but he did not do this graciously and from that point onwards our relationship, which up until that point had been good, was fractured.

The relevance of this encounter was that it occurred prior to the Chaucer team, which Podmore headed, suddenly investigating the charitable activities at Blantyre. I subsequently found out that Podmore had briefed Murtagh, following the Catton investigation that the corruption which had taken place could happen again since nothing had changed at Blantyre. Much had changed but there was no reference to this so Murtagh got a very one-sided briefing. I think that Podmore had also made some derogatory comments about the charity work that some prisoners were involved with and this is why, without any discussion with me, Murtagh instructed Adrian Smith and the Chaucer team to audit/investigate the charity work.

Chapter 12

The investigation into the Blantyre charity work eventually ran its course and the Chaucer team had delivered the verdict that Murtagh wanted. I accepted that some of the record keeping could have been better but did not agree with the conclusion that the charity work was simply a scam being run by the prisoners. The Chaucer team made a huge issue about the time prisoners were spending out of prison on ROTL. One of the investigators, Ron Gooday, was really hostile to the concept of Blantyre and therefore saw everything through that lens. I clashed with him on several occasions during the countless hours I spent being questioned by the Chaucer team. Ron would say things which were not evidence based at all. It was, therefore easy for me to challenge him. I am not proud of how I dealt with some of those situations, I got angry sometimes and just attacked his obtuse attitude in a very hurtful way. I remember on one occasion, after a heated exchange between us, he sneered at me and said, "Would it surprise you to know governor that you have a close associate of a well-known crime boss in your prison?"

I knew exactly who he was talking about - Jack Wells - and his remark was just pathetic. However, what I did not know was what he then planned to do but I was to find out following a phone call that Tom Murtagh made to me on Friday 11 December. The purpose of the Murtagh call was to inform me that on the following Sunday, the Sunday People would be publishing a scoop about how Jack Wells was allowed to "swan all over Kent" when he should have been locked up in prison. Murtagh said that the Home Secretary was furious and that I had to provide a written submission for him by 9 a.m. on Monday morning. He then ended the call abruptly. I was shocked at what I had heard. It meant that Skippy Harmon, the hospital officer who had accompanied Jack on each occasion of his ROTL, must have been compromised in some way.

It took me a few moments to gather my thoughts. I called my secretary, Dorothy into my office and asked her to get Pete Collard, the security PO and Dave Newport to come to my office immediately. While she was doing this, I decided to call the Prison Service press office and try and get more information about what the Sunday People would be printing. When I spoke with one of the press officers he was surprised to hear about this story and he said he knew nothing about it, but he would ask one of the other press officers, who normally dealt with Prison Service affairs. After a minute or two of waiting he said that nobody in the press office knew of the story but they would check it out. He also asked where did I get my information from? My mind was racing, nothing seemed to make sense and then I realised that Murtagh was lying to me. I told the press officer that I had probably made a mistake and misunderstood something I'd heard. I said I would check with my source and get back to them with an update.

A knock on my door signalled that Pete and Dave had arrived. To my surprise, Margaret Andrews was also there, although I had not asked Dorothy to contact her. They sat down and looked worried. Obviously, Dorothy had stressed the importance of their attendance, so they realised something serious had happened. I then told them about the phone call from Murtagh, there were gasps of disbelief from them. I went on to explain that I contacted the press office and that they knew nothing about the story so my conclusion was that Murtagh was lying. Pete Collard said he would immediately make enquiries with Skippy and check the ROTL licences. I then apologised for dragging them away at such short notice and said I'd keep them informed of further developments. Pete said he would get back to me with an update once he had made his enquiries.

By the early afternoon, based on the feedback from Pete Collard, I was confident that Murtagh was lying. At 3.30 pm I called the press office again and spoke for a couple of minutes with the regular press officer for the Prison Service. I said that I had made a mistake and that there was no story. She said that she had drawn a blank too so there was no problem.

At 3:33 pm, I called Murtagh on his office number in London, and his secretary told me he was not there and was visiting John Podmore at HMP Swaleside. At 3:34 pm I called Podmore's direct line. He answered the phone and I said, "Good afternoon, My name is Braggins, a journalist from the Sunday People, and I would like to speak to Mr. Murtagh please."

Podmore immediately recognised my voice. "Tom, it's Eoin on the phone for you," I heard him say. I told Murtagh that I had been in touch with the press office and they knew nothing about the story so could he tell me where he got his information from? There was a short pause and then he said, "I was just winding you up."

So, it was Ron Gooday who had trawled through the ROTL records and seen that Jack Wells had been out on several occasions to visit his wife and subsequently his children. Of course, what is not on the ROTL was the fact that Wells was accompanied by a prison officer. This was a prime example of how the Chaucer team operated.

I took a few days off at Christmas and prepared myself for the meeting with Murtagh on 5 January. It was not a particularly difficult meeting. Perhaps he was still feeling a bit embarrassed over the fake Sunday People phone call. I explained to him how I had been approached by Mike Conway, with Adrian Smith's consent and asked to take Wells on compassionate grounds. He was subsequently transferred to Blantyre and had some visits from his wife before she was admitted to a local hospice. I allowed an accompanied ROTL for Wells on a daily basis to visit his wife at the hospice until she died. Murtagh interrupted me and said, "Well, he can go back to Elmley now his wife is dead."

"That's not fair, Tom," I said. I'd agreed to take Wells at Blantyre and my view was that he should now stay there unless he does something wrong, which would obviously require his return to closed conditions. Also I thought it was important that for the next few weeks he had good contact with his children. It was obvious that Tom had no compassion for Wells or his children, and this was confirmed when he said that if the mother-in-law couldn't look after the children then they would have to go into care. After some lengthy discussion, Murtagh proposed three options, which he set out in a note to me that I received later that week.

Option one – a return to non-resettlement category C accommodation pending his eventual suitability for Blantyre to arise under normal arrangements.

Option two – for me to make the case for Wells to remain at Blantyre since he was already there for what had been compassionate reasons. He would remain ineligible for outside activity until he was risk assessed at the normal point, which in his case would be September 1999. In the interim, he could receive visits in the prison from his children but we would not be allowed to assume the role of primary carer by routine escorted temporary absence. The frequency of such absences would be at the discretion of the governor but must be decided upon in accordance with the norms applicable to other primary carers e.g. women in custody.

Option three – he could be risk assessed and if suitable sent to a category D establishment where he could receive town visits.

I was not unhappy with the outcome of the meeting and I think that Murtagh felt constrained because Adrian Smith, who was acting up for him, had sanctioned the transfer of Wells. My preference was option 2, but I thought it was only fair to put all the options to Wells. He agreed that option 2 would be his preference and he accepted that he would spend just over a year at Blantyre before being assessed for outside activity. There was a provision for me to ROTL him for specific reasons relating to the welfare of his children. However, even that became a point of contention between Murtagh and myself and it involved Murtagh, accusing my deputy governor, Brian Hales, of lying.

There can be no doubt that the combination of Chaucer, Jack Wells and my determination to protect Blantyre's regime was to become a running sore which would eventually poison any relationship I had with Murtagh. It was becoming more and more apparent that Tom Murtagh and his Chaucer team were totally opposed to the concept of trusting prisoners and he simply could not understand how a prison could operate without all the trappings of formal security. This was going to be a battle of ideologies that would suck in a variety of different players.

Chapter 13

My first year of the Master's Degree (MSt) was coming to an end, and I had found the academic workload quite demanding, especially with all the politics going on at the prison.

My relationship with Tom Murtagh was fragile and I was surprised when he told me, in the strictest confidence, that the DG had plans and finances to re-role Blantyre to a juvenile facility. Apparently, the DG wanted me to see the re-role through. I was shocked at hearing this news since Blantyre was almost unique and once gone could never be easily replaced. Nevertheless, I assured Tom that I would not share this information with anyone.

The BOV at Blantyre had, without my knowledge, raised their concerns about what they perceived and described as Murtagh's "bullying" of me, with Martin Narey. They had also alerted Sir David Ramsbotham of their concerns and so there were conversations going on with the senior management of the Prison Service that I had no knowledge of.

In response to the concerns raised by the BOV, Martin Narey came to the prison in June and met with them. I met with Martin after he had seen the BOV and was surprised to learn that he had told them about his plans to re-role Blantyre to a juvenile facility. This information had been given to me in the strictest confidence earlier in the year and I had told no one. I expressed my concern to Martin that he had told the BOV and enquired whether he had made it clear that this was confidential information. He said he had not and so I offered to speak with them to make sure they did not alert the staff to this proposal as it would be very unsettling for the prison. At no time did Martin mention his discussion with the BOV about me being bullied and so I continued to be oblivious to that fact.

Matters really came to a head in September when Wells was due to be risk assessed for external activities. Murtagh contacted me and said that the risk assessment we had undertaken should be sent up to

Commander Gerard, the police liaison officer who worked at HQ, for validation. Never before in the history of Blantyre had this been done and it meant that the local decision I had made could not be implemented until it had been validated by Commander Gerard.

Wells was expecting to hear the outcome of his risk assessment, but it was delayed and not unreasonably he wanted to know why. I explained to him that Murtagh had requested that his risk assessment should be validated by Commander Gerard. Wells was unhappy about this and felt that he was being victimised by Murtagh. He decided to lodge a complaint with his solicitor and with his MP, Jonathan Shaw.

Both of these gentlemen contacted me by phone. The solicitor was under the impression that Commander Gerard had been connected with the conviction of Wells and that he would be prejudiced against him. I was able to assure the solicitor that Commander Gerard was not connected with Wells at all. I believe that it was Commander Gerard's predecessor, who was involved with Wells and so there was no conflict of duty. The solicitor was satisfied with my explanation.

It was very different with the MP Jonathan Shaw. He was very difficult with me on the phone and I could not placate him. As a last resort, I suggested that he visit the prison, and speak with Wells and then if he still felt there was an issue then, he could take it up with the prisons minister. Jonathan Shaw accepted my invitation to visit the prison and he said his office would be in touch to arrange a suitable date.

More than two weeks had passed since Jack Wells should have had the result of his risk assessment, but nothing was forthcoming from Commander Gerard. I happened to be at headquarters with my security PO, Pete Collard on other business and when we had finished, I decided to seek out Commander Gerard and see what the delay was with Wells's risk assessment. I found Gerard's office and he invited me and Pete in. I introduced myself and he immediately said, "Oh, I have Wells's assessment here, but I have been so busy. I have not had a chance to deal with it yet."

I said that I understood that his workload must be high, but the prisoner was waiting for the answer and had been waiting for some weeks. He looked up at me and said, "What do you know about this man?"

For the next few minutes, I gave an overview of Wells based on my initial conversation with him at Elmley the previous year, as well as summarising his progress at Blantyre. Gerard looked at me and I felt that something had happened, like he realised he'd been set up to fail the assessment. Then he smiled and said, "Don't worry. You will have my assessment by the end of the week."

The following week, I received a phone call from Tom Murtagh. He said, "Gerard has knocked Wells back." There was a moment of silence and then he said, "You know that's not true, don't you." I sighed. "I only know what you tell me, Tom."

"Phil Wheatley, (Deputy Director General) is enraged about this," he said. "You saw Gerard and put pressure on him."

It was almost unbelievable that Murtagh or anyone could think that I could put pressure on a senior police Commander into doing something simply on the basis of me having a conversation with him in his office. The truth was Commander Gerard just did his job properly. Below is the summary of his two-page report:

Wells is a very well-resourced professional criminal who has previously demonstrated no other means of earning a living. Formerly associated with the highest level of criminal activity in the south-east of England, there is evidence that he is now no longer highly regarded by his former colleagues. He has had no direct contact with any of these major players since his conviction.

I have been unable to identify any relevant criminal intelligence or indication that he intends to continue his former criminal activity. His domestic circumstances have altered considerably since his conviction and have clearly affected his outlook on the future. His financial resources will not require him to work. At 42 years he is a mature man who has demonstrated his ability to both manipulate and conform with systems where it is to

his advantage. He will be only too well aware of the result of any further criminal activity.

I share the assessment that his risk of reoffending in the immediate future is low and would concur with the proposal to allow him to participate in the resettlement programme.

Murtagh was obviously annoyed about Gerard's report and he was therefore unable to block Wells from participating in outside activities. I then wrote to the Commander and thanked him for his thorough report, which validated the assessment from Blantyre. I closed the letter by saying that if he wanted to visit the prison, then he would be more than welcome. To my surprise, I took a phone call from him, and as a result, we arranged a visit for Friday 22 October.

As usual, for his visit I asked one of the prisoners to show him round the prison and then to drop him off at my office for a chat. He came back genuinely impressed with what he'd seen, particularly remarking on the culture of trust and personal responsibility and the attitude of prisoners he had spoken to whilst on his tour. He admitted that it was not what he originally expected but expressed pleasure that he'd taken the time to accept my invitation. A few days later, I received a letter from him reiterating his positive response to the visit.

A little while after that, Jonathan Shaw MP visited the prison and spent some time speaking with Jack Wells, who also showed him round the prison. At the end of his tour, Wells dropped Mr Shaw off at my office. Over tea, we chatted about the prison and I answered all his questions. He told me that his visit had been an eye-opener and that he was very impressed with the regime and what it appeared to be achieving. "It must be unique," he said. Some days later, I received a letter from him too thanking me for the hospitality he received – and then pertinently telling me that he was so taken with what he'd witnessed he would be writing to Robin, Lord Corbett, chair of the Home Affairs Select Committee (HASC), urging him to also visit the prison.

Sure enough Robin Corbett then wrote to me. In his letter, he asked a number of questions about Blantyre and also expressed the wish to be invited to the prison. I knew that if he visited, like all our visitors, he would like what he'd find. I also realised that he would eventually find out about plans for the prison to be re-rolled whenever the announcement was made and that his Committee may have an opinion on that. And I knew that Tom Murtagh would blame me if the HASC expressed any negative views about the proposed re-role, so I decided that I would refer the matter to him. Murtagh would escalate the request to the Prisons Minister and thus, any decision taken would not be mine.

I also knew of course that it would be very unlikely Robin Corbett's request would be refused and so I expected to be told that I could indeed invite him. This process took more than two weeks during which I fielded a couple of telephone calls from the HASC clerk, enquiring as to when I would reply to Robin Corbett's request. He was obviously keen.

Eventually, the approval was given and Murtagh told me I could write to Robin Corbett but that my letter had to be "absolutely accurate" about anything to do with Blantyre. That presented me with no problems whatsoever.

Despite all this turmoil, it was difficult to think of a more perfect prison; where your staff are content, there are no industrial relations issues, where the performance of the prison, as measured by key performance indicators is excellent, where the prison is absolutely accepted and supported by the local community, where prisoners, who may have been very difficult in other establishments, have changed beyond all recognition. All of this would be any governor's dream.

Despite this level of success, Tom Murtagh failed to recognise it. I remember the Governor of HMP Maidstone saying to me that when he did something relatively ordinary at Maidstone, Murtagh appeared to think it was marvellous. Yet when I did something that the world and his wife thought was quite wonderful he barely mentioned it, unless to criticise it of course. That remark got me thinking that perhaps the official expectations for Blantyre were much higher than for other prisons. Most visitors to the prison formed an opinion based on how everything seemed so nice and peaceful and ordered. It was easy to speak with prisoners and staff and everyone was very polite and the place just had a real good feeling about it. The real purpose of prison, what should it be achieving is keeping the public safe and reducing re-offending and helping to ensure fewer potential victims of released prisoners. Could Blantyre be described as successful if on release the prisoners from it continued a criminal lifestyle? Hardly.

The Prison Service mission statement is all about public safety and keeping prisoners safely and securely in custody as well as preparing them to lead law-abiding and industrious lives on release. None of my performance measures or targets related meaningfully to how prisoners managed on release.

Anecdotally, I knew that many prisoners who were released from Blantyre appeared to be keeping away from crime, I knew this from probation officers who supervised many of them in the community following their release. And many former Blantyre prisoners kept in touch with staff and me and so we knew they were making a success of their lives.

None of this is hard evidence however. So, after having just had a year of quite intense academic study, I decided to see if I could track released Blantyre prisoners and see how many reoffended. In order to do this, I would need access to the police national computer (PNC). I contacted the Research Development Statistics group (RDS) at the Home Office to see how I could gain access to the PNC. RDS wanted to know why I wanted this access and so I explained what I wanted to achieve. To my complete surprise, I was told that RDS already had this information, and in fact had the two-year reconviction rates for every prison in the Country. Furthermore, RDS said they would send me the results they had for Blantyre. True to their word, within a week I had in front of me two-year reconviction rates for prisoners released from Blantyre over the previous four years. The results were stunning. During that time prisoners released from Blantyre had an average two-year reconviction rate of 7%. This is compared to the national average two-year reconviction rate for all prisons of 58%.

To really put this into perspective, it is important to understand the methodology underpinning two-year reconviction rates. The Home Office have a model that predicts the reconviction rate for different groups of prisoners. Young people, particularly teenagers, have a very high reconviction rates, whereas middle-aged long-term prisoners have substantially lower reconviction rates. The model predicted that prisoners from Blantyre would have a 28% likelihood of reoffending within two years, so to be absolutely honest the 7% reconviction rate for Blantyre should be compared to the predicted rate of 28% and not the national average of 58%. Nevertheless, Blantyre was achieving a result which was preventing four times fewer victims than any other prison in the Country – not to mention the economic benefits to society.

I was so excited at having this information that I phoned RDS just to check that the information they'd sent me was accurate and that I had interpreted the figures correctly. They absolutely reassured me on both counts. To say this information was the icing on my lately somewhat bruised cake would be an understatement. It was like having the best winning hand in a game of poker that you could possibly get. Blantyre had a royal flush.

Chapter 14

My letter inviting Robin Corbett to Blantyre was quite lengthy because he had asked several questions based on what he had heard from Jonathan Shaw. Bearing in mind Murtagh's warning to me about my letter being accurate I was meticulous in ensuring that everything I wrote was accurate and could be evidenced. The letter summarised all that was good and successful about Blantyre and I was confident that he would be impressed.

Within a few days, I had an acknowledgement to say my letter had been received and that his office would be in touch early in the New Year to arrange a suitable date for him and members of the HASC to visit. I hadn't realised he'd be bringing other MPs with him and so I thought it would be very useful if I prepared a small booklet summarising the achievements of Blantyre as well as giving an overview of its demographic.

The back end of 1999 was very much a bittersweet experience for me. It had certainly been a very difficult year due to investigations and audits. My relationship with Murtagh was not good because I would not succumb to his intimidating tactics. However, I had fantastic support from my BOV and HMCIP. Many organisations and criminal justice charities admired the work we did at Blantyre. The prison was an integral part of the local community, which supported it brilliantly. Many local businesses and charitable organisations offered employment opportunities to our men and our media profile, both locally and nationally was very positive. To cap it all, the hard evidence of low reconviction rates was indisputable proof of the prison's successful regime. The world seemed a bit topsy-turvy to me. Usually, governors have the support of their line manager and the weight of the Prison Service behind them – but local communities, the media and public opinion are far less supportive. For me it was the complete reverse and I was beginning to feel quite isolated from the Prison Service, which I had served loyally for over twenty years.

Brian Hales, my deputy governor, was due to retire and his last day of duty was Monday 1 November. Brian had been a very loyal deputy. His background had been in security and Murtagh had proposed him to be my Dep, probably believing that he would act as a good restraint to what he perceived as my progressive style of management. Brian had made the same journey as I had. Neither of us knew what Blantyre was about when we first arrived, but within the space of a few months we learned just how different Blantyre was and our view of prison, prisoners and what it is really possible to achieve changed. Yes, he was going to be a sad loss to the prison and a very hard act to follow, and I would miss him.

December was a busy month with a number of external speaking engagements, as well as the two-day area Christmas bash at Flackley Ash. Murtagh had decided that twice a year, all the Kent governors and his area staff would meet for a two-day area conference. The conference would also double as being a Christmas get-together for everyone so it tended to be a boozy occasion. This was more enjoyable than I thought it might be – it was a bit like a wartime Christmas truce, although I wouldn't be playing any Christmas games with Murtagh and his Chaucer team.

I knew January would be an interesting month since we were due to have an announced full inspection of the prison by HMCIP. Earlier in the year, with the help of prisoner Greg Peters, I put together a PowerPoint presentation about Blantyre. The presentation included video footage of interviews with prisoners, managers and myself as well as statistics about the performance of the prison and of course the superbly low two-year reconviction rates. Peters and I had used this presentation on a number of occasions at external engagements and we had even presented it to the postgraduate Criminology cohort of students who were embarking on their Masters degree at the Institute of Criminology at Cambridge University. In fact, on that occasion, Peters and I swapped roles in as much as our introductions did not identify who was the prisoner and who was the Governor. I introduced myself with a South London accent and immediately the audience wrongly deduced that I was the prisoner and smartly suited Peter the Governor. It was only as the presentation progressed and a few red faces that they realised their error – making the point of how easily we tend to stereotype people, groups and individuals we don't really know.

I had decided to use the PowerPoint presentation at the introductory meeting with the inspection team when they arrived on Monday 17 January. Normally, Governors prepare a written report for HMCIP prior to their announced visit. I had told HMCIP that I would not be preparing a written report, but there would be a presentation for them. The other thing I did was to ask twelve former Blantyre prisoners to return to the prison and meet with HMCIP so that they could say what they thought was good or bad about their time at Blantyre – and give some testimony on how it had helped or impeded their resettlement. To the best of my knowledge, such a thing had never been done before but I believed that these former prisoners were the product of our work at Blantyre and if we were to be inspected then surely their views would be relevant.

I hadn't discussed either of these things with Murtagh since I thought it would likely antagonise him, especially since he had indicated to me that I should not try and impress HMCIP unduly. Every Governor tries their best to show their establishment in the best possible light and so I decided not to pay any attention to Murtagh's comment. Every one of the twelve former Blantyre men agreed to attend the prison and meet with HMCIP. Before taking a few days off over the Christmas period, I felt that I had done everything I could to prepare for the inspection and I knew that the New Year would be very interesting since I had been notified that the HASC would be visiting on 1 March.

At about 10 AM on 17 January, the Inspection team arrived. After the usual introductions and tea we convened in the boardroom and I, along with Greg Peters, co-presented our PowerPoint presentation. It appeared to set a good tone for the commencement of their inspection. They would soon discover if what we had presented was a genuine reflection of the prison.

There are always issues that crop up during an inspection and I was challenged by one of the inspectors about an adjudication I had done the previous year. We did not have many adjudications and so in order to assess the quality, the inspector had to trawl back over a couple of years in order to have a number to look at and judge. I was being challenged about a fine I had imposed on a prisoner who had abused a condition of his ROTL. I had fined the prisoner £200 and the inspector thought this was unacceptable as it far exceeded anything she had experienced before. I explained that most prisoners earn prison wages and these can range from £2.50 to £30 per week. However, prisoners at Blantyre who are working in the community earned real wages and this particular man was making £200 per week. It is not uncommon to fine a prisoner one week's wages when an adjudication has been proved - and this is all I had done. The inspector accepted my explanation and agreed that it was a proportionate punishment.

Another issue which arose was when I transferred the prisoner out who had failed the breathalyser test on his return from outside paid work after drinking two tins of 'alcohol free' lager. The inspectors felt that I was being too harsh in transferring this man back to closed conditions when the reading had been so low. But I stood my ground as No Alcohol was one of the three golden rules at Blantyre and I was not prepared to make an exception that would undermine these rules for the rest of the men.

The other really major issue that cropped up was when the inspectors said that they had heard the prison might be re-rolled to a juvenile facility. Apparently, they received this information from a source based "somewhere in the North of England." Although I have no direct evidence, I believe the information came from the BOV at HMP Kirklevington who probably were informed by the Blantyre BOV. This sent shock waves through the prison and I spent a frantic day reassuring staff and prisoners that nothing had been decided yet and that I would keep them informed of events.

On Friday, I met with the inspectors along with Murtagh to receive their initial feedback on the inspection. It was glowing and I basked in their praise of the prison. Tom just sat there expressionless.

After this meeting, one of the inspectors spoke with me in confidence and asked why it was that Murtagh seemed so unhappy about the great feedback they had given. I said that it was a mystery to me as well and simply shrugged my shoulders. HMCIP left the prison and Murtagh stayed on since he would use this day as one of his monthly visit days. We reviewed the performance of the prison and Murtagh said that the figures he had for our Mandatory Drug Tests (MDTs) were different to the figures I had submitted on our monthly return. Our figures were lower than his and his inference was that I was falsifying the Blantyre results so that they looked better than they really were. I challenged him on this and dispatched one of my staff to get the original records of the tests so their authenticity could be verified. Despite producing this evidence Murtagh was having none of it and still insisted that his figures were correct and accurate. Eventually, I said, "Look Tom, even if I accept your figures are the correct ones, they are still the best in the area and probably in the Country, so if you want to use your figures that's fine by me."

I couldn't help but feel that after the glowing feedback from HMCIP, Murtagh had to try and do something to knock me down. He didn't stay long in the prison that day and in all honesty, I was glad to see the back of him. I just wondered what the hell was coming next.

Chapter 15

The annual Prison Service conference was held in early February 2000 at Harrogate in the North of England. It followed the usual format and was quite enjoyable as it's the one occasion in the year when you can meet Governors from other prisons, far from your own area. I took the opportunity to catch up with the Governors of the other two resettlement prisons and, in fact, arranged to visit another resettlement prison, HMP Kirklevington Grange, in North Yorkshire at the end of the month. The Governor of Kirklevington was Suzanne Anthony, a self-assured individual who shared my passion for resettlement prisons.

The regime at Kirklevington was similar to that of Blantyre, but they accepted prisoners serving very short sentences. Many of the prisoners had paid jobs outside the prison and several of them had the use of a car and mobile phone. Unlike me, Suzanne had no interference from her area manager in the day-to-day running of the prison and the use of cars by prisoners was not an issue. I must admit to being a little envious of the relationship she had with her area manager, and it was supportive and understanding of the risks associated with large-scale ROTL.

After my visit, I felt more reassured about how I was managing Blantyre since there was so much commonality between Blantyre and Kirklevington. Suzanne's area manager was relaxed about how the prison was managed and obviously did not see the risks and dangers that seemed to flood through Murtagh's mind. When you are being constantly criticised and berated by your line manager it is not surprising that you begin to doubt yourself. The reassurance I gained from visiting Kirklevington confirmed in my mind that I was not some kind of out-of-control Governor. I was just unlucky to have an area manager who struggled with the concept of trusting prisoners and lacked the imagination to consider that there may be alternative ways of protecting the public other than by using security and coercion.

1st March was a really interesting day. Robin Corbett and three other MPs from the HASC arrived at the prison for their visit. I'd planned the day carefully so that they had an opportunity, not only to see around the prison, but to be able to speak with groups of prisoners, and groups of staff, including the Prison Officers Association committee and the BOV. The day started with the same presentation that Greg Peters and I gave to HMCIP and then we both responded to questions. Each member of the HASC was given a copy of the booklet that I had prepared which contained facts and figures about the prison, its performance and its prisoners. The committee members were then free to roam around the prison and meet the various groups.

At the end of the day, I had scheduled a meeting between the HASC and my Senior Management Team. I got a strong impression that the visitors were impressed with what they'd seen and after a very enjoyable 30 minutes Robin Corbett said, "Just one last question Governor. Who is the bloody idiot who wants to re-role this prison?" I hadn't expected such a direct question. "That is a totally inappropriate question to ask me Robin and I suggest you take that matter up with the prisons minister." He gave me a wry smile before he thanked me for my hospitality and reiterated how useful and informative their visit had been. He and his colleagues then left the prison and I felt very pleased with how the day had gone - but wondered what might come from it.

It transpired later that Robin Corbett wrote a personal letter to the Home Secretary, Jack Straw urging him to reconsider the re-role of Blantyre House. Straw wrote back confirming the reversal of the plan to re-role: "Following the assessment of options for Blantyre," he wrote, "you will be pleased to learn that we have concluded it should remain as a resettlement establishment for the foreseeable future."

It would be these raw ingredients that convinced Martin Narey that I was the orchestrator of the HASC visit and their subsequent intervention which derailed his planned re-role of Blantyre. It was this that had to have led Narey to believe that I had betrayed him and been disloyal - this was what must have laid behind the remarks that he made to me at our meeting with Lynne Bowles. I believed then it was primarily for this reason that he authorised the raid on Blantyre. It certainly could not have been because he thought I was corrupt, something he acknowledged at our meeting and confirmed by the fact that he'd planned to send me as deputy governor to a very secure prison in a role that would put me in charge of the prison security. Little did I know then about the outrageous allegation that had been made to him about me by the Chaucer Team.

March would prove to be a very busy month. On the 3rd, I had to attend Cambridge University to receive my diploma in criminology and prison studies. This marked the halfway point of the Master's degree and the coming year would entail me undertaking some original research within prisons and then writing up an 18,000 word thesis. There would be the three blocks of two-week residential courses at Cambridge, culminating with a viva where I would be questioned on my research by the professor of criminology. If all went well, then I would get my Master's degree at an award ceremony in the summer of 2001.

It had been a tradition at Blantyre to stage a pantomime in March where elderly residents from the local community were invited into the prison to see the performance. Local schoolchildren and Blantyre staff family members were also invited for other performances. It may seem odd, staging a pantomime in March, but there was some method to this madness. Pantomimes are traditionally staged at Christmas time and Blantyre is involved in either lending or borrowing costumes and props for pantomimes being staged in the community. In order not to compete with these events, the Blantyre pantomime was staged in March. Admission is free but visitors can make a donation to the Stir Crazy Day, which was held later in the year.

One of the big challenges governors face is how to keep their staff up to date with training in a variety of things such as first-aid, fire procedures and C&R (Control and Restraint.) Much of this training is mandatory and so governors struggle to release staff from their operational duties to attend such training. When the prisons are resourced, there is an allowance for annual leave, sickness and training. Many prisons have high sick rates amongst their staff and because everybody generally takes their annual leave entitlement, the allowance for staff training is squeezed. Most prisons are unable to meet the training needs for their staff and it is a continuing battle with staff associations about the appropriate resourcing of a prison. At Blantyre, it was a very different story. Our sick rates were among the lowest in the

Country and with the cooperation of the local POA, I was able to set aside a whole week in March for staff to receive all the mandatory training required.

It was at the beginning of this training week that I took a call from Tom Murtagh. In this call, he was blaming me for getting the HASC involved with Blantyre and strongly inferring that the director general, Martin Narey, viewed me as being obstructive to his plans to re-role Blantyre as a juvenile establishment. I could scarcely believe the accusations he was making, but more worrying was what he was saying to the director general. Had Murtagh not interfered in local decision-making over Jack Wells' risk assessment, then no complaint would have been made to Jonathan Shaw and in turn, he would not have contacted Robin Corbett, chair of the HASC and the committee would never have made that fateful visit. The irony of this could not escape me, Murtagh had brought all this on himself, but now he was casting me as some kind of grand conspirator who had engineered a visit by the HASC simply to derail Narey's re-role plans for Blantyre. The invitation to the HASC predated the comment about the re-role made by HMCIP during their inspection of Blantyre.

I decided to write a very frank note to Murtagh, setting out the facts and the chronology of events. I thought it was important to set the record straight and have something in writing, which recorded that. I knew my note was strongly worded and I faxed a draft to a close friend and colleague, Peter Hanaway, who worked at HQ. We had a conversation about the draft because I wanted to know whether someone independent would view it as being offensive and disrespectful to a line manager. Peter thought it was a very hard-hitting note and was surprised that things had gotten to the stage where I had to write such a note. However, he could not find anything in it which was offensive or disrespectful. Below is the text of that note, which was dated 22 March 2000.

Re: Home Affairs Select Committee visit to HMP Blantyre House

Following your telephone conversation with me on the morning of Monday 20 March. I believe it is necessary to formally set out the sequence of events leading up to the visit by the HASC. In September 1999 a Blantyre prisoner complained to both his solicitor and MP (Jonathan Shaw) about a specific issue. I was contacted by both of these individuals and assured them the prisoner did not have any justifiable complaint. During the course of my conversation with Jonathan Shaw I invited him to see the prison and speak with his constituent in person. Jonathan Shaw subsequently visited the prison on 2 September 1999.

On 24 September 1999, I received a note from Jonathan Shaw thanking me for his visit to the prison and also informing me that he had contacted Robin Corbett, MP, Chairman of the HASC and advised him to visit Blantyre house. Prior to receiving this note, I had no knowledge of Robin Corbett's interest in Blantyre.

On 4 November 1999, I received a note from Robin Corbett explaining that he had been contacted by Jonathan Shaw, who had urged him and members of the HASC to visit Blantyre. Robin Corbett asked me to formally invite the HASC to visit Blantyre and also to provide some general explanation to expand on some specific points Jonathan Shaw passed on to him.

At this stage, I notified you of events and, following your advice, drafted a letter dated 23 November 1999 to Robin Corbett, which was forwarded to you.

On 9 December 1999, you returned the Robin Corbett letter to me and said that it could be sent. You also warned me to ensure that the content of the letter was accurate.

During the early part of the New Year, Liz Booth phoned me on a number of occasions to confirm visiting arrangements and obtain a draft programme for the visit.

Four members of the HASC visited on 1 March 2000 and met prison staff, a volunteer, BOV, a comeback representative, prisoners and ex-prisoners.

Other issues:

The future role of Blantyre House is a totally separate issue from the HASC visit. In fact, arrangements for this visit preceded any public announcements about the future role of Blantyre.

When you phoned me on Monday 20 March, you repeatedly told me that you had warned me not to lobby the HASC. You inferred that the Dir general viewed me as being obstructive and antagonistic towards his policy on juveniles. You advised me to keep a low profile and not to become involved. Finally, you made it clear that you were stepping back from this issue as well.

Blantyre House is a resettlement prison. As Governor, I am committed to lead and manage the prison to the best of my ability. The prison is very good at what it does, and I am very good at explaining what it does. To suggest that I should keep a low profile and not become involved is to deny my role as Governor. I have no choice in the matter, and my job is to lead and manage the prison to the best of my ability. I would fulfil this role irrespective of whether Blantyre cared for juveniles or some other section of the prison population.

It appears to me that because other parties, whether they be BOV or HASC, see the merits of what Blantyre House does. I'm in some way blamed for that. If you, or those above you, did not want the HASC to visit Blantyre House, then the opportunity was there to do something about it. To allow the visit and then blame me for doing my job is totally unacceptable.

As I told you on the phone, I made it clear to the HASC that I and my staff are public servants who do and will continue to follow Prison Service instructions and policies.

It appears to me that you believe I'm colluding with others to try and undermine any plans to change the role of Blantyre House. I'm doing no such thing, but I'm leading and managing Blantyre House in accordance with current Prison Service instructions and policy. It would be of some reassurance to me if I thought you believed that. However, your phone call of Monday 20 March suggests the contrary and I would be very disappointed if you were reflecting that misleading view upwards.

What I find particularly of concern about the current situation is the absolute lack of any evidence to suggest that I am orchestrating or colluding with others to obstruct the Dir general in his policy on juveniles. Despite no evidence, I am subjected to a continuing wall of suspicion, peppered with warnings from you. Despite your declared support for Blantyre, you have made no attempt to understand my position as Governor; you have never indicated any desire to represent my position to those above. What you have done is to ensure I feel totally isolated and unsupported by the line.

It so happened that Murtagh was attending the training unit at Blantyre later that week. I decided to personally walk round to the training unit and hand my note to him. As I gave him the brown envelope containing my note he said, "Is this your resignation."

I looked directly at him and said," When you read it Tom you'll wish it was." I then left him and returned to my office.

The other major event for me in March was attendance at the annual Prison Governors' Association (PGA) conference. This is always an enjoyable event and takes place over three days in the Grand Hotel in Buxton, a spa town in the Peak District. Invariably, the Home Secretary and or the prison minister attend to give a keynote speech and take questions. I took the opportunity to relax and chill out at this conference and it was a wonderful distraction from the turmoil that was unfolding at Blantyre.

On returning to work after the conference, I noted that Martin Narey's wife, Jan, was visiting the prison on Thursday 6 April. This visit had been arranged sometime before following a presentation I had given to Jan and some of her friends at her home in Tunbridge Wells. I thought the timing could be awkward and I wondered whether she would cancel the visit. To my surprise, there was no cancellation and she had an enjoyable visit and there was no mention of anything relating to tensions between me and Tom Murtagh. It crossed my mind that if her husband was so angry with me, then why would he allow his wife to visit? Could it be that Murtagh had lied to me when he said, in his phone call of 20 March, that the director general viewed me as being obstructive and antagonistic towards his policy on juveniles?

For the next two weeks, I was away at Cambridge on the MSc course and returned to Blantyre on 25 April which happened to be my daughter's birthday. The first week back after Cambridge was always busy and is really just a catch-up week in the prison. The following week would only be four days due to the May Day holiday and I had no external commitments, although on Friday 5 May, I was expecting Murtagh's visit. I could never have imagined it would be such a catastrophic day.

Chapter 16

In the weeks and months after the raid, I tried to concentrate on continuing with my Masters Degree and Prison Studies which I had applied for in 1998. It was funded by the Prison Service and formed part of the career development for senior Governors. Before I could be accepted onto this course I had to have the support of my line manager, Tom Murtagh. He had given me this support but then been very critical of me for being out of the establishment whilst participating with the course in Cambridge.

I had completed my first year of study successfully and in my second year, I was required to undertake an original piece of research which would be written up as I said, as an 18,000-word thesis. So, I decided that my research would look into why Blantyre House appeared to be so successful at reducing reconviction rates. Central to this would be selecting six new prisoners to Blantyre House and six new prisoners to HMP Standford Hill, an open prison on the Isle of Sheppey. Both groups of prisoners would have to be interviewed soon after arriving at their respective prisons and then again three months later. The interviews would be semi-structured and use a psychometric tool, Crime Pics, which would establish the prisoner's attitude towards offending. The Crime Pics tool was developed in the 90s with the help of the Probation Service and is used to evaluate the effectiveness of interventions that prisoners undertake.

I contacted Chris Bartlett who had taken over running Blantyre after I'd been removed - and John Robinson, Governor of Standford Hill, to seek permission to visit their prisons for the purpose of interviewing the two sample groups. Both Governors gave their consent and over the coming weeks, I arranged to conduct my interviews.

During one of my visits to Blantyre, I was in the Board room interviewing a prisoner when the door suddenly opened and Tom Murtagh appeared. He must have been on a routine visit to the prison but judging by the expression of surprise on his face he had not expected to see me in the prison. Without saying a word he disappeared as quickly as he had appeared and I don't know whether Chris had told him that I was visiting the prison. At the time, I thought little of this event and had no knowledge that something far more ominous was awaiting for me at Standford Hill.

On 23 May, I visited Standford Hill to conduct some of the interviews with the six prisoners I had identified for my research project. I was met at the gate of the prison by a Principal Officer who took me to a room that had been set aside for me to use. Arrangements had been made for the prisoners concerned to come and see me at prescribed times and from my point of view the prison and its staff were being very accommodating. The morning passed without incident and at lunchtime I joined one of the prisoners in the communal dining room and we ate together. After lunch, I continued with my interviews but around mid-afternoon the Principal Officer who had met me in the morning appeared. He apologised for interrupting my interview and asked to speak with me alone. He looked uneasy and appeared to be very embarrassed.

"I'm really sorry sir," he said, "and I don't know quite how to say this. But you have to leave the prison immediately." It took me a moment to understand what he had said, and he could tell by the look on my face that I was totally shocked. "It's come from the Governor," he said. But I knew John, the Governor was not in the prison because when I had spoken with him to arrange the visit he told me he would be away that day.

"Is there a particular reason why I have to leave?" I said. I said it very sternly and I could see that the PO, conscious of my rank, felt very awkward. "I don't know why Sir; it's just a direct order and I have to take you to the gate."

There was absolutely no point in trying to argue with this man, it was not his fault and he obviously felt very uncomfortable. I spoke with the prisoner briefly and said that we would have to continue the interview at a later stage. I left the prison and back in my car phoned the deputy governor of Standford Hill to find out why he had ordered my removal. He refused to speak with me so I contacted the PGA and Lynne Bowles said she would get to the bottom of it and come back to me. She didn't get back to me until the following day but when I arrived home I got a call from the Governor of HMYOI Rochester, Colette Kershaw. "I'm just phoning to see how you are Eoin," she said.

"That's kind of you but is there any particular reason why?" I was still puzzled by what had happened. Colette was a colleague and we had developed a good friendship but this was the first contact I had from her since my removal from Blantyre House.

"I'm worried about you, especially after what happened today at Standford Hill," she said. I could hear the real concern in her voice. "What have you heard then?" I said. "They say you have had some kind of breakdown and were impersonating a prisoner." I was speechless. After an awkward pause, I reassured her that I was perfectly okay and I had no idea why I'd been evicted from Standford Hill.

The next morning, Lynne Bowles got back to me and said that she had had difficulty getting hold of the deputy governor at Standford Hill and when eventually she spoke with him he told her he, "wasn't having that maverick Governor in my prison." It was clear to me that my reputation had been trashed in some quarters following my humiliating removal from Blantyre and that there were some senior staff in prisons who believed the damaging stories put out by the Prison Service press office about me.

When I wrote to Martin Narey on 25 May thanking him for the two weeks special leave he had agreed to, I mentioned this Standford Hill incident and cited it as a reason why I should not go back into prison until my name and reputation had been restored. I never received a reply to this request which made me even more unsure as to my future within the Prison Service.

Despite this apparent setback, I then had a call from Standford Hill governor John Robinson, apologising for the actions of his deputy and said that I was welcome to return to the prison any time to complete my research project. I subsequently visited on two more occasions without incident.

During late May, I was beginning to feel quite isolated from the Prison Service. More colleagues across Kent, with the exception of one or two, were keeping their distance and information from the Prison Service to the media was still painting me out to be the bad guy. My anxiety was further fuelled by the Prisons Minister Paul Boateng telling Parliament that "a frightening amount of contraband" had been found during the raid. This was being said, despite the fact that I'd told Martin Narey much earlier in the month that most of what had been found was not contraband - and almost everything that had been seized from prisoners on the night of the raid had been returned to them. Furthermore, I was amazed when Paul Boateng told the Home Affairs Select Committee (HASC) that, "a criminal investigation was underway."

Jack Wells you will recall was one of the prisoners removed from Blantyre on the night of the raid - because of "intelligence received," according to a report that Tom Murtagh produced after the raid:

"Following a detailed briefing from the Chaucer team, the incoming governor, Mr Bartlett, asked for three prisoners to be removed to more secure conditions in the interests of protecting the public."

As I said in earlier chapters, Murtagh's desire for Wells to be removed from Blantyre and my resistance was one of the reasons for the breakdown in our professional relationship. So it seems to be no coincidence that the new Governor, based on information from Chaucer decides that Jack Wells should be transferred out. I believe the new Governor did not come to that conclusion himself. Bearing in mind Murtagh, in the same report, stated that the new Governor had requested the full search of the prison:

"Mr Bartlett's first action as the new Governor was to request a full search of the establishment and to have every prisoner drug tested. Mr Bartlett's request was based on the intelligence briefing he had received from the Chaucer team on the current activities of individuals at HMP Blantyre House."

However, it was later revealed that this decision had been taken some days before the new Governor even knew of his appointment. The

Executive Summary of another investigation into the raid by Ian Truffet, a serving prison Governor gave specific details:

"**Operation Swynford was the code name given to the planned search at HMP Blantyre House, a Category C prison with a resettlement function. The plan was commissioned in late April 2000 by the area manager for Kent, Surrey and Sussex, Tom Murtagh, following authorisation by the Director General, Martin Narey.**"

And what about Jack Wells? Apparently his transfer, according to what Martin Narey told the HASC on 16 May 2000 was, "Subject of the intelligence gathered both from the police and other prisoners about their involvement in potentially illegal activities while in Blantyre," and that, "the intelligence over a period of time, was discussed at length with the governor." This was simply untrue - nothing of the kind had ever been discussed with me.

In relation to Wells, I had already risk assessed him and found him to be suitable for temporary release to work in the community. Tom Murtagh was unhappy with my decision which was why he arranged for Commander Gerard to do a thorough risk assessment on him. After his assessment, Commander Gerard wrote to Murtagh on 9 September 1999:

"**You asked for an assessment in respect of the above prisoner (Wells) and the proposal that he be allowed to participate in the resettlement programme from HMP Blantyre House. I am sorry that it was not possible to provide a response within the original timescale, but this has allowed me the opportunity to discuss this case fully with the various agencies involved, including the officers involved with the original conviction.**"

He continues:

"**None of the intelligence sources which have been consulted had any relevant information on Wells, nor is there any subsequent** to his conviction. Enquiries with NCIS revealed no active interest or recent contact from his former criminal associates."

He then concludes:

"I share the assessment that his risk of reoffending in the immediate future is low and would concur with the proposal to allow him to participate in the resettlement programme."

And a criminal investigation? Three weeks after the raid I received a note from my Head of security, PO Pete Collard:

"Dear Eoin, you will no doubt remember, after the last enquiry at Blantyre, the main reason for the action (raid) was given as 'intelligence received' and 'police investigations'. At that time, I asked Nick Bramwell, our police criminal intelligence liaison officer what he knew about such things. He assured me that he and his unit had no knowledge or involvement in that operation.

On Tuesday 23 May, I attended an area drugs meeting in Blantyre training unit. There were two members of the criminal intelligence unit in attendance, at the end of the meeting. Detective Sgt Chris Tomlin went out of his way to speak to me. He went to great lengths to assure me that neither he nor any of his squad had any knowledge of this operation or any current intelligence that warranted the actions that took place. He went to great lengths to reassure me this operation had nothing to do with his squad and they wanted to distance themselves from it.

I asked him if he knew of any current intelligence involving staff or inmates that would justify direct action of any sort and he said no. He expressed the personal opinion, as an outsider, that the actions appeared to be political.

I felt you should have this information, Yours sincerely - Pete Collard"

Yet on May 16, Paul Boateng tells the Home Affairs Select Committee:

"You will understand that there is an ongoing criminal investigation into matters that stem from the search. There was close police liaison around this operation, close use and detailed use of intelligence sources; and they are, and remain, serious causes of concern in relation to security, and there is an ongoing criminal investigation."

In actual fact no prisoner or member of staff at Blantyre House was interviewed by the police and no charges were ever brought against anyone.

I was beginning to receive copies of letters that had been sent to MPs from individuals who were clearly supportive of Blantyre House. Although these letters helped to counter my feelings of despair and hopelessness, I was infuriated by the replies which continually referred to these "frightening amounts of contraband" and "criminal investigations." It seemed clear to me that the service was determined to hide the truth and were prepared to pass on false information to the prison minister to cover up their own mistakes and poor decision-making.

Martin Narey had told me when I met him with Lynne Bowles on 9 May that there would be a non-disciplinary investigation into the search of the prison and I would be able to comment on emerging findings. At the time I took some reassurance from this as I believed an independent and impartial investigation would clear me and Blantyre of any wrongdoing. However, it transpired that Murtagh would in fact be commissioning a disciplinary investigation into the management of Blantyre, and that the former Governor, Brian Pollett, the same man who had presided over the only two of the most serious failings at Blantyre and had escaped with barely a slap on the wrist, would be the Senior Investigating Officer (SIO).

Within a moment, any reassurance I had about an independent investigation vanished. Murtagh was the man who dreamt up the raid and I had inherited the outcome of a tragedy and scandal at the prison from the former Governor who was now investigating me. Were these two individuals about to criticise their own actions? I very much doubted it and so once again, I phoned Lynne at the PGA.

"I don't know if it's just me, but I think it is totally wrong that Murtagh can commission a disciplinary investigation into the management of Blantyre House and appoint Brian Pollett as the SIO. It's like they are investigating themselves."

Lynne couldn't believe it. "You are joking! She said. "This is bloody madness. Look don't worry Eoin we'll get hold of Narey and put this right."

True to her word, Lynne and the President of the PGA Mike Newell, took it up and I was later notified in a letter, dated 12 June that Martin Narey would be the commissioning authority and Adrian Smith, who often deputised for Murtagh, would be the SIO. The letter also made it clear that it was not to be a disciplinary investigation and that I should be able to comment on emerging findings. I had hoped for a truly independent investigation. Adrian Smith was line managed by Murtagh and had been used before to undertake a disciplinary investigation into me which provided an outcome that Murtagh wanted. I always believed that that investigation was deeply flawed and challenged it vigorously. I was never charged or disciplined and I believe this was because the investigation was so defective that a proper case against me could never be made.

During those last days of May and for the bulk of June, I was involved in being interviewed and responding to countless written questions relating to the management of Blantyre House. As I was enduring this process it felt more like a perverse witch hunt rather than an independent investigation. Adrian Smith was always of the view that it should be a disciplinary investigation but Narey had given me his word that it would not be and confirmed that in his letter of 12 June.

Adrian Smith had decided to sequentially follow through on four lines of enquiry. In brief, these were my failure to follow security procedures, my non-compliance with a lawful order, my abuse of the ROTL system - and finally my mismanagement of the charity funds raised by the prison. Smith and his team of helpers, who were also part of Murtagh's Chaucer investigation team, tried their best to make a case against me. On each of their lines of enquiry, I was able to demonstrate that I had done nothing wrong or illegal and that I had complied with all prison policies and instructions. Since this was a non-disciplinary investigation I did not feel that I needed support or assistance from the PGA and although annoyed and angry with how the investigation team behaved towards me I did my best to be cooperative and open.

While this investigation was continuing, I was also writing up my thesis for the Master's Degree and preparing for the viva. I was also in regular contact with members of the Blantyre BOV who were writing to the prison's minister and local MPs about the inaccuracy of information being given both to the media and government. There was a debate raging between Sir David Ramsbotham (HMCIP) and Martin Narey over the content of the preface to the full inspection of Blantyre that took place in January 2000. Narey was unhappy that Ramsbotham had directly been critical of Murtagh and named him in the preface. Narey wanted all references to Murtagh to be removed and there was a stand-off which was causing the publication of the report to be delayed.

On the home front two of my children were sitting their GCSEs and A levels and Dorit and I did our best to keep my problems away from them. June was a fraught month for me and my morale and mood oscillated in accordance to what information I received or read in the media.

Apart from my interaction with the investigation team, I had no other contact from the Prison Service and June slipped into July. The Prison Service had decided to give the HASC an interim report on the investigation into the management of Blantyre House although it felt more like that it was into me. The HASC had not requested this interim report and I never saw a copy of it but I am sure it was designed to try and undermine whatever credibility I may have had with the HASC.

At long last the deadlock between Narey and Ramsbotham was broken and the inspection report on Blantyre House was published (26 July). Below is the original preface of the Inspection – and then the preface that was published:

HMCIP Sir David Ramsbotham:

"Following his inspection of HMP Blantyre House in 1992 my predecessor described the prison as: *'An example of all that is best about the Prison Service'*

In the preface to our follow-up inspection in 1997 I wrote:

'The whole ethos of Blantyre House and the excellence that it represents is that of a resettlement prison, and I strongly recommend that it should be so treated and regarded"

Following his visit to the prison in May 1998, the then director general of the Prison Service, now Sir Richard Tilt, wrote in the governors visitors' book:

'My first-ever visit to Blantyre house and I was delighted to see such a constructive atmosphere and purposeful establishment. The Governor and staff are to be congratulated of what they are doing'.

In June 1998, the then Director of Regimes, Mr Martin Narey, wrote in the same book, following his visit:

'If any establishment is delivering the government's manifesto commitment on constructive regimes it is Blantyre House. Its offending behaviour programmes, education and general atmosphere - with singularly impressive staff/prisoner relationships – are likely to make a real difference'.

However, these views appeared not to be shared by the area manager for Kent, who continued to regard Blantyre House as just another Category C training prison, with a resettlement function, and judge it according. The resulting tension so alarmed the very active Board of Visitors, that they wrote expressing their concerns to the Director General, Mr Martin Narey - who had succeeded Sir Richard Tilt - who revisited in July 1999, after which he wrote in the Governor's book:

'Blantyre House performs a valued role as a resettlement prison within the service. Its general ethos supports its special function, and I am committed to protecting this.

However, the Area Manager continued to believe otherwise, as did other parts of the Prison Service Headquarters. It was audited recently by the Operating Standards Team, and, unsurprisingly, to us at least, failed miserably as a category C prison, the level of security being nowhere near what is required of such an establishment. It is clear that the Lifer Management Unit regards Blantyre House as a category D/open prison equivalent, allocating life sentence prisoners there in response to Parole Board recommendations that they should go into open prison conditions.

The version that was finally published was identical to the above with the exception of any reference to the Area Manager of Kent being substituted with the words:

'other parts of Prison Service Headquarters'.

Perhaps this gives an indication of how protected Murtagh was by the senior management of the Service. Nevertheless, it was an excellent final report and concluded with this paragraph:

"Therefore, I conclude by praising the consistent, innovative and courageous approach of the Governor and staff at HMP Blantyre House to their very difficult and challenging task, on behalf of the public. It has established a reputation for excellence as a resettlement prison, a most difficult role, in which the recognition and support of the Minister and the Director General—and HM Chief Inspector— needs to be confirmed not only by official endorsement but early clarification of its future."

Two days later on 28 July, the HASC announced that they would hold a Select Committee enquiry into the raid at Blantyre House.

Chapter 17

I had been off work for nearly 3 months before the HASC announced that they would be holding a Parliamentary investigation into the events that took place at Blantyre on 5 May. During that time, I had not been idle. Despite the initial setback at Standford Hill, I was making good progress with my research project and had virtually completed the literary review, as well as the practical elements of my prison research.

I could not divorce myself from all the background noise relating to Blantyre and this was only to intensify now that the HASC had announced their investigation. Since the raid, there had been some Parliamentary activity, as well as various media comments. I was still bound by the gagging order and therefore was unable to make any comment to the media despite the fact that I had had several approaches.

I am indebted to those individuals, many of whom I did not know, who sent me messages of support as well as copies of letters/documents that had been leaked from Prison Service HQ. Colleagues in the PGA were a continual source of support and would draw my attention to various matters that were being discussed in Parliament.

Even before the HASC investigation got underway, Parliament was continuously being misled with the information given to them by Martin Narey and the prisons minister, Paul Boateng. An example of this was when on 16 May Narey/Boateng told the HASC that they had, "serious intelligence on Blantyre and the Governor" and that there was "a police criminal investigation underway," which clearly they could not make any further comment on. Not surprisingly, the HASC asked for an update on this criminal investigation but all they got was an inaccurate management report on the investigation into me that had been originally commissioned by Murtagh and subsequently taken over by Narey. The other notable deceit was under reporting the true financial cost to the fabric of Blantyre caused by the search staff during the raid. On 16 May Narey told the HASC that the cost of the damage to the fabric of the prison was in the region of £400, in fact, because the repair work had been undertaken by prison Works staff it was nearer £6000 – the true figure if staff wages had been factored in and if the repair work had been undertaken by outside contractors would have been in the tens of thousands.

As upsetting as these things were, I managed to immerse myself in the MSt but this became less possible once the HASC announced their investigation. Various members of the Blantyre BOV, Molly Tipples, David Smith, Lady Rosie Clark and Dr Brian Hugo played an incredible role in providing information to the HASC and unstinting support towards me. Behind the scenes, Mike Newell, David Rodden and Lynne Bowles from the PGA were doing their utmost best to make Narey realise that he had been duped by Murtagh into authorising the raid. They were able to demonstrate how Murtagh had misled them about the financial cost of the damage done during the raid and completely undermined Murtagh's claim about the amount of contraband found.

Although trade union officials are supposed to be free from any kind of retribution from senior managers relating to them undertaking their lawful trade union activities, even if it showed the Service in a not very flattering light, Mike Newell, president of the PGA was to pay a heavy price for his condemnation of the raid and his support for me. Through a series of subtle, and sometimes not so subtle, managerial manoeuvres, Mike was forced into a position where he felt he had no option but to take early retirement.

In the early weeks of August, it was clear that the Prison Service was on the back foot as more and more truths came out about events on the night of 5 May. From documents passed on to me from fellow civil servants at HQ it was evident that Narey realised he would not be able to continue with his offensive action against me because it was based on information provided by Murtagh and his Chaucer team. The Prison Service Secretariat was instructed to formulate a strategy that Narey could adopt with the HASC during their investigation. Various tasks were given to senior operational managers and main grade civil servants, and the Prison Service Secretariat went into overdrive in order to coordinate this strategy.

One of their strands was to ensure that I should be charged under the code of discipline investigation that was being undertaken by Adrian Smith. On 3 August, Phil Wheatley wrote to Smith to say that he will now be the commissioning officer for the investigation since Narey will be involved with the HASC investigation and this will avoid any conflicts of interest.

On 4 August, Smith served me with a DAPS-F.2. This is a form issued to staff when they are to be interviewed under caution. So, it is now a disciplinary investigation and a letter from Narey of 11 August confirms that he has gone back on his word that it would be a non-disciplinary investigation, and I could comment on emerging findings. August proved to be a very busy month for me. I had to attend Adrian Smith's investigation interviews, answer countless written questions, deal with requests of information from the HASC clerk, Andrew Kennon and continue with the write up of my MSt thesis.

There were lots of stories in the local media and they all were supportive of Blantyre, me and my Head of Inmate Activities, Dave Newport. Dave had joined the service as a trades officer and worked his way up through the ranks to become a very competent Head of Works. Following a major restructure of the rank system, Dave opted to leave the Works function and become a generic operational governor grade. He had worked at Blantyre for several years and was a fantastic member of my SMT. He was highly regarded by all the prisoners and well respected by the staff. I could not have wished for a better colleague and his support to me was both immeasurable and invaluable. Dave had told me that he would retire when he was fifty seven and a half and that was going to be in the Autumn of 2000.

Murtagh tended to be hostile to my SMT because they were all so supportive of me and Blantyre. He would mask this hostility under the banner of humour, but it was not difficult to see through that. When I was removed as governor so was Dave Newport removed from his post and he was dispatched to another prison to take on the Head of Works position until he was to retire three months later. Moving to prison is like starting a new job and Dave was expected to pick up Head of Works duties immediately despite the fact that he had not done that type of work for several years. This decision it smacked of punishment and Dave did not deserve it. Not surprisingly, Dave lodged a complaint against Murtagh which was investigated by a senior manager, who was close to the upper echelons of the Service. His complaint was not upheld.

Murtagh was certainly being supported by the most senior managers in the service. I knew that if it was not for the BOV, HMCIP and the HASC, I would be dead in the water. When senior management closes ranks you become powerless and it matters not what is right or truthful. Unlike others who have been treated unfairly in the service, I gradually garnered some very powerful allies who helped me to get the truth out to the media which had a field day highlighting the untruths and inconsistencies that had become a trademark of Prison Service modus operandi. The satirical magazine Private Eye was on the case and exposed so many embarrassing issues that the story ran for 12 consecutive editions.

The investigation into me rumbled on and it was clear that they were desperate to charge me with something. Fortunately for me one of the lead investigators was Ron Gooday of the Chaucer team. He was so intent on trying to nail me that his research into Prison Service polices on ROTL was scant and he made basic errors and completely misunderstood the Categories of ROTL. I was relieved to have been able to expose his ignorance and close down any further investigation into that area. Having unsuccessfully tried to get me for disobeying a lawful order, abusing ROTL, and failing to comply with security requirements they were forced to revisit the audit undertaken into charitable work two years before. It was a bit like déjà vu but I had no choice, I cooperated with their disciplinary investigation.

All the positive media reporting made home life easier now because some friends, who had originally been wary of me due to the initial wave of negative publicity now realised what the truth was. Documents sent to me from someone at HQ revealed that Clare Checksfield and Tony Watson, from the Prison Service secretariat, were coordinating the preparations for the Service's appearance before the HASC enquiry. It was interesting to note which operational managers were assigned to various tasks and it was clear that they knew they were in for a rough ride. One of the operational managers tasked by the secretariat was a woman called Claudia Sturt. I did not know her at all but she was to surface again in a rather bizarre and unhelpful manner later on in my career.

Written evidence had to be submitted to the HASC by the end of September and on the 26th of that month, I got a phone call at home from Michael Spurr telling me to report to HQ the following day at 10 am. Other than the investigation team, I had not been contacted by anyone in the line to check to see how I was. There was no duty of care, not that by then I particularly wanted that from them. I was being well supported by my family, the PGA and of course the BOV. Michael Spurr had been a Governor but was now the Area Manager for the Eastern region and although I knew of him, I did not know him at all.

"What do you want me to come up to HQ for?" I asked.

"I need to charge you under the code of discipline for financial irregularities and you need to sign for the papers," he said.

I was annoyed at his nerve. No one in the line makes any effort to contact me and then, out of the blue, I get a call saying get to HQ so that I can be charged under the code of discipline.

"I'm not coming, "I said. "You can post them to me, and I will sign and return them to you."

Michael was a bit surprised at my response.

"I don't like doing business like that," he said

"And I don't like the fact that no one in the line has contacted me for months and then you just phone me out of the blue and expect me to come into HQ so that you can charge me. No - you post them," I said.

There was a pause, I could tell that Michael had not expected my response and I broke the silence by asking him if my Head of Management Services, Margaret Andrews would be charged as well. Margaret was responsible for the day to day finances of the prison and so it would be very difficult to charge me without also charging her.

"Yes," he said, "and I was going to call her after you."

Margaret was a career civil servant who had worked at Blantyre for many years. She was excellent at her job and dedicated to her work. She was totally signed up to the Blantyre ethos and played a full part in all SMT decisions. I knew she would be devastated to get a call telling her that she was to be charged under the code of discipline. I explained this to Michael and suggested that he should let me speak with Margaret first so that she was prepared. Michael agreed to this and before our call finished, I asked him what the sudden rush was to lay these charges.

"Written evidence has to be into the HASC by the end of the month and we want them to know you have been charged under the code of discipline."

So that was their game. I was not surprised by his response to my question and in a strange way, it made me feel more confident about the HASC enquiry. To do this to me must be the actions of desperation. They would do their best to undermine any credibility I had with the HASC. It was a character assassination plot and poor Margaret would just be collateral damage.

I phoned Margaret and explained what was going to happen. She was no fool and she expected something like this. She asked me if I would assist and support her during the disciplinary hearing. Of course I agreed to that and I knew we would work well together in defending ourselves against what we both knew were trumped-up charges.

I was notified by the HASC clerk that they would be taking oral evidence at Blantyre House on 17 October since they wanted to hear from some prisoners. I could attend as an observer since I would be required to give evidence the following day at the Palace of Westminster. I had never been involved with a Select Committee before and I was a little anxious. The proceedings would be televised and everything would be subject to the scrutiny of the media. In essence, I would be fighting the organisation I had worked for loyally during the last 22 years and I knew they would stop at nothing to damage my reputation and criticise my managerial style. All I could do was prepare myself for what was to come and simply tell the truth.

Chapter 18

I woke early on Tuesday, 17 October, a bit apprehensive about the day not knowing what to expect. It was odd driving to Blantyre again, a journey I had not done for months. I had arranged to meet David Roddan, General Secretary of the PGA at the Blantyre training centre, a barn-like staff facility where the HASC would convene. When I arrived, the HASC members were already assembled and all those who were to give oral evidence were congregated outside the centre or in the waiting area by the kitchen.

Apart from those who were to give evidence, there were some members of Blantyre staff who were off duty, including Dave Newport, my trusted colleague and friend. There were also one or two main grade civil servants from HQ, who were obviously there to observe and report back to Martin Narey.

I chatted with Dave and the off-duty Blantyre staff who were excited about the HASC enquiry since they firmly believed it would expose the truth about the raid. They reassured me that things would work out okay and that I and Blantyre would be vindicated. I knew that it was not possible for them to know that, but I happily accepted their reassurance in the spirit it was given.

When the HASC were ready, we entered the room and took our seats. As I walked in one of the HASC members commented, "Good afternoon Eoin, don't worry you are among friends." This immediately put me at ease. David Roddan looked at me with a big smile plastered across his face. I certainly felt more relaxed after the brief conversations as we waited.

The Home Affairs Select Committee members taking evidence comprised of the Chair, Lord Robin Corbett, accompanied by Ian Cawsey MP, Janet Dean MP, Gerald Howarth MP, Martin Linton MP, Humphrey Malins MP, Paul Stinchcombe MP and David Winnick MP.

The former prisoner

The first witness to give evidence was a former prisoner, Steven Jones. Jones presented as your stereotypical East End villain, tall, stocky with a gravelly voice. He had committed armed robberies and subsequently moved into the class A drugs trade. He had spent the best part of four years at Blantyre and for a significant part of that time he had been working as a drug counsellor having gained the necessary qualifications while at Blantyre. He had been paroled and was now working for the local Health Trust in their addictions unit at Tunbridge Wells.

He nodded to me as he stepped forward to give his evidence. He had very clear views about why the raid took place and he spoke so eloquently about the trust that existed between staff and prisoners. As he answered the panel's questions and spoke so positively about the difference Blantyre had made to the lives of so many prisoners I felt a distinct sense of pride beginning to return to me about what I had been trying to achieve at Blantyre.

Lord Corbett welcomed Jones to the proceedings and explained that other panel members would also be asking him some questions. He acknowledged this and then Robin began taking his evidence:

LC: Some of us had the pleasure of meeting you and your colleagues when we were here earlier in the year. I wonder if I might start by asking you to give us your views as to how you think the changes that have been made as a result of the raid on 5/6 May have affected the ethos of Blantyre House and how you feel that prisoners have reacted to this?

SJ: I think it has got to have an impact. If you were to try and sum up Blantyre House in one word it would have to be "trust". Excessive security is not needed at Blantyre.

LC: What would you describe as "excessive security"?

SJ: The raid itself and the way they conducted it and the way they searched the premises and kept the prisoners awake all night, and drug-tested them. If you look at the history of Blantyre and the results it has achieved, there is no way they can justify what they did and how they did it. That has got to have an impact. If you were to strip-search prisoners every time they go out of the prison then, arguably, you should not be letting them out anyway, if you do not trust them enough. Trust is a funny thing as well. It is not just one-sided, it is not just about the Governor and the staff trusting us as prisoners, it is about us actually learning to trust them as well and trust their judgment.

LC: We have been told by the Area Manager, Mr Murtagh, of his full and continuing commitment to the resettlement role of Blantyre House. Since the removal of the former governor and these other events, do you feel confident you can rely on that?

SJ: No, I do not. I think resettlement is a totally alien concept to the Prison Service itself; nearly 65,000 prisoners and only three resettlement prisons. They have got away with paying lip service to resettlement for donkeys years now and it looks like they are going to continue to do that. As far as I understand, Mr Narey told the Committee when he was called before you how precious Blantyre was and the regime. That is laughable when, over a period of years, they have consistently tried to destroy the system. Up until the visit on March 1, they were going to change Blantyre into a young offenders institute. No, I have got little confidence, if any at all, that Blantyre will survive. If you take the element of trust out of Blantyre you destroy it, it just folds in on itself. At the beginning, I said I believed they were going to destroy Blantyre by stealth, and I think that is what they are doing, bit by bit. It will become an ordinary C-cat prison.

LC: There have been all sorts of allegations that on the night of May 5 keys could not be found, which is why an enormous amount of damage was done around Blantyre House. You have good knowledge of this place. Is it conceivable that keys, which were supposed to be in the gatehouse and checked three times to see whether they are there or not every 24 hours, that that position could arise—that no one could find the keys that they said they wanted?

SJ: I would say no. Prison officers and staff have got their own little boxes on the gate and it is pretty routine for them to put their keys in there. I have been on the receiving end of raids in different prisons by Mufti squads, armoured up, and the adrenalin starts going and there is a gung-ho attitude. I think that is what happened here. I think this was a lesson.

LC: So are you suggesting that they were not bothered whether there were keys or not because they were going to get in another way, with brute force?

SJ: Yes, absolutely. I am suggesting that, yes.

Humphrey Malins MP

HM: You are a drug counsellor?

SJ: I am, yes.

HM: As a lead-up to this raid on May 5, one would have imagined that the authorities suspected that all the prisoners were on drugs. Am I right in saying that all prisoners were tested and none of them tested positive?

SJ: Absolutely remarkable, is it not? It is true.

HM: They did not know the raid was coming?

SJ: No, of course not.

HM: So the result is either they had no such intelligence or they had intelligence which was absolute rubbish.

SJ: First of all, it is remarkable—I actually drug-test, maybe, 30 or 40 people a week as part of my job—to pick 120 people at random in any community anywhere in this Country and get a totally 100 per cent negative test back, let alone a prison. The fact is there is not a drug culture within Blantyre House; there is not and never has been since I have been there. What drug use there was occasionally was done very, very secretly.

HM: Any suggestions to the contrary by the authorities was entirely erroneous?

SJ: It comes back to the point of "Where's the evidence? Prove it." Blantyre's figures have consistently been the lowest in the service.

David Winnick MP

DW: Do you take the view that the whole purpose of the exercise to search on 5 May was to change out of all recognition this institution?

SJ: I believe it is that and, also, a mixture of two prison governors who would not toe the line on "bang them up and shut them up" policies that dictate the Prison Service in general.

DW: Why do you say that?

SJ: I say that because in every other prison I have been in, there is an air of despondency, despair, no hope, prisoners sitting about, basically, planning future crimes and making new friends to commit them with. Blantyre is different. There is an air of enthusiasm about Blantyre. You will find groups of prisoners sitting down and talking about college, university, their families, and what job they are doing. I am still in the same job now that I started at Blantyre House in March 1996. I am still there now and I started there as a volunteer. Yes, I think the idea was not just to destroy Blantyre once their plans to turn it into a young offenders institute were thwarted. Not just that, but I also see it as an act of revenge, to some extent, on the two governors involved.

DW: Do you feel, particularly, as far as the last governor is concerned, that there was a feeling in the Prison Service that he was too soft and that he did not know how to deal with those who had been convicted by the courts?

SJ: First of all, I would like to go on the record and say that there is no such thing as an easy prison. There really is not. Ninety-one people committed suicide in our jails last year; 91 people thought that the circumstances they were in were so bad they preferred death to living. That is all our fault for doing little or nothing about it. There is no such thing. As far as calling Blantyre a soft option, what it does is challenge our past behaviour, and behavioural change, as I know in my occupation, is one of the hardest things for human beings to do. It is very difficult to change that behaviour.

DW: It is not that I disagree with you, but do you feel that the Prison Service felt that the previous governor was soft?

SJ: He was not soft in any description at all. Do I think? Yes, I do think that, but in the 3 years and 4 months I was at Blantyre he certainly shipped out upwards of between 70 to 100 prisoners, I should think, to other prisons for not conforming to the regime at Blantyre.

DW: Would it not be right to say that he worked on the basis that he expected full cooperation from prisoners and once they acted in a way which he believed betrayed the confidence he put in them they were asked to leave or told to leave?

SJ: I was going to say "asked" is, perhaps, a polite way of putting it but, yes, shipped out to a more secure prison.

DW: That happened on a number of occasions?

SJ: Yes, absolutely, yes.

Ian Cawsey MP

IC: You said in a previous answer that the thing that made Blantyre stand out to you was the feeling of enthusiasm and perhaps optimism as well. Since 5 May, to what extent has that changed amongst the prisoners, staff and voluntary workers as well?

SJ: I have had contact with all three parties. Obviously security has been rearranged and upped. Again, it is not the same Blantyre, and there is not that same enthusiasm, that same feeling of trust. It is so hard to explain because it is such a big thing. It is not just the matter that you are being trusted and let out of the door to come back, Blantyre instils in you over a matter of months a feeling of not just trust of the prison governor and staff who are letting you out but responsibility for coming back, responsibility for not offending while you are out. It becomes a collective responsibility within the prison, not just an individual one.

IC: There is always a natural resistance to change but do you feel that this is much more significant than that and this is not going to settle down? There is going to have to be some change to the regime if Blantyre is going to return to its former glory, for want of a better phrase.

SJ: I feel very despondent. I do not think it will go back to what it was. I think whatever the outcome of this inquiry, the Prison Service has won, they have done what they wanted to do and that is destroy the regime at Blantyre House. Blantyre House has found a very successful way of reintegrating prisoners back into society but doing it in a very controlled way. If you have lived, as I did for most of my adult life, outside the law and outside of society's rules and norms, it is very difficult to get back into that, especially if society rejects you, as they often do, for being an ex-offender. At the end of the day if you will not let people like me reintegrate back into society then I am not likely to respect it or want to contribute towards it. That is how important the work is that happens at Blantyre.

Gerald Howarth MP

GH: The Area Manager told us this morning, that intelligence had come to light towards the end of April which meant they had to move and had to move quickly. The implication was quite clearly that there was a threat to public safety. Can you tell us whether in your experience there ever was a realistic threat to public safety, particularly the security of people living nearby and those organisations with which prisoners were working?

SJ: Not to my knowledge but again, what we have got to accept is even though the Prison Service prefer risk aversion to risk management, they are in the risk business. That is the business they are in. They are dealing with offenders and ex-offenders, that is the business they are in, and they do have to take risks. It seems funny listening to your statement that there have been no follow-up charges or investigations by the police. How good was this intelligence? That must be the question.

Board of Visitors

The next witnesses were five members of the Board of Visitors - David Cottle, Molly Tipples, (Lady) Rosie Clarke, Dr. Brian Hugo and Helen Warriner. They entered the room together and sat opposite the panel. Lord Corbett welcomed them and thanked them for agreeing to give evidence. Their evidence was clear and straightforward and nothing they said surprised me. They described the excellent relationships that existed between Blantyre and the local community, commented on the fact that vocational training had all but been abolished since the raid and talked about the so called 'escape equipment' that was found on the night of the raid.

Lord Corbett asked David Cottle: Do you detect big differences in the way the present governor thinks it is his responsibility to run the prison from the earlier governor, the former governor? DC: Absolutely, yes. You need imagination, you need to understand resettlement, you need to understand people, risk management and so forth to take it forward. With the governor who is running the place at the moment, it is very difficult for him because obviously everyone is watching the place. The changes which are going on are bringing the security measures round to a sort of Category C basis, which generally means you have control. Well, Blantyre was not run on a control basis, it was run on a trust basis. Break the trust and, yes, you go.

LC: We understand that the new governor has clamped down very severely on inmates taking driving lessons, either standard driving lessons or HGV or whatever, which have been useful, it has been put to us by many people.

DC: Yes.

LC: Were you consulted over that?

DC: No.

LC: Would you have expected to be consulted? If not, would you be able to make representations if you felt you wanted to?

DC: We said we were not happy beforehand, but we were told this was not in line with Prison Service policy; it would not be acceptable to the public. We have made…

LC: Forgive me, but you know they are encouraged at Kirklevington apparently? (Kirklevington was then one of the three resettlement prisons in the Country and actively encouraged the men there to train and learn work skills including HGV driving.)

DC: Yes, we have quoted that. Even on the basis of Blantyre or driving lessons in general, we have talked to Martin Narey about it, and we have talked to the Prison Reform Trust because the board thinks it is important; it is a very important base skill. Certainly in a resettlement regime there are no security threats, it is not costing the Prison Service money because it is funded either by the men themselves or the Blantyre Voluntary Fund. As far as the risk goes, if the man is out anyway, the risk is even less when he is on a driving lesson because he is picked up at the gate and dropped back again.

LC: Are you aware of unspecified plans to reorganise the education department and to treat a large part of the work it does now, which leads to some form of accreditation, as purely recreational?

DC: Yes, I have heard of this. Lady Clarke has our education brief on the board, and she understands what is happening in education.

Rosie Clarke then interjected: The education and vocational training is absolutely fundamental to the work which Blantyre is doing. It gives individual attention to each man to find a job for when he is released. It is not just a token gesture to get a man painting in the art studio, it is actually working towards a life after prison, which is what this place is all about.

LC: Have you heard of proposals or plans to reorganise it?

RC: Yes.

LC: But unspecified?

RC: Unspecified and specified. We have an excellent vocational trainer here whom the men trust and believe in. He offered his resignation some while ago but said he would stay on until he was replaced and I understand under the present regime no efforts are being made to replace him. As the funds in the vocational fund are administered by him and applied to the men, and the men are encouraged to take up training, without him there is no future for these men. He works in close contact with our education officer so they can tailor-make a programme for each man.

LC: Do you have views on the governor's decision—I think he said on security grounds—to discontinue the photography classes and club?

RC: My understanding on that is that during the raid a photograph was found of a key, and it has all spun off from that.

LC: Do you happen to know where that key normally lives?

RC: I think it was a man's door key. (All prisoners at Blantyre House held their own keys to their rooms.)

LC: It lives in one of the prisoner's pockets, yes.

RC: Yes. I think in photography the idea was you pinned on something, a specific object, and then did a project on it, and he—quite rightly in my opinion—thought the key was rather big in his life and did his project on that.

Damage

David Winnick MP then asked David Cottle about the damage he found when he returned to the prison on the Saturday morning:

DC: I came in in the morning and there had obviously been a massive disturbance.

DW: Tell us in your own words, what did you discover?

DC: I think I am right in saying I came into the prison at approximately 11 o'clock in the morning, went round to the men and was told, "Why weren't you here last night?". I said, "I was", and they said, "Have you seen the chapel?" I said, "What has happened to the chapel?" and they said, "It's sacrilege, they have broken down the doors."

DW: The door was broken down?

DC: Yes. I therefore conducted a complete tour of the prison, looking at the damage and reporting on it into a pocket memo which I carried with me. The chapel door into the chaplain's room had been smashed down and two other doors. I was astonished; it was quite unnecessary. I then later heard the medical centre doors had been broken down and sure enough, they had.

DW: Were you shocked?

DC: I was appalled. In fact later, when I saw the new governor, I told him and his second governor that I was shocked at the chaos I saw and it appeared to me totally unnecessary.

DW: One of the prisoners said that the search was carried out as if it was by storm-troopers.

DC: It was an appalling mess. If our men had rioted, which they did not, it would have been a lovely story for the press.

Bullying

David Winnick MP then asked David about his perception of the relationship between myself and Tom Murtagh.

DW: I just want to ask, if I may, about the relationship between the previous governor and the area manager. The area manager of course was the person who was responsible for initiating the raid, and the search, which was of course given authorisation by the Director General of the Prison Service, and we asked questions about that in the House of Commons when we had the witnesses before us. What was your impression of the relationship between the previous governor and the area manager?

DC: There was certainly, I think, a difference. This is subjective but certainly a difference in the way they viewed prisons, and resettlement prisons. I think that the area manager likes control, as do most people in the Prison Service, and when you have a special unit, a special resettlement unit that is actually doing pioneering work, innovative pioneering work, the two do not quite meld together in the way they should. So I would say there was probably a professional difference. Although we were aware of a difference of opinion in maybe how Blantyre should be run or the way you should run a prison, there was certainly no animosity that we were aware of or tension because Mr McLennan Murray always spoke well of Mr Murtagh as a professional. Equally, Mr Murtagh—

But then, as David Cottle was being questioned Rosie Clarke brought the colour to my cheeks when she interjected again and said: "Can I just say that the Board had the impression that the governor was being bullied by the area manager and he had a strong enough personality to cope with it."

At this my heart started to race, I could feel that people were looking at me.

DW: He did have?

RC: Yes, but we were concerned about his state of health and for that reason we wanted to get in the Director General of the Prison Service, we were worried about the state of bullying of the governor.

DW: Lady Clarke, that is a very serious accusation to make.

RC: It was one which was discussed at meetings many times.

DW: I am not suggesting for one moment you should not say it, but you are quite clear in your own mind—

RC: Quite clear.

DW: —that the governor was being bullied and was that the impression of your other colleagues?

David Cottle: I think I would have to go along with that, yes.

Molly Tipples: It was not the governor who came to us saying, "I'm being bullied", It was Dr Hugo, as a professional doctor, who came to the board and said he was worried about the state of the governor's health because he felt the pressure being put on him amounted to bullying and he came to us as a board. I and the then chairman saw Martin Narey and said we were worried. He then came down and the results which followed are well-known.

Brian Hugo: A letter was sent by our chairman at that time in fact, because we were very concerned that there were being very heavy pressures put on the governor.

DW: Bullied?

BH: I would have said that, yes. That is accepted by various other persons we have spoken to who have been in similar—

DW: Thank you very much.

The issue of bullying came as a shock to me. It was totally unexpected. I could only think about what I would say if I was asked the next day about whether I felt I was being bullied by Murtagh. Should I say no and contradict the BOV or were they right? I thought about how Murtagh spoke to me, not just in private but in front of other staff as well. I thought about the wind-up telephone call he had made to me about the Sunday People story of Wells, 'swanning all over Kent'. But admitting to being bullied is not easy, it makes you feel inadequate, a victim that has no control. I just didn't know what I would do.

Everybody knew Tom Murtagh's reputation, but all the Kent governors just accepted it and it was described by senior managers, such as Narey, as 'a robust style of management'. I knew that if questioned the next day about bullying I would have to give examples. Often, bullying takes place in private and so there are no witnesses to corroborate any allegations that may ensue. However, I could remember occasions when Murtagh acted in a manner which could be described as bullying in front of witnesses and so I decided that I would use such examples if asked by the HASC the next day. I remembered a couple of memos I received from an officer support grade (OSG) and a Senior officer in May of the previous year.

SJ:

MEMO from O.S.G. Newton to S.O. Golding dated 20 May 1999;

"On the 19/5/99, I received a phone call at approx 18:00 hours. The person on the other end of the line, demanded to know who I was, I replied 'Who do you want'. He wanted to know if there were any duty governors on, I told him that they had all gone home, and then he wanted to know which SO was on duty. I told him it was S.O. Golding; I found S.O. Golding's location, which was the officers mess, I asked this person if he wanted me to 'drag him out', but the reply was 'No, it's the area manager you can deal with it, ring the governor at home and tell him to make sure he gets his backside in his office at no later than 8.30 in the morning ready to receive an urgent phone call ref: clarification of some paperwork. You can tell him in those words'. With that he put the phone down.

I informed S.O. Golding, and commented on the attitude of the area manager; I contacted the governor at home and relayed the message to him.

The governor said that he would ring Mr Murtagh at home because he had an appointment on the morning in question.

I feel that he (Area Manager) was using his authority in an unreasonable and unprofessional manner.

Signed by Angie Newton.

Memo from S.O. Steve Golding to the governor dated 20 May 1999.

"Sir,

I would like to bring to your attention a memo from O.S.G. Newton regarding a telephone call she received from our area manager. I am appalled that firstly O.S.G. Newton had such difficulty in obtaining the identification of the apparently irrate person who was demanding to know which staff were on duty, and secondly that an area manager should talk about the governing Governor in such a derogatory and disrespectful way to any member of that governor's staff.

How can staff be expected to treat their governor with respect when he is belittled in such a way by his superior?

Signed by Steve Golding

I could think of other examples as well, but then my mind focused back in on the evidence being given by members of the BOV.

Local Community

Gerald Howarth MP asked about the attitude of the local community towards Blantyre House and the prisoners. Their answers were emphatic.

GH: Are you in any sense, as it were, the representatives of the local community?

DC: Yes.

MT: Yes.

RC: The eyes and ears of the public.

MT: The eyes and ears of the public.

GH: So you are the eyes and ears of the public and therefore to a large extent the public looks to you to make sure all is well in this establishment.

MT: Yes.

Gerald Howarth: What was the local reputation of this establishment, in your view?

MT: Excellent.

DC: Excellent.

GH: So people were not concerned about fears for their safety?

MT: No. People locally are very proud of their prison, or they have been up to now, very proud. They know the results, they see the men around, they come past, they can see in, there is no fear, they think they know what is going on because they cannot see anything amiss, and the people in can see out.

RC: There is not a village hall or a church or school round here that has not been supported by men from Blantyre House.

GH: So the trust that we have heard so much about today applied as much to the local community putting their faith and their trust in the regime at this prison?

RC: We are all from the local community, so we are in touch with our—

GH: It would be wrong, in your view, to suggest that there was a risk to public safety from the regime being run here.

MT: When they put on the pantomime, which they do brilliantly, in March—because that is when they can get the equipment—the local brownies, the local schools, they all come and bring their children in to see this. There is no fear at all about what is here, and there are long-term criminals.

Escape equipment

Gerald Howarth: Can I ask you if the public's attitude to this establishment has changed since the events of 5 May?

DC: I think the public wonder what is going on. They have read newspaper reports about escape equipment which was in the building, building tools and things like this. Yes, there was a perception—

GH: I am sorry. Escape equipment?

DC: That was in a Prison Service press release that was published in the local papers. It was stated that there was escape equipment found in the search.

GH: Was it escape equipment?

DC: It was a chap's spirit level and trowel, and so forth. Building equipment.

GH: A spirit level to spirit him away?

GH: We agree it should not have been there, but it could not be described as escape equipment.

DC: It was an interpretation because I rang the Area Manager and asked him about escape equipment, thinking that we might not have been told something and it was building equipment.

MT: He had come in from work one day and was going out to work for Mencap for free at 6 o'clock the following morning. He should not have taken it into his room but he had taken it into his room, instead of leaving it at the gate, because he did not think anyone would be at the gate to give it to him the next morning.

GH: Was this, perhaps, just one example of an element of lax security at the prison?

MT: Yes, probably. It should not have gone into the prison.

DC: Certainly the Board—no one—has questioned the fact that the stuff should not have been in there, but that it would be used for escapes, no. If you want to find something to dig your way out of Blantyre you can find something.

BH: If you work outside, why take it in?

DC: Even the ones who do not go outside, you are not going to dig your way out with a bricklayer's trowel. There are better pieces of equipment around, or you could find a way out of Blantyre.

GH: What is your view? Do you think the events of 5 May were justified? Do you feel that you were kept as informed as Prison Service regulations require Boards of Visitors to be kept informed?

DC: No, on the first two counts. We were not informed properly, especially before, on the night. We do not feel—unless anything else comes to light—that it was justified.

Next to give evidence were the chaplaincy team and the Education department. Ironically, Rev John Bourne, the part-time prison chaplain and Rev Dave Adkins, from a church in Tunbridge Wells, had both been police officers prior to their ordination. Their evidence was sincere and measured and clarified the issue of keys allegedly not being available on the night of the raid.

Lord Corbett welcomed the witnesses:

LC: Good afternoon, again, to you. Can I just ask a question of those of you who represent the Chaplaincy? Again, I think most of you, if not all, have a long connection with Blantyre House and those who work there—and I mean work there—both the prisoners and the staff. Would you give us, please, a couple of opinions about what changes you detect have taken place since that raid on 5/6 May?

Rev JB: Certainly. I am John Bourne, and I am the Anglican part-time Chaplain at Blantyre and, also Vicar of the Parish of Marden, the nearby village. The effect of the raid has been, as you have heard so well put by others, a tremendous loss of morale amongst staff because their conduct and the way they were running things has been called into question—their judgment and integrity. For the men, where they come from a system where there was an "us and them" culture, they come into a culture where through working together there was trust, there was responsibility and there was respect. They have certainly seen that shattered. Their perception is "Well, it was all a dream, it was an illusion. This is reality. It is us and them".

LC: Do you have experience in other prisons?

Rev JB: No, my background is that I was in the police for 18 years, so coming into the Prison Service and coming to Blantyre as Chaplain, I took an awful lot of convincing about what was going on here. However, seeing the work that the then-governor, Jim Semple, was doing I was enormously impressed.

LC: You had spent a large part of your life trying to get them put in there, as it were.

Rev JB: Yes. So there was an enormous culture shock in seeing how well they were treated and the respect they were given. I began to see the enormous value of it and, in the community of Marden, of which I am the vicar, we have seen men come down and work in the church, help old ladies and doing work in the school.

Lord Corbett then turned to Dave Adkins: Reverend Adkins?

Rev DA: I have not had experience of the Prison Service since the raid but prior to the raid, I came here a number of times. I am an ex-police officer, too. I spent 25 years in the Metropolitan Police, and I was on the team that arrested the Kray Twin gang, so I have experience with prisoners and the like. So to come here was quite a culture shock for me because I had been in closed prisons where there was an awful atmosphere. To come here and see the respect there was on both sides, and the fact they did seem to work together so very clearly, and the governor was willing to let his men come out to the church and do work, I was so impressed with these men because they could be trusted. They had a keen sense of self-discipline, by that time, instilled in them and they work exceedingly hard. One Christmas, we were hard put to staff a place for the homeless—a homeless shelter. They totally staffed it for a week and, actually, the money came out of their own pockets to pay for some of the food—turkeys and so on. It was not asked for, they actually volunteered. It was brilliantly done. I have stayed friends with four men, in particular, who worked so well in the church. They are now out of prison and they have not re-offended. Some of them are still working in the church, I am in contact with all of them, and I am proud to call them friends. They do mix with my family. I think the work the previous governor did is brilliant.

Janet Dean MP

Janet Dean then turned to Francoise Fletcher, Head of Education at Blantyre, and Mike Duff the photography teacher, who gave damning evidence about the callous behaviour of the search team and their total disregard for the educational work of prisoners involved in the photography class.

JD: Can I turn to Francoise Fletcher and her colleagues from the education department and ask what changes there have been, or are planned, to be made in the education department, with particular reference to the lack of photography now?

FF: Yes. That is a good question. We do not know what changes are planned for us. The governor who is in charge of education at the moment has told me several times "If it is not working you do not need to mend it". The governor in charge of security tells me the education programme is going to be changed totally, and this has been said to me several times. As a result of it I have absolutely no idea what is planned. What has changed is that in the past the programme of education was discussed and negotiated with the head of inmate activities. Now, the programme is imposed, pretty much as the photography class was cancelled. The photography class was cancelled on Friday. I was told "This class is closed. There is no discussion." The previous Monday— the Monday of the same week—the Governor, Mr Bartlett, had asked me to explain what the photography class was about, how the accreditation was gained and how we were keeping track of the cameras, and so on. I explained it all to him. I brought one of the booklets that the men have because this class is accredited, and, in fact, I was told on the same day, "This is fine, there is no problem". On Friday I am told "Close it". No discussion. Since then I have been told "It has gone. Do not even talk about it". Now this is a class where, this year, men were accredited not only at level 1 but up to level 3. We have had, in the past, a number of men who have discovered photography here and gone on to higher education and finding jobs involving photography and doing degrees. We also, as was mentioned before, were represented at the Koestler Awards. I went to the awards this year and there was a photography section. I questioned the reasons why the class was closed. I was told the class was closed for security reasons. Reasonable alternatives, in my mind, were offered. For example, the photography tutor would dedicate the first hour of each of his sessions to going round taking pictures and then coming back, the cameras would be taken away from the men and, therefore, nobody would have a camera in-hand, or if, because of the nature of the work required, (at times they have to take pictures early in the morning, or late at night, or different times of the day), I would have gone with the men and the cameras would never have been out of my sight, and then taken away again from the men. This I was told, "No discussion. The class is closed. There is no negotiation".

JD: What you are saying is that other prisons have photography classes?

FF: Yes. Not many, I gather. Wandsworth has a class. Certainly, photography was represented at the Koestler Awards, so there are photography classes at other establishments. Mike Duff: We have won the Koestler Awards practically every year—in fact, every year. We also had a student who won a national competition, and I took him up to London to present him with his prize—all those kinds of achievements. What puzzles me is that I ran the photography class for seven years and there was never a problem with security. The rules were tightened up at one point because worries were expressed about security, but we made that work and, as Francoise has said, we were quite willing to tighten up even more, if necessary.

Lord Corbett

LC: Mr Duff, did any of these classes lead to jobs where people used photography, or was it for other reasons?

MD: Yes. One chap is working, I believe, for the national press now. We had a chap who went to Greenwich to do media studies at degree level. Various people have used photography to enhance other work as well. So it kind of spreads out. Also, we found that people came into photography because they found it a friendly subject, if you like; it was not a subject they felt intimidated by and, very often, because you get to know people and you discuss things with them, people would go on to do other subjects they might not have felt able to do. In that sense, it was very positive. It seems to me that no—what I would call—proper reason has been given for closing the class.

JD: Going back, are there problems with other subjects? Do you foresee changes in the way you are able to teach other subjects in the future?

FF: Yes, I do foresee problems. One of the problems is that the Home Office only monitors results in literacy and numeracy. None of the other subjects, although they are accredited by Blantyre, are seen as having educational value, and I have been told that the wide range of classes that we run—i.e., art, pottery, woodwork, decorative painting techniques and languages—are all seen as recreational classes with no educational value.

JD: Can I ask you by whom you have been told that?

FF: By one of the governors.

Humphrey Malins MP

HM: Just arising out the education issue, Ms Fletcher, I think all of us would agree that education is an absolutely vital aspect for all prisons, in that qualities of hope and enthusiasm are essential qualities in prison staff. With that backcloth, has it ever been said to you about Blantyre prisoners that "these men are all beyond redemption"?

FF: Yes, it has.

HM: Who said that?

FF: Mr Murtagh.

HM: The Area Manager?

FF: Yes.

David Winnick MP

DW: Can you tell us when he said that?

FF: He said that on 5 July.

DW: In what context? It seems odd that suddenly, out of nowhere, he should make such a comment.

FF: We had, on that day, a visit from Mr Paul Boateng. (Then Prisons Minister). Mr Boateng spent quite a long time in education. Also, his visit took place after the classes had finished. Therefore, he did not have a chance to see the students or to see classes in action. But he did spend a lot of time in education and was very interested in the fact that the education department at Blantyre is unique and offers a lot more classes than normal education departments would in a normal prison. Mr Boateng came to visit and when he came around the department he had Mr Bartlett, Mr Spratling and Mr Murtagh with him. After he had gone I was called to Mr Bartlett's office and Mr Murtagh was there. He wanted to discuss the visit, and I actually brought up the photography class again, as I did not want to give that one up very easily, and my other concerns about the education department. I brought up—with the photography class in mind—the subject of trust and the men. He told me that they were not to be trusted because they were all beyond redemption.

DW: What is your view?

FF: I disagree strongly with this.

DW: Did you tell him that?

FF: Yes, I did.

DW: Or was it difficult to do so?

FF: I did tell him that and we disagreed. Because I have not got a prison background and because I have only been in this employment for a short while, I was told I was naive.

DW: Were you shocked that someone in such a senior position in the Prison Service should make what many believe to be a somewhat outrageous remark?

FF: I was, particularly as when I first came to Blantyre, I live locally and I had heard of Blantyre, I did not quite believe that this regime was as good as it was. It was very simple, and the simple rules were: no alcohol, no drugs, no violence, and the men were given trust and they were given respect. There was a very strong message coming from the Governor, and our Head of inmate activities who was responsible for education. It answered all my beliefs on how people should be treated. I felt, at the end of a sentence, this is how men should be treated; respect given and trust given was being paid back ten-fold.

DW: What would you say, Ms Fletcher, if it was said that the person who made the remark has had many, many years of experience in the Prison Service? You have not, you might be naive and he understands human nature better. What would be your response to that, with your experience at this institution?

FF: With my experience at this institution I would say that he was wrong because, yes, perhaps this is the view of somebody who has seen other prisons, but Blantyre is unique, and the ethos at Blantyre was unique. I would say that it is the view of somebody who fails to understand what the ethos was here and, also, who fails really to understand human nature.

Paul Stinchcombe MP

Paul Stinchcombe then asked Mike Duff about the facilities he had for running the photography class:

MD: I had better give you the history of it. It started off as an activity day or during activity week, where people are brought in to teach subjects that are not normally provided here to stimulate interest in things. Anyway, I came in to do a day on photography and it was so well-received that I was contacted by the education manager and asked to come in one day a week to do this as a subject. At first it was not accredited, it was more like a camera club, and then after a couple of years I wrote a programme and had it accredited at the Open College Network at three levels. In the early days we used to use a room that was also used for decorative paints and before I started class, we had to blank all the windows off, and it was very tedious. We did that for years and years and years, and then in the last couple of years I finally got a room. It is very, very small (it is a little dark room, about 8 feet by 3 feet) with an enlarger in it, and then a little tiny room next to that where I keep all the paperwork.

PS: So two rooms?

MD: Yes, two very small rooms.

PS: What did those rooms look like after the raid?

MD: There is a little cupboard in the dark room, and the door of that was literally ripped open and the lock broken. In that I had work that was waiting for verification—several level three folders and quite a few level ones. They were thrown all over the floor.

PS: Level 3 is equivalent to what level?

MD: A level.

PS: A level. Thrown on the floor?

MD: They were thrown on the floor, and they seemed to have been trodden on as well, which added insult to injury. I was completely appalled and could not believe it.

Paul Stinchcombe thanked Mike Duff and then turned to Rev Bourne and asked him how the chaplaincy had been affected by the raid.

Rev JB: The chapel has two offices, the Roman Catholic Priest's office and my office, which were locked offices, and both doors had been broken down. My door was taken apart at the frame, and part of the wall and rubble and the doors left all over the floor. The drawers had been searched quite tidily and some money removed. In another room, there was a locked, 4-feet-high cupboard that I have never had a key to, but that remained untouched. It seemed a rather strange search.

PS: Was there any need to break the door in that manner?

Rev JB: The keys to the chapel are kept, as they always are, in the gatehouse. I had been in the prison that day and left at 5 o'clock, after all the unfortunate events regarding the removal of the two governor grades, and I had replaced my keys so that they were there available for anyone who wanted them in the night.

PS: So you left your keys at the gatehouse?

Rev JB: I left my keys at the gatehouse.

Gerald Howarth MP

GH: Can I ask if there has been any explanation given to either the Chaplaincy or to you, Mr Duff, for what has happened, or whether you have, perhaps, had an apology?

Rev JB: No.

MD: No, none whatsoever. Incidentally, there was a key for the photography cupboard in the photography room, and it is well-labelled; it is actually labelled "Photography keys, cupboard".

GH: It was unjustified. Would it come as a surprise to you if I said that in answer to my questions to Mr Murtagh this morning, the Area Manager, he said he did not know anything about the photography—

MD: I do not believe that. I do not believe that.

As the afternoon progressed, I was feeling more and more optimistic about the enquiry. Everyone so far had been so supportive of the Blantyre ethos and recognised my enthusiasm and commitment to it. The next witness called to give evidence was Jim Semple. He was the Governor who created the Blantyre regime and, in comparison, all I did was to stand on his shoulders. Jim spoke eloquently and with passion about his vision for the prison. He'd written a very strong letter to the Committee.

David Winnick MP asked him about it:

DW: Very briefly, if I may, you describe in your letter dated today, Mr Semple, the previous governor was removed in a humiliating and disgraceful manner. You stand by that obviously, you have just written it.

JS: Yes.

DW: Why humiliating and disgraceful?

JS: The Prison Service is a very personal organisation, really quite small, there are very few governing governors. If I could just give some flavour to that, very quickly. Martin Narey said in the press when he removed Eoin McLennan-Murray that he promoted him to Deputy Governor at Swaleside in the same grade.

DW: Yes.

JS: Tell me when a Deputy is a prize? I would say never. I would say about that, to actually lose one's command without the staff having an inkling, other than they thought that this man might be very effective in terms of Blantyre and the prevailing climate, one knew, certainly within the area, everything that had a purpose was an uphill battle. I can only suggest that was what lay behind that, therefore humiliated.

DW: Thank you for your very concise answer. Can I ask you if you feel that someone should be held responsible for what you have now described as humiliating and disgraceful removal?

JS: Absolutely, yes.

DW: Who?

JS: The Director General of the prison is responsible for the culture of the organisation, no-one else. Tom Murtagh, is his appointment, not anybody else outside the service.

DW: The Director General?

JS: Absolutely yes.

DW: What would you say about the Area Manager?

JS: The Area Manager is the Director General's appointment. He has a controller in between. Certainly the Director General would be looking very hard at the advice to the Area Manager, from whom I believe these days must be called the Director of Operations.

DW: You see we have heard evidence that the previous governor was subject to bullying by the Area Manager. This is my concluding question. Do you have any comment on that?

JS: Yes, I have. I am not surprised by what you have heard. One has close personal friends, that is the nature of the service, who are governors elsewhere who have said in a social setting to me, people who I would regard as quite tough personalities who actually belong to the middle ground of sound progressive, not excessive, who perhaps might have come the way of Blantyre, but maybe not, they find it a struggle to hold on to what they believed in under his management.

After Jim Semple stepped down Lord Corbett explained that we would have to leave the room as the next group of witnesses were serving prisoners and they did not want their evidence to be given in public or televised. One of the prisoners had been one of the men shipped out on the night of the raid only to return some days later. We learned later that Lord Corbett opened up the questioning asking this prisoner, Frank Driscoll about how he thought things had changed at Blantyre since the Raid:

LC: You know why we are here, to have a look at the impact upon the ethos of Blantyre House of the raid on 5/6 May and other related events and the investigations by Kent police into alleged criminal activities by prisoners. I think the immediate thing we would like to hear from you is the changes those of you who were here before May feel have happened since and what you think it has done to the whole role and purpose of Blantyre House?

FD: You have heard from all the various departments so far. You have heard from the education department, you have heard from most of the works departments, etc. We can tell you about the morale changes here. The trust that existed before has gone completely. The inmates here do not know where they stand from one day to the next. They do not know who to approach, or who is leading the place. There is no control, there is no management. Decisions are coming not from the Governor, we believe they are coming from the area managers of other departments with self-interests to protect. At the moment we are being governed by a puppet Governor, somebody who is taking his lead from above. He is not being allowed to govern. Mr Bartlett is probably an excellent Governor but he is not being given the opportunity to do exactly that. Perhaps that is what is wrong at the moment.

LC: Forgive me, what about relations between you and the staff below the Governor level?

FD: The staff up to the PO, and PCO level are tremendous, in fact it has brought us closer together. We are so solid. We are speaking for them now when we come before you today. The relationship is tremendous, it could not be better. It is unusual in the prison system to find staff and inmates so solid, so united, so in favour of the prison establishment. We are here today because we are passionate at Blantyre about its resettlement function and we want to encourage that and build upon it. The difficulty comes at the higher level, the management level, that is where the problem is arising. At the moment, people do not know where they stand and there is no enthusiasm for this place anymore. There is no enthusiasm to go to education, to go on courses, to do work placements, to do community work, things which people looked forward to and enjoyed and thrived upon before, they think "Why bother now? What are we going to get out of it now" and it has all gone, the trust has gone.

He then spoke about his 'ship out' experience:

FD: Could I return to the raid itself again? I was one of the five inmates who were shipped out that night. I was taken out of my bed at twenty past five in the morning, and I was fast asleep, my room had been searched, I did my drug test, and I was having a quiet night's sleep. Six officers in riot gear burst in, dragged me from my bed, looked at me, stripped me naked—they stripped me naked, I was not asked to undress—checked me out, took me down to health care, stripped me naked again, and I was in Elmley within 40 minutes; the segregation unit at Elmley. I was given a reason for my removal, and I have a little slip here, the slip I was actually given. "You have been transferred from HMP Blantyre House to HMP Elmley. The documents found in your room amount to significant financial transactions. The documents appear to have originated from police intelligence sources." My removal received quite a bit of publicity, not that I had escape equipment but that substantial financial transactions had been transacted. I have brought before you today the evidence bag. It is still sealed by the Prison Service. It is the original bag. These are the documents which were taken from me which resulted in my removal. This has never been opened. I am quite prepared to open it in front of you now. Inside that bag you will find my telephone address book, a paying-in slip for my national insurance contributions, and a document from my solicitors showing how money which they had got on my behalf had been paid out. Those are the financial transactions they referred to. I am quite prepared to open it now. It is still sealed.

LC: How did you get this bag?

FD: I went to Elmley. I knew the system, as a former solicitor I knew how to play the system, so to speak. I petitioned them, and I got complaint forms, I made a nuisance of myself, to be honest. I demanded to see the evidence. They could not produce it and within a week, I was told, "You have been exonerated completely, you can come back." That was what got me out.

***

As I drove home that evening I had quite a mix of emotions. The day's events had all been good, everyone who had given evidence was supportive of the Blantyre ethos and of me. Even the committee members seemed to be rooting for Blantyre but I was anxious about the following day, when I was sure I would be asked about the bullying allegation. Also, I knew that my adversaries would be there in force and from the secretariat papers that had been leaked to me from HQ I knew they had been busy looking for anything they could use to discredit me and the Blantyre Ethos.

When I got home I told Dorit how the day had gone and she just hugged me and said, "We will all be there tomorrow with you." I went to bed that night playing the events of the day over and over in my mind and almost daring not to imagine what the next day would bring.

From right to left Board of Visitors members John Smith, Dr. Brian Hugo, Molly Tipples and the governor.

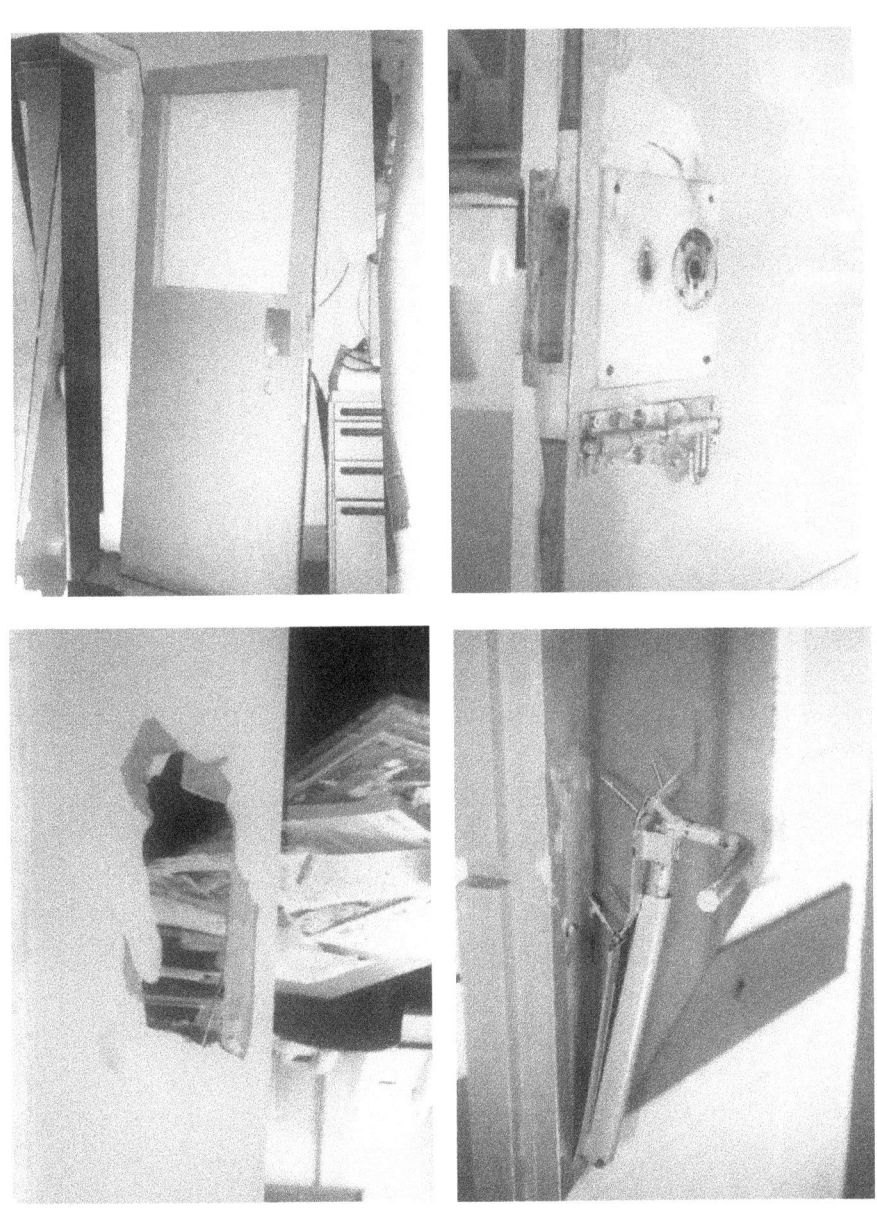

Damaged doors that could simply have been unlocked with a key.

This was scrawled on a blackboard by one of the search team.

Chapter 19

Wednesday 17th October morning session – Palace of Westminster

The clock radio sprang into life at 6 am and I awoke to the distinctive voice of John Humphries introducing the Today programme on Radio 4. While I was showering, Dorit was getting the children organised and preparing the breakfast. It was like any other day's routine, albeit an earlier start than normal. Over breakfast, Dorit said that she had arranged to meet my sister Lesley at the exit of Westminster tube station opposite Big Ben at 9.30 am, that would give us plenty of time to get to Committee room 8 in the House of Commons for 10. 30 am. Having dispatched the children off to their respective schools in Tonbridge, we walked to the station to catch the train to Waterloo. As usual it was full of commuters and we had arranged to meet Dave Newport in the last carriage of the same train as this is usually not so full. Dave had picked the train up from Staplehurst, where he lived, and fortunately that part of our plan went smoothly. I only hoped it was to be an omen for the rest of the day. We chatted about the previous day's events and speculated on what the outcome of today would be, but to be honest, we really had no idea.

The train arrived at Waterloo on time and then it was simply a matter of catching the 211 bus which runs from Waterloo and passes Westminster tube station. The traffic was heavy but our bus lane enabled us to cut through the London congestion and we met up with Lesley, who had decided to bring a close friend of both of ours, Glenda.

Having negotiated the Parliament security, we made our way through the great entrance hall into the heart of Westminster Palace. I asked one of the ushers where committee room 8 was and he led us up a wide staircase which led to an open vestibule area from which a long corridor ran in both directions. "Committee room 8 is down there on the left sir, you can't miss it, all the rooms are numbered", he said.

This was my first time in the Palace of Westminster. It is an impressive building with distinctly patterned blue carpeting and dark stained wooden panelling adorned with oil paintings of various parliamentarians past and present. These paintings have ornate golden frames, and although not to everyone's taste, they look quite grand. As we passed various committee rooms, I noticed that each one had two entrances, one for committee members and one for the public. Outside committee room 8, there were a few people gathered already, none of whom I recognised. We took our seats and sat in silence just taking in the grandeur of our surroundings. Suddenly, a familiar, gravelly voice said: "Hello Eoin, well this is the big day and I've got a good feeling about it".

It was Steven Jones who had decided to take another day off work and come to the House of Commons to support me. I introduced him to my sister and Glenda, he already knew Dorit from Blantyre and obviously he knew Dave. He said that Jack Wells was also here, but he didn't know if any other former Blantyre prisoners would be coming.

As we were chatting, I saw Sir David Ramsbotham, now Lord Ramsbotham with his deputy, Colin Allen and another inspector, Geoffrey Hughes. Sir David greeted me warmly, as did his two colleagues and after I had done all the introductions, he said to me, "I'm sure this committee will get to the bottom of things and discover what we all know to be the truth". I felt reassured by these words and before I could say anything, the large panelled door for committee members opened and an usher informed us that we could enter the room through the other entrance door.

By this time, there must have been about twenty of us, and as we filed through the door there were two or three rows of seats for public use and in front of these were several tables laid out in a horse-shoe configuration. At one end sat Lord Corbett, flanked by the other committee members. Directly opposite Lord Corbett at the far end of the horseshoe was where HMCIP would sit. There were place names for them and each seat round the horseshoe set of tables was served with a microphone, bottled water and glasses. The room was panelled in the same style as the corridor outside and it had the same carpeting and the sumptuous leather chairs all had a House of Commons logo on them.

Opposite the entrance doors to the committee room. There were large leaded windows that overlooked the river Thames. Various paintings, similar to those I had seen in the corridor were hanging on the walls. In the middle of the horseshoe sat a woman who was obviously there to take a verbatim record of all that was said.

Our little group was sitting in the front row of the public area directly opposite Lord Corbett and right behind Sir David Ramsbotham, who was flanked by his Deputy Colin Allen on his left, and Geoffrey Hughes on his right. In all there were seven committee members sitting around the horseshoe including the chair. Within a few minutes Robin and other committee members were quizzing Sir David and his colleagues about their views on the raid, on the allegations of bullying and on the role of Murtagh and Narey. After some exchanges about reports and inquiries after the raid Lord Corbett asked Sir David about risk regarding prison security, before going on to talk about the issue of me being 'bullied'. Martin Linton MP asked Sir David about the risk of letting criminals back into the community – Sir David wanted to make some wider points. But I was incredibly pleased with what he had to say:

SDR: I think that the person who has got to take the greatest risk is the governor of the place concerned. If you have got a brave governor, like Eoin McLennan-Murray at Blantyre House, who is prepared to take these risks and he got the response from the prisoners - which is the most important thing because they understood and they appreciated the trust that was being placed in them and the opportunities they were given—, the chances are that you are probably going to succeed. It is a very difficult balance. Personally, I would always like, certainly with long-term prisoners, for this risk to be taken while they were still in prison because if the system breaks down while they are there they can always be returned to the system. Of course, if it happens outside, the same is not so possible. The important thing is, if governors are going to be expected to take that risk—and there is a no more testing risk to take— then it is desperately important that the governors themselves are supported in taking that risk. Everyone is a member of a chain of command which goes from top to bottom, and a chain is used as a very appropriate description because everyone has got to pull in one direction or another. Governors can only take this risk in confidence if they feel that they are supported. I think, going on down this mutual trust, once the governor is confident he is supported (therefore, he is taking his risk and the prisoners and the staff understand the processes by which the risk assessment is made, and it is explained and there are checks and balances in the system so that if there is a failure or a person goes back) then you have a system, but without that I do not believe that you have, and that is where you get problems.

ML: Do you imply that this was the case at Blantyre House?

SDR: Mention was made yesterday to you about the feeling that the governor had that he was not necessarily supported by his Area Manager in the resettlement role. That is very uncomfortable for a governor because his immediate source of help, guidance and advice is his line manager, who is his Area Manager. If he is involved in the risk assessment business and being successful at it he has got to feel that he is supported in taking those risks, otherwise he may be tempted not to, in which case the system will not work.

ML: And he was not, is what you are saying?

SDR: The evidence you have had, I know, shows that people did not think that that trust was meted out to the Governor in the way he might have had reason to expect.

Colin Allen, Sir David's deputy then interjected:

CA: I add something to your question? It is about the culture of the Prison Service and it relates to something I was asked just now. I think I would be very doubtful about whether, if Blantyre House did not exist, it would be created in the climate of today's Prison Service. The reason for that is the aftermath of the escapes at Whitemoor and Parkhurst, the ramifications of which, with regard to physical security and preventing escapes, are still very heavy with the Prison Service. The Director General and his colleagues are quite clear—and governors are quite clear—that if they lose prisoners that is the biggest sin they are capable of committing.

ML: Do governors not feel that just keeping your nose clean by having no escapes is not enough, and that having a low re-offending rate might be a better guide to your success?

CA: There is a lot of talk about that, but I do not actually think that we see evidence of it, except in particular people in the Prison Service, who are self-motivated. I do not see a culture yet developing in that way. I think if you are looking for an explanation about the apparent nervousness of the Prison Service towards Blantyre House, then what I have just said about the implications of post-Whitemoor and Parkhurst are the answer.

ML: This dilemma they have, that actually increasing security may, in the end, be counter-productive.

CA: At the end of the day, I think governors are quite clear, and certainly senior Prison Service personnel are quite clear, that it is losing prisoners or losing control of prisoners that is the thing by which they will be judged, not whether prisoners commit offences after release.

ML: Is there a problem—again, taking the Prison Service standpoint—or a dilemma in having a category C prison, which, as I understand it, means people who still might escape, and having a resettlement function? I think the motto of Blantyre House is something like (and I am sure somebody will correct me) "A Category C prison with a resettlement function". There seems to be a tension between those two as much as there may have been between the Area Manager and the Governor. To have a category C prison means that you have to have a certain level of security, but to operate a resettlement policy effectively means you need a different level of security. Maybe the answer is that Blantyre House should have been upgraded to a Category D prison, or an open prison. Maybe that is what is necessary to allow it the space in which to operate the kind of security policy that they really need. That, in turn, might mean that certain categories of prisoners who currently go to Blantyre House would not be eligible. Is there a solution in that area?

SDR: I think, if I may say so, this comes back to the problems of categorisation. Is A, B, C and D absolutely appropriate? In many ways, you could say that an open prison is a contradiction in terms. A resettlement function exists in every prison. Prisoners are released from the segregation unit of dispersal prisons and so they have got a resettlement function as well. If there are some specialist resettlement prisons then the whole ethos of the place is of letting people work in the community rather than being constrained within a closed training prison. I think that this is a dilemma which was exemplified very clearly when we went to Kirklevington Grange where the Prison Service Operating Standards Audit described the regime at Kirklevington Grange as being "idiosyncratic", because they could not understand exactly what it was that they were meant to be judging because there was nothing like it anywhere else. If you are judging a category C prison, a resettlement prison fails on every count on security, and if you are judging a resettlement prison, of course, category C is inappropriate. Again, I come back to this business of essential policy, which I think is so important to define to help everyone. As far as this case is concerned, if we learn the lessons from it, it is a confusion which we could do without, but as Colin says, it is absolutely understandable, given the past record of past years that have been bearing on the Prison Service.

LC: Your colleague, Colin Allen, was telling us about the pressures on governors not to lose the prisoners. Can you just remind the Committee how many prisoners were lost when Mr McLennan-Murray was governor of Blantyre House?

CA: Hardly any at all, I think. I cannot remember the exact—

LC: Was it one in two-and-a-half years?

CA: Something like that, yes.

Gerald Howarth MP

GH: How many have been lost since 5 May?

CA: Again, we have not been back, so I cannot answer that.

David Winnick MP

DW: The information we have is that during the regime of the previous governor there were no escapes at all in two-and-a-half years.

CA: Yes.

DW: Since the new governor there has been one escape?

Martin Linton: And four or five abscondments.

Gerald Howarth MP

GH: By Prison Service standards (and I know you are not here representing the Prison Service but by their standards) Mr McLennan-Murray was a huge success and Mr Bartlett, regrettably, is not such a huge success.

SDR: I do not think we can say that precisely. We can certainly say that by our standards Mr McLennan-Murray was a huge success in what he was achieving on behalf of the prisoners to whom he was sent. He was a huge success on behalf of the public, by the figures of recidivism that resulted. As we have not been back since then I cannot comment about Mr Bartlett.

David Winnick MP

DW: You were full of praise, Sir David, when you wrote your preface to the report on the institution, which we are now looking at, of March 2000. You concluded your preface, if I may quote, by saying: "Therefore, I conclude by praising the consistent and courageous approach of the Governor and staff at Blantyre House to their very difficult and challenging task on behalf of the public." You wrote that and I think you stand by it.

SDR: Absolutely.

DW: What do you say, Sir David, to the attitude of the Prison Service, who clearly took a very different attitude and who, less than two months after you wrote that, removed him and offered him another position?

SDR: I have a concern about this because I have a huge admiration and respect for the current Director General. I think he is a very thoughtful man who is moving the Prison Service forward, and I think the Prison Service is better for his leadership in many ways that we see going around. To be quite honest with you, the reported events of 5 May do not seem to me to be fully in line with what I understand to be the way that the Director General wishes the service to go and the sort of standards that he wishes it to achieve in its statement of purpose. Therefore, I wonder how much of what happened actually was really Prison Service policy or whether it was the policy of the Area Manager for Kent, Sussex and Surrey. The regime which was so successful, as I say, was not treated in the same way by the Area Manager for the North East in respect of Kirklevington Grange, which was doing exactly the same things. On the other hand, I am not aware of whether there was any police evidence to suggest that something needed to be done in this way. So that is something that I am in ignorance of.

DW: We will come, in a moment, to the search which took place on 5/6 May and which, as you know, caused a tremendous amount of controversy, and we will be hearing evidence later from the Prison Governors' Association and, indeed, from the former governor. What about the relationship which you have just touched on between the Area Manager and the previous governor? Did you have the impression it was a tense relationship?

SDR: To be quite honest, yes. The evidence we got (and some of it is recorded in, I think, the flavour of the inspection) was that the governor had a very clear view of his mission, which had been endorsed by successive Directors General and which we looked at in the context of a resettlement prison and which you, as a Committee, yourselves went and saw and reported on. You received the same treatment as we did, such as the meeting with former prisoners and being shown round by prisoners, and the feeling of the place. You experienced it as well as I did. I do not think that that was actually shared by the Area Manager. I get the feeling that the Area Manager, for reasons best known to himself, did not actually support what the governor was doing or why. I think that is thoroughly unfortunate, if I may say so, and I think the body of evidence there supports what we felt during the inspection. You were there during that week and the Area Manager was present at the debrief. I do not know if there is anything you want to add.

Geoffrey Hughes MP

GH: It was certainly left unresolved, and we have touched on it already, in that the governor, the Board of Visitors, staff and prisoners, for that matter, were quite adamant that it was a resettlement prison. There was no doubt in their minds whatsoever about the role that they thought they were carrying out. However, in discussions with the Area Manager there was absolutely no doubt in his mind either that it was a category C prison first and foremost, with a resettlement function. We left with that being unresolved. That was, perhaps, the main issue of contention and tension between the two.

SDR: And it was unsettling to staff.

DW: Sir David, when we were taking evidence yesterday at the prison from the Board of Visitors—and I think you would agree with me that the Board of Visitors, be it at this institution or elsewhere, do a very fine job and dedicate much of their work to helping in the way in which they do—we were told that there was a clear feeling that the former governor was the subject of bullying by the Area Manager—sustained bullying. Perhaps the word "sustained" was not used but that was certainly the impression, but the word "bullying" was. Do you think that was an exaggeration?

SDR: The thing about the Board of Visitors (and this is why I rely on what they are saying) is that they are in prison every single day of the week, every day of the year, and they can see this at first-hand. I have learned to respect what they say. The first experience I had was when they had been talking about Holloway for nine months, and when I went into Holloway, I found that what they were saying was absolutely correct. If the Board of Visitors observed what they describe as bullying of the governor by the Area Manager over a considerable period of time—bearing in mind the sort of people who are members of the Board of Visitors—I would be inclined to accept their view.

DW: It is a very serious accusation. Is it not?

SDR: It is a very serious accusation indeed.

DW: Would there be any possible justification for it?

SDR: You spoke to them yesterday, and the justification of it by a member of a chain of command, I do not think, is there. If it was in the Army I would certainly deem very suspect a chain of command which contained a relationship between two people in key positions like this, because it would seem that the chain might break at that point.

DW: When did you first know that the previous governor was being removed?

SDR: I knew absolutely nothing about it until I heard that he had been removed that afternoon. In fact, I did not hear about it until the next week because I was away that day.

DW: When did you learn about the search on 5/6 May?

SDR: At the same time. It may have been that I saw something in the newspaper to say that it had happened, but it was not until the following week that I heard.

DW: There was no reason, presumably, for you to be notified?

SDR: No.

DW: You are not criticising that?

SDR: I am responsible for the treatment and conditions of prisoners. This was an event to do with the treatment and condition of the governor, which was not really in my bailiwick, as I understand it.

DW: The criticism has been made very strongly from the Board of Visitors and from prisoners and other people that the search was conducted in a way which was not the correct way; doors were broken down, the Chaplain's door was broken down (apparently no attempt was made to find the key which was available) and money was taken from the Chaplain's office which was later returned (it was said there was nothing wrong in the way that money was located in the Chaplain's office), and a great deal of damage, I think £6,000, was done during that search. Does that surprise you at all?

SDR: It more than surprises me, frankly, I find it extraordinary. It is rather horrifying, frankly, that that should be necessary. When I look at this objectively I have to ask "What was the purpose of the operation?" and "What were the results of the operation?" As I am led to believe—and I do not know what the police evidence was because that has never been shared and there is no reason why it should—the results of the search did not actually seem to indicate a great deal of contraband. What had happened was that the governor had been moved, which was followed by this search. Then, of course, there were two other inquiries, one into the management of the prison and then, later on, this turned, as I understand it, into the examination of some financial dealings and work with charities and so on. So the end result is that the governor has been moved and there was an inquiry into a financial irregularity. When I am responsible for the treatment and conditions of prisoners then, I wonder why similar searches and similar treatment of governors might not have happened at some of the failing prisons that I have been to, like Wormwood Scrubs, Wandsworth, Brixton, Feltham, Chelmsford and others—Birmingham—when this happened to the governor of a successful prison. If there was police information, to be quite honest, I would have expected that any information about a prisoner in my prison, if I was governor, was shared with me, and that I would be responsible for having something to do with the checking of whether or not people were breaking the rules, because I am the governing governor and I would expect the Prison Service to do everything it can to support governing governors in the governing of their prisons. I have strayed slightly away from the question, but what worries me is the impact that this sort of removal of a governor, who has been successful, has on other governors in the Prison Service about the support they can expect. We were concerned to find that the governor of Kirklevington Grange, when we went there soon after the event, was understandably somewhat concerned about her position, because she was doing exactly the same as the governor at Blantyre House.

DW: One of the witnesses giving evidence yesterday described the search as rather like "stormtroopers", acting in that way. Whether that is an exaggeration or not one does not know. However, are you aware of the deep controversy over the way in which the search was conducted?

SDR: Oh certainly. People have written to me and people have told me about it: the numbers of the people, the time that they arrived, and so on. Certainly, these have incited comments.

DW: Should the Prison Service or the Home Office hold an inquiry into the way that search was conducted?

SDR: The Prison Service has held its own internal inquiry.

DW: I mean more than an internal inquiry.

SDR: I am not aware of any others.

DW: Should the Minister, Sir David, hold an inquiry?

SDR: To be quite honest with you, I was surprised that an event like this was not actually controlled by Prison Service headquarters. It is a fairly serious event to produce 80 people in the middle of the night to descend on a prison. Presumably, they put the numbers there because they were concerned that something serious might happen as a result. It did not, in the event, but I, personally, am rather surprised that this was not something which was handled by and from Prison Service headquarters rather than left down to the local area, in the same way that I have to admit to some surprise that the person who conducted the subsequent inquiry was the person who had been a previous governor at the prison, who had been in charge at the time of previous events there, and who was, at the time, the governor of Elmley Prison, which was one of the prisons responsible for sending people to Blantyre House in the first place. I would have hoped for something rather more external and independent in terms of an inquiry, to be quite honest with you, but that is because I come from an independent and outside viewpoint on all these things.

DW: As always, Sir David, you have been very forthright in your responses. Thank you very much.

Lord Corbett: I take it you would not be surprised to learn, as one of the inmates told us yesterday, that while all this mayhem was going on, one of the prisoners asked the guys doing it "Would you like a cup of tea? I am just about to make one", and he got a mouthful of bad language as a result.

It was fascinating listening to the questions and answers and it seemed to me that various committee members already had a gut feeling about the truth. Some of the questions and responses clearly suggested that they were sceptical about some of the official responses given by senior managers in the Service and the Prisons Minister, Paul Boateng.

When the committee had finished with Sir David and his colleagues, a clerk changed the place names and invited Mike Newell, (President of the PGA), David Roddan (Gen Sec of the PGA) and myself to take our seats. Mike was sitting in the middle and I was on his right, with David on his left. My heart was in my mouth and as I poured some water out my hand was shaking a little. I don't know whether Robin noticed this but in his brief introduction, he said: "We are especially pleased to see you, Mr McLennan Murray. As you know, we were at Blantyre House yesterday. I do not want to cause you the slightest bit of embarrassment, but you have one or two friends left there. I may say, in some extraordinary way, the rapport between staff and prisoners there was demonstrable, you could feel it, so we thank you again".

This really helped put me at ease and Lord Corbett then went on to begin questioning Mike Newell about whether it was usual for the governor not to be informed and involved with a search of his prison.

LC: Can you help, Mr Newell? Whose authority is required to carry out a search on the scale of the one which was carried out at Blantyre House?

MN: It is a very difficult question.

LC: How many fingers are in the pie?

MN: The normal process would be that something of that magnitude would be discussed with the governor of the establishment, plans would be put in preparation and, as was said by Sir David, would actually tend to be commanded from the centre.

LC: When you say "on that scale", do you mean by that a full search of the prison?

MN: Yes. Quite simply because in normal circumstances, if I was carrying out a search of my own prison, if I could do it within my existing resources, it would be within my power; if I required assistance in terms of resources, then obviously they would be authorised from Area and HQ, and that would be dependent on the level of threat and intelligence.

LC: Just come down a peg, as it were. What kind of searches need to be authorised by anyone other than the governor?

MN: The sorts of searches are the sort where we would report any intelligence which was of a significant nature. Say, for example, if there were rumours there may be firearms within the prison, then the level of that search—the resources which required additional arms and explosives dogs—would be such that that authority would all come from headquarters, but it would come as part of an intelligence reporting process.

LC: What scope in that process is there for concerns to be expressed about what is being planned; a search of this scope, the kind of raid which took place on Blantyre House?

MN: The difficulty about this search is that this is, in my experience, and this goes back 26 years, unique. We do not do these sorts of searches without discussion with the governor. That was from our point of view one of the features about this particular incident.

LC: Forgive me, but you are not buying the explanation that it was almost a coincidence, an accident, that the Governor was transferred on promotion from being governor to a deputy governor—some promotion—that was quite accidental and then, hey presto!, the new man arrives and quite out of the blue he says, "I want a full search of this place"? You are being a bit sceptical about that, are you not? MN: I am just not buying that it is even practical to have done it that way. I think it is open knowledge that the planning for that search went on for several days prior to the actual search.

LC: How are governors appointed? Does a notice go on a board or in a house magazine? How is it advertised? Or does the fickle finger of fate tap you on the shoulder?

MN: Perhaps increasingly it does, but the usual procedure is that if anybody is moving on for career reasons there are discussions about that, the future posting is sorted out, and the particular post would then be advertised through the Prison Service internal vacancy system, suitable candidates would be interviewed, an appointment made and that would be announced. The governor would obviously be announcing within the establishment that process as well.

LC: Do you happen to know when Mr Bartlett was appointed to that job as Governor of Blantyre House? I have a date, I think, of 3rd May.

MN: I am not aware of the exact date that individual was told they were taking over Blantyre House. We believe from the planning of the raid that a few days before the new Governor was involved in that process, he was clearly aware they were going to be the new Governor, and I think that is made clear in the search report done by the Prison Service.

LC: There is some confusion about this. I think from memory Mr Murtagh said it was decided, because of the severity and concern over the intelligence which the Chaucer team had got, that a decision to mount the raid was taken—I think he said—on 28th April and it was going to be carried out as soon as possible but with them saying the Friday night was the best time to do it because they wanted to do it when everybody who should have been in the prison was in the prison. So certain senior people in the Prison Service knew what was going on. Can you think of an explanation as to why the new Governor, Mr Bartlett, felt it necessary then to sign a piece of paper saying he wanted the prison searched from top to bottom?

MN: No. I simply cannot explain any of the events, based on my experience of the service, in that week.

LC: If you put it in the context, as we were discussing earlier, where it would normally be expected that the governing governor would be informed that such a search, a raid, was going to be mounted?

MN: More than "informed". The governing governor would be the leading player in that process.

LC: Yes, so this confusion, if confusion it be, between April 28th and the arrival of the new Governor, the appointment of the new Governor, on 3rd May, in those circumstances would not have arisen, would it?

MN: No.

LC: Are you aware of a raid on such a scale involving 84 officers, all of whom apparently drove there in their own motorcars, arriving there mid-evening and staying until 5 or 6 in the morning, on any other Cat C prison in the estate?

MN: I find it difficult to remember a raid of this type and certainly I cannot think of anywhere, as I say, it was done without the knowledge of—well, I will rephrase that—where the previous governor or the governor had been removed the day before and was done with the knowledge of the new governor in the way of this raid. I certainly cannot remember anything co-ordinated outside Prison Service headquarters of that magnitude. That is what seems very unusual to me.

LC: Is it not the case that a former Home Secretary, Sir Kenneth Baker, made quite clear that the governing governor of an institution, where there were anxieties or suspicions, would be informed of those?

MN: Yes.

LC: Except, as we were saying earlier, where the circumstances were the allegations were specific to you.

MN: Exactly. The position is that our own security manual makes it quite clear that it is the duty of any member of staff to report intelligence to the governor. That extends simply because of the interpretation following the Brixton escapes where, I am sure you were aware, there was a covert operation going on in relation to IRA prisoners, where things were happening in the prison of which the governor was not aware. Following that investigation, which was carried out by Judge Tumin, it was made clear by Kenneth Baker that there would be no further situations where governors would not be aware of what was happening within their prison, for the obvious dangers and risks and, as you know, in that particular escape people were injured.

The questioning eventually then moved on to me and I had to answer an allegation that I had not followed instructions issued to me by Murtagh.

LC: Obviously, the difference in views which were taking place between the Area Manager and Mr McLennan-Murray, which we have heard about from various witnesses, meant that there were instructions given, as we understand it, by the Area Manager before the search. Why were the Area Manager's instructions not carried out? Is there any evidence of breaches of security which occurred over the two years prior to May 5th?

MN: I think it might be most appropriate if the former Governor answered that question. Eoin Mclennan-Murray: In relation to instructions not carried out, I do not believe that is the case. Following the security audit which was carried out in the establishment earlier that year, an action plan was produced and we followed through with the elements of that action plan. Some of those elements required additional resources, in my view, to enable us to do them. You have to understand that if you say Blantyre House is a Category C prison, you have to ask yourself what security provisions does a Category C entail. It usually requires the outside fences to be clad, and it usually requires there should be S-wire (Razor Wire) there should be secure cellular accommodation, there should be a sterile area, there should be a proper gate, there should be clean and dirty areas for reception. None of these things are present in that establishment and physically it is well below the requirements of Category C. To suggest, therefore that we should try and comply with Category C standards, I think, is patently absurd. I have heard Kirklevington Grange mentioned, and that is a Category C prison, it has the same security deficits as Blantyre House and it was not subject to a security audit because there is a provision in the security manual to allow that dispensation to occur in recognition of the fact that resettlement prisons which operate nominally as Category C clearly cannot meet the requirements. So when there were additional searching requirements imposed upon the establishment by the Area Manager and he set targets, I continually resisted these targets because I said they were unachievable, I was not resourced to produce them and it was setting a target I could not achieve; I would fail. I pointed that out. There has already been mention of the staff repro-filing exercise from the consultancy team which did not go ahead. I knew that within our own resources I would not be able to come up with a solution to overcome this problem which did not have a solution locally; it just did not. So the targets which were set were imposed upon the establishment. I did not disobey the order at all, I set in train a series of actions that we would do our best to achieve, but in my heart I knew that we would fail. That is the honest truth.

LC: It has been said by the Board of Visitors that you were being bullied. Have you any comment to make on that?

EM-M: It is a very difficult question really to respond to. Perhaps it is more obvious to people who are outside observing the situation than it is for the participants themselves. I was under a lot of pressure in that my approach and how I wanted to run the prison, I know, was at odds with the Area Manager. We had different philosophies. He wanted to exert control over me, and it is fair to say I was resisting that control because I could not see any rhyme or reason for it. That sets up a tension clearly. I suppose the line between exerting managerial control robustly and bullying is a fine line. I think if I am able to stand back, having had the benefit of other people's observations, I would say, yes, I was the subject of bullying. I resisted that and perhaps that is why I am in the position I am in at the moment. I can think of a number of occasions where there were specific instances which I think could be defined as bullying which I and other members of my staff were subject to.

Gerald Howarth then asked me for examples.

EM-M: The way I was referred to sometimes or spoken about by the Area Manager was not in my view professional. It did generate actually a formal complaint from a member of my staff which I kept within the establishment because I did not really want it to go out, I did not think there would be any benefit in that. This was an occasion where the staff felt that the Area Manager publicly humiliated me and undermined me in front of the staff and they took exception to that. The Area Manager, while we have been in conversation and sometimes in the presence of other people has said about me—his expression—that "I am wired up to the moon."

LC: Wired up to the moon?

EM-M: Wired up to the moon, which really is an indication, I think, he did not share my judgments on certain elements of risk, if you like, and that perhaps I was not really on this earth, so to speak; I had a different sense of reality and naivety about me. That is his view and I guess he is entitled to have it but I think you need to be careful how you express such views in the custodial setting. There were accusations that he had made against me and members of my staff. We have a number of men who work out in the community and there was a train cleaning contract in which a number of men were involved. One of the non-prisoners working in that industry had either left or had been sacked, I am not sure, but he went to the media and claimed that prisoners were taking over the jobs. One of the prisoners had been promoted as a foreman and it was not right, so there was a little flurry of activity in the local media about that. There was a follow-up article which put the other side, and then various members of the public wrote letters because it was an issue. A particular letter was published which was a very supportive letter and articulated the arguments for resettling prisoners and getting them back into work very eloquently, and I and my management team were accused by the Area Manager of writing this letter and pretending we were somebody else, which I took great exception to and so did the other members of my team. There were occasions where—I choose my words carefully here—I was lied to. I would have a phone call and something would be said to me like, "There is an exposé in the *Sunday People* coming up this weekend about Prisoner X swanning all over Kent with close associates who are well-known criminally outside." Then demands were made of me and all sorts of accusations were then made about why I had let this prisoner out, or whatever. I would investigate these matters only to find there was no such article coming out and when confronted he would say to me, "That was just a wind up." I see that as intimidation and exerting pressure unnecessarily and I think it is quite calculated why it is done.

David Winnick asked me why I thought it was calculated:

EM-M: By the Area Manager.

DW: Yes, but you say you know why it was done.

EM-M: To make me feel intimidated and to try and make me feel more vulnerable and to weaken me.

Janet Dean asked if it was to undermine me:

EM-M: To undermine me, yes.

DW: To try and get rid of you?

EM-M: Well, subsequently that is what happened, but at the time I just saw it as a way of trying to continually undermine and knock me down. Other members of my management team have been subject to similar experiences and I know one of them has formally put in a grievance procedure about it and we are waiting for the outcome of that. As was said yesterday, these are serious matters. So I was the subject of bullying. I think in most of the cases I resisted. There are times when I caved in because the pressure was such that I made decisions which I did not believe were right, I believed they were wrong, but I did them because at the end of the day I was frightened, I suppose frightened of losing my job.

Janet Dean asked me if I had any inclination of what was going to happen on 5th May. Did I have any warnings or threats I was going to be moved from being Governor?

EM-M: No. About four weeks before—and I have the date in my diary—I bumped into someone who was another senior manager in the service and he enquired how I was getting on in my new position. I played dumb because I suddenly thought, "Hello, what is this?"

Gerald Howarth asked me when it was:

EM-M: I can give you the date, I have my diary here. It was in the week commencing 17th April. I cannot remember exactly what day it was. I was up at Cambridge and that is where I bumped into this individual. I could not coax out of him where it was I was, but I just knew I had moved. I kind of let him know and he felt very embarrassed and I said I would not say anything about it. I made one or two additional enquiries through the grapevine and everything I heard seemed to confirm these rumours.

GH: What position was this bloke in the Prison Service?

EM-M: A senior manager in the Prison Service.

GH: At headquarters?

EM-M: At headquarters.

GH: Not at the Area Manager's level?

EM-M: A similar level but at headquarters.

GH: So this was being plotted on high, as it were?

EM-M: That is the only inference I could draw from that. I noted that there had been a meeting scheduled with the Area Manager earlier in April which was a three-line whip meeting. We all had to be there, but that had been cancelled. When that meeting was rescheduled for 5th May and it was a three-line whip meeting and all the management team had to be present, I put two-and-two together and thought, "I know he is going to tell me I am going to be moving from the prison." I mentally prepared myself for that and I began to try and wind things down a little. I did not share this extensively with my management team. So I was prepared for that but what I was not prepared for was the way in which it happened and the speed of it. I just thought it would be a normal transfer, and we would talk about where I was going to go and what I wanted to do. It would be a career move. I had no idea.

LC: In normal circumstances, are you able to say, "I'm not sure this is a good career move for me. What I thought I might do next is this or that"?

EM-M: Yes. Earlier on, as part of what I suppose comes under the category of bullying, I had been threatened on numerous occasions with being moved from prison over the last two years.

LC: By the Area Manager?

EM-M: By the Area Manager.

David Winnick then asked:

DW: No one else? Was it the Area Manager who was the constant person?

EM-M: After a time, when you are continually told the same thing time and time again and it does not happen, it loses some of its impact. Nevertheless, that was the history of it. We had discussed it. He had said to me, "I think you should go and be deputy governor of a big prison, then you can learn how to govern a prison properly", sort of thing, that was the inference. I will be quite frank with you, I treated that with the disdain I thought that kind of remark deserved.

LC: When you went to this meeting on the 5th, what were the actual words he used to indicate you were going to have the governorship taken away from you?

EM-M: I was expecting him to arrive around 2 o'clock because he had had a meeting in the morning in the training centre with a lunch—I think it was an NHS bilateral meeting. I had visitors in the jail and I was with them and he arrived at about 12.30 I think and my Head of Management Services said to me, "There's something not right here, he seems to be very nervous. I have left him in your office but I think you should cut this short and go and see him." I did cut it short and let others finish off with our visitors, and when I went in he was standing up, and as soon as he saw me he just walked up to me and thrust this envelope into my hand and said, "Sit down, read it, it is bad news." I said, "Tom, I don't need to sit down and read it", and I walked round to my desk, I took my letter opener and I opened the letter. It was a short letter from Ivor Ward, who is in personnel at headquarters. I do not have it with me but I paraphrase it. It was something like, "On the written instructions of the Director General with immediate effect you are being moved from

Governor of Blantyre House to Deputy Governor of Swaleside." It then said something about I might be entitled to some expenses in terms of additional travel expenses and I might want to take a few days' leave before taking up my new post. So I read it, I went and sat down and just said, "Why?" He told me it was a career move. I would rather not repeat here what I had to say to him then but it was a fairly forthright response from me.

Humphrey Malins interjected:

HM: This career move, you were told about it on what day exactly?

EM-M Friday, 5th May at about 12.30.

HM: Would you normally expect to be consulted about a career move?

EM-M: That has been my experience to date. I have had six different postings, and every time there has been a run-up period and I have often had discussions about where I am going.

Gerald Howarth moved on to question me about resettlement and risk. I felt very comfortable with these areas and gave what I believe to be a very coherent response:

GH: On the question of resettlement policy, you will have heard earlier there are no resettlement policy guidelines. How was it that you managed to operate Blantyre House? Were you flying by the seat of your pants, to use a northern expression? Did you have a handbook? Did you take the bible according to St Jim Semple? How did you approach the task? Were you given any guidance from the Prison Service?

EM-M: I was not given any guidance. I was not given any particular steer at the handover or a briefing from the Area Manager. I did get a handover from the previous Governor whom I succeeded. You will know that Blantyre House did have some history in terms of one or two serious incidents which occurred in the previous years to my taking over command. I decided to look fundamentally at what Blantyre House was all about. I rediscovered a lot of the work that Jim Semple had originally done, and that impressed me enormously. I decided that my way forward with Blantyre House, particularly in light of what happened previously, was to rediscover and renew the values on which the establishment was first set up. That is what I set about doing. I transmitted that very clearly to the staff and to the prisoners. I heard someone talk about the logo before, and it was enabling resettlement. Blantyre House Enabling Resettlement, that was our logo. That is what our mission was. That is what we did. We had it embroidered on uniforms, and all sorts of things. We had a real sense of purpose, very much guided by those initial principles that Jim Semple put in place when he set up the establishment.

GH: Have you been aware of Blantyre House before and what it was doing? What did you think of it from the outside? Did it enter your consciousness as being something different from the rest of the Prison Service?

EM-M: I had visited Blantyre House. I was the Staff Officer to the Director General for an early time in my career.

GH: Which Director General?

EM-M: Derek Lewis. I visited Blantyre House with him and met Jim Semple. It struck me as being a very different kind of establishment, and it just feels different as soon you walk into the place. To understand Blantyre House takes considerably longer. My background has been in secure prisons. I have worked in dispersal prisons. I have worked in big locales. The model I carried around in my head about how prisoners behave and what they do was very much shaped by the experiences I had. Those experiences and that model did not fit with what I saw in Blantyre House. I was certainly confused when I first got there. You are just presented with such a different culture, and you either reject it and be cynical about it, and say, "It cannot be real, it is a con", or you say, "Hang on, is there another explanation that can help me understand what is going on here?" I chose that latter route and looking at Jim's previous work helped me. It took me probably four to six months before I began to understand how Blantyre House worked. Although I had seen it before I had no real understanding. It was very superficial. You have to be there and be part of it to make sense of it.

GH: Do you think, as Mr Semple suggested to us yesterday—and the question I put to Sir David Ramsbotham—that there ought to be a separate category to take away from the constraints that are imposed by the current categorisation? Sir David suggested that somebody ought to be responsible and accountable for this particular type of prison. Do you think that would be a way forward?

EM-M: Yes, I do. I have been doing a research project at Cambridge University on resettlement, trying to understand some of the mechanisms that are working to produce the results we had at Blantyre House. If you have security within a prison—you do need secure prisons, I have no doubt about that, particularly when men are in the early parts of their sentence—you have to have control, you have to have some kind of rigour. We know that people get damaged by that process, however that is an artifact of imprisonment, it is a sad fact of life. We also know that these people are going to be released. It seems to me when you are looking at people to be released we need to undo some of the damage, some of the pains of imprisonment—as Gresham Sykes described it—that they have acquired through their process of imprisonment. Blantyre House is very much about undoing some of that damage and re-socialising people, so that when they go out they are going out with pro-social attitudes and not anti-social attitudes. As Sir Alexander Patten said, "You cannot train men for freedom in conditions of captivity." You have to stand back and if that means we have to re-look at how we classify resettlement prisons, I very much support that as an issue.

GH: There are only 120 places in Blantyre House, and there are something like 63,000 prisoners in the total prison population. If you were to have a free hand, how many such institutions do you think the Prison Service could use? Consistent with some recognition of the financial costs, do you think 120 places is the right sort of size?

EM-M: Just dealing with the last point first, I think the size of the establishment is very important. Once you get above a couple of hundred you cannot maintain the intimacy and the levels of trust and the intimate knowledge that we have of one another, above that it becomes too impersonal. There has to be a limitation on size. In terms of the number of people that could benefit from a regime like Blantyre House, unlike Kirklevington—and, perhaps, not quite so much with Latchmere House, which caters for long-term prisoners, Kirklevington takes short term prisoners—Blantyre House specialise in long-term prisoners. Long-term prisoners are making an ever-increasing large proportion of the average daily population. In the last fifteen years, the numbers have rocketed from something like literally a few thousand to tens of thousands of prisoners who are long-term. As research has indicated long-term have different needs from short-term prisoners. There is no blueprint for resettlement, to say one size fits all. You have to tailor it to the needs of the prisoner. We have not defined what resettlement needs are. Most people think it is accommodation and employment. My own research at Blantyre House demonstrated that most of the men were in full-time employment prior to conviction and most of them had stable accommodation. Just having a job and a place to live did not prevent them from committing further crimes. There were other needs that they had. Those are the needs we need to address. Some of those needs come about because of the process of imprisonment in our secure estate. We have to recognise that problem. I could not put a figure on how many people could benefit from the Blantyre House experience, that in itself would require a little bit of research, and I have not undertaken that. I would be reluctant to guess what those figures might be.

GH: You mentioned that the Area Manager sought to wind you up by suggesting there might be press reports, that somebody was hanging around. It is very easy for the tabloid press to pick up some of these matters and really wind up the public, not to mention Members of Parliament. The idea is that people who have committed some absolutely disgusting crimes are able to enjoy the freedom of a mobile telephone, bank card and a job when their victims are still suffering. How do you address that? Are you confident that the kind of regime you were operating was as secure as it could possibly be for the protection of the public?

EM-M: I can never make a guarantee that it was as secure as it could possibly be.

GH: Was it consistent with the regime you were applying?

EM-M: It is a bit like chicken and egg. I monitored the outputs of the prison. I monitored what our temporary release failure was. I monitored what our police interest was. I had regular information from the police liaison. I kept an eye on what the media were saying. These inputs, if you like, moderate what we do in the prison. If things were going very well, if everything was going superbly well I might think I can be a little bit more adventurous. I can take a little more risk here because it seems we are in acceptable bounds. It is very much a dynamic situation. The whole concept of risk assessment is quite a complex business and it is not an easy thing, so much of it is subjective. You cannot go and say, let me score this prisoner and see how many points he presents. A lot of it is very, very judgmental. People have different judgments about these things. My prime aim was to protect the public. I took that very, very seriously. I knew that if a prisoner was to do something that he should not do when he was outside that the consequences for me and for the prison would be enormous. The prisoners also understood that. There was a great deal of self-regulation, self-control and self-discipline. They had a stake in what was going on. They were ambassadors of Blantyre House.

GH: The taxi driver who drove me to Goudhurst on Monday night said they had no problem with the prison system in Blantyre House. He said they are extremely courteous. They do not like to wait for the bus to get back to prison because the bus often gets them back late and they do not want to be late, so they club together to get a taxi. They always pay promptly and they give you a good tip. Unlike the ladies' prison, where the chap said they dish out all sorts of change they have in their pocket, very often foreign coins. Can I just ask one final question on your own personal position? We have been impressed, you know that. We have heard that the ethos of the place has plummeted since your departure. Do you think that it is possible to recover from this present position? Would you like the Prison Service to recognise what you think you have achieved there? Do you think you have a role to play and do you want to play it in trying to take forward the project that you managed, some would say, so successfully between 1996 and this year?

EM-M: I think that sometimes events happen and they are defining moments. It is very difficult to put the genie back in the bottle. I think Blantyre House can recover. I think it needs to have very clear and highly motivated leadership. It needs to have the support of people above the governor level as well. There are many individuals in the Prison Service that could fulfil that role. For me to play a part in that, although it pains me to say so, I think we are just too far down the road now. It would never be the same. I have been changed by what has happened.

GH: Do you think you have experience, backed up by very hard empirical evidence of the genie? We heard earlier that the litmus test by which prison governors are judged is by the number of escapes. I put it to Sir David earlier that you were rather successful.

EM-M: Yes. I would like to think I could make a useful contribution to the formulation of policy in terms of resettlement. I have a number of ideas which have been shaped by practical experience. I have first hand knowledge of that. It surprised me greatly that I was not invited to be a member of the Committee that was looking at this. When that Committee was convened, I had been the longest serving governor of a resettlement prison at the time. I was very surprised I was not invited to join that Committee. What I deduced from that was that my experience was not valued and would not be welcomed because it might be going against what others might see as the future for resettlement. I am a firm believer that what we do should be evidence-based and it should be based on the empirical outcome. I spent some time developing or helping to develop cognitive behavioural programmes in the Prison Service. I was a passionate advocate for that. Those programmes were based on research outcomes. They were evidenced, very much based, on the "what works" philosophy. I believe there is a similar philosophy to be developed for resettlement. I have a number of ideas supported by evidence which should be taken into account. Some of it needs to be validated by further research because the research that I have done is very small-scale. As you know, small-scale projects can be very misleading, I accept that. There is a call for more things to be done and I would certainly like to be part of that process and, therefore, help the development and resettlement of prisoners.

Gerald Howarth then asked me a couple of specific questions:

GH: Apparently, there were ten prisoners who had been out with their own cars whose insurance was defective. One of those people, indeed, had a job as a chauffeur, chauffeuring around personalities, and had that prisoner been involved in a crash the insurance company would have voided the policy. Do you have any comments to make on that? With the benefit of hindsight, do you think that there was inadequate supervision of the insurance arrangements?

EM-M: Firstly, I think it is a very serious breach. I am ashamed that it has happened. I am responsible for that. I set up the system for actually rigorous checking of insurance two and a half to three years ago, where I insisted that every prisoner disclosed that he was a serving prisoner. It crossed my mind if that was not the case there may be some difficulty in any claims. I think I came to that conclusion, because of the history of the establishment, where there had been a previous driving incident, and I knew there was some insurance wrangle. It is a valid criticism and something that I take full responsibility for. It has slipped and some prisoners were able to manipulate things, so they were not disclosing accurate information. I have no defence against that and I regret that. I would also say that I have read in one of these Reports that we did not check the driving records of prisoners. Again, that is something that I set up and we did check rigorously the previous driving records of prisoners. I was the first governor in the service to set up breathalyser testing. It was not the legal limit but zero tolerance, because I thought it was an explosive cocktail to have alcohol and prisoners driving. It would be indefensible if a prisoner was ever involved in an accident under the influence of alcohol. I took those responsibilities seriously. It was always my intention to safeguard the public. I feel really bad about that report that is the one thing that struck me.

GH: It struck me, I have to say.

EM-M: I feel I have to say if the Prison Service wanted to charge me for that, I would put my hands up and say guilty.

GH: It is a big issue, but it is only one. What about the bank cards? Can you explain the policy there? I think, again, there has been some misunderstanding. When the Minister responded, again to a Parliamentary question in the Lords, it was said twenty-five bank/credit cards were found. There was a clear policy on this and it was an acceptable policy.

EM-M: We used to insist that prisoners set up bank accounts if they did not have one. There has been a lot of difficulty in prisoners setting up bank accounts and we tried to negotiate a local arrangement so they could. This facility meant they were not issued with a chequebook for some time but they were issued with a cash card to withdraw small amounts of money so as to give the bank greater control. I also instigated a control. We saw the original document and have copies of their pay slips and their bank statements. We could monitor what expenditure was taking place. Using that process, we were able to detect one individual who was taking small amounts of cash on a regular basis to buy drugs. He was dealt with appropriately and sent back to closed conditions. Resourcing is the key to this. It was an attempt to control, regulate and monitor what we set up. It is a big task. I know that the Report has been critical of the attention to detail that we paid to that but it was a planned activity in the same way that Kirklevington have the same procedures in place. I do not think they did the checking in terms of bank accounts.

GH: What about the suggestion that there was potential corruption of prison officers? The allocation of transfers to Blantyre House. You may have heard the Chief Inspector say earlier today he felt that the selection decision should be removed from Blantyre House to the providing prison, if you like. Do you agree with that?

EM-M: Firstly, the corruption. People buying their way into a place like Blantyre House, that was something that occurred in the past, some six years ago, or longer than that, possibly. They were the allegations anyway. I do not know whether it was ever proven or not. We have a written selection criteria list, that men have to adhere to before we will take them. Staff from Blantyre House physically go out and check the men that are being proposed by the sending establishment. The sending establishment identifies the men through the sentence plan process or some other means. They say to us, Blantyre House, "These are the men we want to send you". My staff go out and they would check them against our published criteria. On many occasions, they would say, "This man does not fit, he is serving too long, he has too long left to serve or too little left to serve", and he would be discarded. We only selected men or took men from a menu that was provided to us by the sending establishment. All we were looking for was that the men they were putting up met our published criteria.

GH: Okay.

EM-M: I was confident that that process itself was not being corrupted from the Blantyre House end. I was given no information in my tenure as Governor to make me believe anything else.

GH: Let me revert to my first question, it has been suggested to us that the raid that was conducted on 5th May was not so much to find evidence of wrong doing in the prison amongst the prisoners but was a fishing expedition to find evidence to justify the decision made earlier in the day to remove you from post. In the aftermath of what happened, what do you think of that?

EM-M: I find it difficult to comment on that.

Chairman

LC: We respect that response. It is an important point and we may get an opportunity later on today.

Lord Corbett then thanked us and asked me if I would share with the committee any published results from my research at Cambridge. "We would be fascinated to see that," he said, "This Committee have a continuing interest in this area, beyond this particular inquiry. Thank you for your patience and help." He then adjourned the session until 3.30 in the afternoon.

Chapter 20

Wednesday 18th October 2000 afternoon session – Palace of Westminster

I was glad to have a break from the session, it had been quite intense and I was ready for a bite to eat. We went to the cafe in the House of Commons and over a sandwich, chatted about how the session had gone. I felt that the committee members had really understood what Blantyre was about and were both sympathetic and supportive towards me.

Of course, the afternoon session would be very different from what had happened in the morning. All of the witnesses so far had been, at best, supportive of me and Blantyre and at worst, neutral. The next session would be very different and I knew I would feel as if I was under attack. We made our way back to the Committee room at 3.30 pm and this is where I saw Tom Murtagh with Martin Narey and John Podmore. Fortunately, as we arrived the doors to the Committee room were opened and we filed in and took our seats in the public seating area. There were only 3 seats set out for the 4 witnesses and I remember Murtagh having nervously to find a 4th chair. It struck me as being a bit comical and it probably wasn't the kind of start he wanted. He looked a bit embarrassed and everyone's eyes were on him.

The room went quiet and there was tension in the air only broken when Lord Corbett spoke to introduce the afternoon session. This was to be the most interesting evidence session as apart from the then Prisons Minister Paul Boateng MP, these were the main players involved in planning and initiating the raid. The chairman welcomed the witnesses and explained how he wanted the session to run:

LC: Good afternoon, gentlemen. You will know that we are inquiring into the impact of the raid on Blantyre House on 5th and 6th May and related events, and the results of the criminal investigation carried out by Kent police. Perhaps I should explain the way in which we would like to do this. We would like to start with some questions about the career change which had been planned for Mr McLennan-Murray and the appointment of the new Governor, Mr Bartlett. Then we would like to ask some questions of Mr Podmore and Mr Murtagh about the briefing that proceeded the events of 5th and 6th May, and then go into the search itself. I am just explaining this to you, Mr Boateng, because, clearly, neither you nor Mr Narey were actually there when all this happened and your two colleagues, Mr Murtagh and Mr Podmore, were.

Paul Boateng: Of course, Chairman, and in relation to decisions as to the deployment of personnel, that would be an operational matter which you will understand Mr Narey will want, first of all, to respond to, and I will be happy to add anything that I usefully can.

LC: Thinking of past events, I know how important the distinction is between operational decisions and ministerial ones are, not least in the Prison Service.

PB: Quite so, Mr Corbett.

Gerard Howarth MP

GH: Mr Murtagh, can I just pass you this document? Can you tell me if that is your document?

TM: It is a document that was prepared following the search. It was not actually prepared by me, but it was prepared on my behalf.

GH: It was prepared on your behalf?

TM: Yes.

GH: It has your name on the bottom?

TM: That is correct, yes.

GH: Who was it prepared for?

TM: It was prepared to brief the Director General.

GH: It was for the Director General?

TM: Yes.

GH: This was the basis of the information upon which the Director General was—

TM: I am sorry, that is the brief following the search, as I understand it. Can I just look at the document?

GH: It says, "A report of the events of 5th May 2000", and it says, "Kent, Surrey and Sussex area office report of events at HMP Blantyre House, 5th May 2000." So it was after, but it was for the Director General?

TM: It was a report on the search immediately afterwards, the following day.

GH: You may recall that in the document, you said that in paragraph two, "Chris Bartlett was appointed as the new Governor of Blantyre House. Mr Bartlett's first action as the new Governor was to request a full search of the establishment and have every prisoner drug tested." You said, "I accepted Mr Bartlett's request."

TM: That is correct.

GH: Is that not somewhat disingenuous? We were told just yesterday, in answer to my question to Mr Bartlett, that you only approached him on 3rd May, two days before the raid. He knew absolutely nothing about his promotion and you only approached him two days beforehand, and suddenly he should come up with a request for this draconian search, and that you had requested this request. You had been planning this thing for weeks, had you not?

TM: The search was authorised on 28th April and the request was a formality from the Governor. Having taken charge of the prison, he then formally asked for us to carry out the search, which was already planned, which he, as the Governor, had to formally approve, and which he did.

GH: You had been planning this for weeks, had you not?

TM: No, we had not been planning it for weeks. We began planning it on the weekend prior, it was the Bank holiday weekend. It was given formal approval on 28th April, if I remember, and I briefed Mr Podmore to begin planning the search over the Bank holiday weekend.

GH: When did you first discuss this with your so-called Chaucer team, that conditions in Blantyre House were such that it warranted this kind of SAS style raid?

TM: I did not actually discuss it with my Chaucer team. The Chaucer team are a support group who are investigators. They report to us, but I did not discuss it with them at all. I discussed it with my superiors.

GH: In your report, you refer to initial planning meetings. When did they take place?

TM: Can you repeat that?

GH: You said, "I also attended the initial planning meetings to provide advice based on my experience of similar operations in the past."

TM: That is correct.

GH: When did they take place?

TM: I attended the meeting at Rochester. That was on the Wednesday prior to the search.

GH: That is the 3rd.

TM: The 3rd or the 4th, I think.

GH: Is this before or after you had advised Mr Bartlett of his exciting new appointment?

TM: It was on the same day. He attended the meeting.

GH: Was it before or after?

TM: I am sorry?

GH: Was it before or after?

TM: It was after I had told him.

GH: You told him in the morning, "I've got this exciting new job for you. You have got a briefing. The first thing we are going to do is go and raid the place because I was authorised by the Director General on 28th April to do this."

TM: I did not refer to it as a raid, I briefed him that he was to take over as governor and I invited him to the meeting where he became aware of what was planned. That was all the detail that was given to him at the time. He understood that it was a confidential matter at that stage.

GH: Can I move to the actual promotion of Mr McLennan-Murray from being a governor of a prison to being a deputy governor of a prison, which I am told was a promotion? In answer to questions taken in the House of Lords by Lord Mayhew, the former Member of Parliament for the area, Lord Bassam said, "Mr McLennan-Murray's career move to a different type of prison had been planned for some time." Is it normal for the area manager to serve a notice on a colleague that he is to be moved forthwith?

TM: It does happen.

GH: That is a planned career move, just to say, "You are out this afternoon"?

TM: I did not plan his career move. I was merely the courier of a letter from somebody else. I did not decide when he was to move or where he was to move to.

GH: Who did?

TM: That decision was made by the Director General.

GH: On whose advice?

TM: I did discuss it with him.

GH: I think you will find that in the evidence that the Director General gave us it was upon your own advice, Mr Murtagh. So you were not a by-stander in this.

TM: I am sorry, I did indicate that I was quite happy to have Mr McLennan-Murray as part of my team in the area.

Martin Narey: Mr Corbett, can I clarify this particular line of enquiry?

Chairman

LC: If you can help, sure.

MN: Mr Howarth, I take every decision on the appointments. I take all those decisions personally, each and every one. I take them, generally, on advice from the area manager and personnel department. I had decided to move Eoin on from that post some months previously. He had been there for four years and he was ready for a move. Indeed, there were one or two jobs he had personally applied for. So the decision to move Eoin and where he was to be moved to—although I later, on appeal from Eoin, revised that—was taken by me on advice from Mr Murtagh and by personnel.

David Winnick MP

DW: To being a deputy governor of Swaleside?

MN: That is correct.

DW: The Governor of that particular prison was the very person who was given responsibility for carrying out the search on 5th and 6th May, John Podmore.

MN: No. The person who carried out that search, Mr Podmore—who is here today—had been the Governor of that prison. He had already left that prison, or was in the process of leaving, and Eoin would have moved to Swaleside to work with a completely new governor who had just moved into that post.

Gerald Howarth MP

GH: There was a bit of musical chairs going on all of a sudden on 5th May whilst the raid was under way, or had been planned to be under way that night. Is this good management?

MN: I do not think it is musical chairs, Mr Howarth. Eoin had been at Blantyre House for about four years. I think for the majority of that time he did a very good job. He is a man I hold in high regard. I believe he needed alternative experience and I believe, and still believe, he needed experience in a more secure prison. Eoin is a man of some potential and I expect him to govern larger prisons than Blantyre House in the future, and I think he needed the experience of—

GH: Mr Narey, I accept that entirely. I accept that you were well disposed towards him. I accept that you were not totally critical of what he was doing at Blantyre House, but you cannot honestly sit here and tell us that a planned career move was notified to this bloke all of a sudden—although he had, through his own intelligence, got wind of it some three weeks previously—and on the very day that you knew that this bloke and his team were planning this Rambo style raid.

MN: There is a distinction to be made between the decision to move a governor on—I might say that I have, since being the Director General, which is 20 months, moved, I think, 12 governors on at very short notice from prisons that have sometimes been failing. The decision to move Eoin was taken by me sometime before. I think I could produce a letter I sent to the Chief Inspector telling him this some time previously, because he had taken a personal interest. The timing of the move is another matter. I was persuaded, because of intelligence, which I hope I am able to convey to you in closed session, that we needed to bring forward that move and at the same time, following that move, we needed to engineer a search, not a raid, a search of Blantyre House Prison.

GH: It is extraordinary that this planned move should have taken place on the very day that you were planning a search of the establishment. Surely there is no better way to signal to a man that you have no confidence in him than by removing him on the very day that an exceptional move takes place, because everybody who has come before us today has said that it is most unusual to have undertaken this kind of lock-down operation with an outside force and to combine the two. Surely this was not a well disposed move towards somebody to whom you were favourably disposed?

MN: It is an extraordinary move made in extraordinary circumstances. Once I had decided that there was a need to effect a search of Blantyre House, which in itself is not exceptional—there have been six lock-down searches of category C prisons in the previous six months—

GH: By outside forces?

MN: All of them, including outside forces.

Chairman

LC: With sledgehammers and crowbars?

MN: No crowbars were used. No sledgehammers were used.

LC: Maybe I have the tool wrong, but you insert a metal instrument into the gap between the frame of the door to prise it open. Is that a crowbar or is that something else?

MN: A metal instrument is used, which we obtain from the police, especially for our purposes. No crowbars and sledgehammers were used.

GH: You are playing with words. - I think, Chairman, I have finished.

Chairman

LC: Let me just ask another question about this planned career move. It was so well planned that within a few days, it was withdrawn as not being appropriate. What kind of planning is that?

MN: That is not quite fair, Mr Corbett.

LC: Did that happen or did it not happen?

MN: If I may explain. I moved or offered Eoin a move, to be deputy governor of Swaleside Prison. I would not have done that if I did not have confidence in him. Swaleside is a very large and difficult prison. It would have meant that for many weeks of the year, and at least four days in 14, Eoin would have been in charge of that prison, and I still think that in career terms it would have been very good for him. Eoin, with the support of his trade union, protested against that and asked if I would consider, in the circumstances, an alternative move, and sympathetically I did and he is now doing a very important job for me in education services. I remain of the view that the best career move for Eoin, the best way of ensuring that he governs a larger prison sooner rather than later, would have been to take the first job I offered him at Swaleside.

LC: Mr Narey, I have to tell you that you are totally and wholly unconvincing. I accept everything that you have just said to the Committee, but you are totally and wholly unconvincing as to why that had to be done that day with the man given two hours notice to leave the prison. It simply does not make sense.

MN: I think I need to explain later on the extraordinary intelligence which led to that decision and why, once the decision had been taken to affect the search,—

LC: Just a minute. Let us get this clear now, just a minute. So this was not a long planned career move then, it was done on other grounds, was it, which you are going to tell us about later?

MN: No.

LC: It cannot be both.

MN: Mr Corbett, I have explained. It was a long planned move. The timing was the thing that was special to this particular day. I had planned Eoin's move on from Blantyre for some time. The timing of the move was consequent upon the need and the decision to search the prison and I thought it better that the two things should happen at the same time.

LC: We will come to that later.

Martin Linton MP

ML: I do not doubt for a moment that a career move was planned for Mr McLennan-Murray, but what I do not understand is for what reason was the security intelligence that you had gathered not shared with the governor at the time? This intelligence was with the Prison Service for some weeks before the search. As we understand it from every other witness, the normal procedure in these circumstances would be to inform the governor of the prison about intelligence about his own prison. I accept that there may be information that we do not yet have that may shed a new light on this. If it was information about drugs that required a drugs search or if it was information about contraband, all of this, in the normal course of events, would have been imparted to the governor and would not explain a lock-down search carried out at night or carried out at such short notice.

MN: I think I can only adequately explain that in a closed session.
Chairman: Okay.

David Winnick MP

DW: I want to ask you, Mr Narey, if you knew of what can only be described as the tense relationship between the Area Manager, who is present today, and the previous Governor. Were you aware of that?

MN: Yes, I was aware of that.

DW: How long were you aware of it?

MN: I had been aware of it, certainly, since becoming Director General right at the beginning of 1999.

DW: In evidence that we heard yesterday when we were at the prison, it was said by more than one witness from the Board of Visitors that the previous Governor had been the subject of bullying by the Area Manager. Have you heard of that?

MN: I had not heard that either from Eoin or from his union until I was told it yesterday and I heard Eoin say it this morning, nor do I agree with it.

Chairman

LC: Had the Board of Visitors not conveyed this to you?

MN: I do not recall the Board of Visitors conveying this to me. The Board of Visitors have certainly used words such as "robust" to describe Mr Murtagh, but I do not remember them ever conveying to me that Eoin had been the subject of bullying. I find it surprising that he would, because it is only a few months ago that Eoin applied to work for Mr Murtagh in another job as the Governor of Dover Young Offenders Institute.

David Winnick MP

DW: So you were totally surprised yesterday when you learned that he had been the subject of bullying?

MN: I do not believe he was the subject of bullying. I know Mr Murtagh has a robust management style. Frankly, in the Prison Service that is frequently necessary. I think the evidence shows that it is perfectly reasonable to argue that if anything, on occasions, Mr Murtagh had not dealt with Eoin as firmly as he might. When there had been recommendations as long ago as 1998 of disciplinary action against Eoin the Area Manager chose not to follow that. Mr Murtagh has 13 governors working for him at the moment, 11 of them have worked for him before and have volunteered to work with him again. That does not suggest an ogre.

DW: In evidence today Mr McLennan-Murray reported to us one incident which had taken place and the explanation from the Area Manager that he was "winding him up"?

MN: I was not party to that conversation. I do know that clearly Mr McLennan-Murray and Mr Murtagh had slightly different views. I shared Mr Murtagh's view that Eoin had not got the balance between security and resettlement right. I recorded that formally in the Commissioner's book in June 1999 and wrote in extensive terms to the Board of Visitors to convey that view. I do not think that Mr Murtagh's instructions to the Governor, for example, to have prisoners searched on entry to the prison and for visits to be supervised and so forth were unreasonable and I think the Governor should have carried them out.

DW: You were aware of a tense relationship which existed between the two?

MN: Certainly, Mr Winnick.

Humphrey Malins MP

HM: Do you share Mr Murtagh's view that the men at Blantyre were "beyond redemption"?

MN: That view has never been made to me by anyone, and certainly not by Mr Murtagh. No, I do not share that view, if anyone were to make that comment.

TM: May I respond to that?

HM: You should know first that it has been given in evidence to us that you have said that to one of the volunteers.

TM: I have certainly not said anything of the sort. I am a professional prison governor, that is my background. I am in a business where if I had that belief I could not continue to do my job. I categorically deny it.

David Winnick MP

DW: Clearly, both witnesses cannot be telling the truth. You may be telling the truth or the witness yesterday, but you cannot both be telling the truth.

TM: I do not know what the witness said. All I can tell you is the statement that you have made there as quoting the witness I certainly did not say. I do not know what else was said, but I am certainly happy to respond to that.

Gerald Howarth MP

GH: Can I put it to you, Mr Narey, that given you were aware right from the start of this hearing of your responsibilities as Director General, which I recognise are wide ranging, you knew there was this tense relationship between a man who you are well disposed towards, the Governor of Blantyre House, and the Area Manager. Given that Blantyre House was quite different from the other prisons that were then in the Area Manager's command, surely it was unwise to have allowed this mistrust between the two to build up, and surely it would have been better to take Mr McLennan-Murray's career move decision rather earlier than it was taken?

MN: If you remember, at one point in the year, there was talk of changing the role of Blantyre House to become a juvenile institution. I wanted to keep Eoin there. I think he would have been an exceptional governor of an institution looking after boys. I wanted to keep him there. Once that decision had been made between the minister and myself that that was not going to happen, I considered that it was time for him to move.

Paul Stinchcombe MP

PS: If I might go a little further in respect of the statement given to us yesterday in evidence, Mr Murtagh, that you had said that the residents, or inmates, of Blantyre House were beyond redemption. That was told to us by the education manager of Blantyre House and she gave a date upon which you said it to her.

TM: And the date was?

PS: 5th July. It was the date of the minister's visit.

TM: I did speak to the education manager on that date and I spoke to her in the Governor's office in the presence of the new Governor. The subject of the conversation was to pass a reprimand to her for the behaviour of one of her contract staff who, in my view, behaved totally inappropriately in the education department in the presence of prisoners. I spoke to her and asked her to deal with the situation. That was the gist of the conversation that I had with her. At no other time did I make any such comment. There is a witness who was in the office at the time.

PS: Did you say that inmates and residents of Blantyre House were beyond redemption?

TM: Of course, I did not say that

.

PS: You would accept, would you not, that any such statement would be completely out of keeping with the ethos of the establishment?

TM: Absolutely. Can I add that I set the objectives for the establishment, I set the business plan with the Governor for Blantyre House, and if that was my belief then, presumably, it would be reflected in the business plan. I have reinforced my desire that the ethos of Blantyre continues, even with the change. My first briefing to the new governor was to make that explicitly clear to him that the whole ethos of Blantyre had to be maintained.

PS: That was a lie. Was it that we were told yesterday?

TM: Well, all I can tell you is that I did not say that.

David Winnick MP

DW: She was lying?

TM: Well, I did not say that.

DW: You are saying if the evidence given to us yesterday by the lady in question quoted you as saying that and now you deny it, clearly she was lying?

TM: If you like, then she is lying.

Paul Stinchcombe MP

PS: Can I take you back to the document that Mr Howarth referred you to and the questions that he asked you about the second paragraph of that document?

TM: I do not have the document in front of me.

PS: This is a document bearing your name and prepared on your behalf and sent to the Director General.

TM: Yes.

PS: It says in the second paragraph that Mr Bartlett's first action as the new Governor was to request a full search of the establishment and have every prisoner drug tested.

TM: Yes.

PS: That was a request that you mandated of him, was it not?

TM: Yes, it was.

PS: It does not say anywhere in this document that you actually told him that his first action would be to request you and others a full search of the establishment, does it?

TM: I indicated to him when he was informed of his appointment that it was our intention to carry out a search of the establishment.

PS: This document does not make it clear at all, does it, that you told him that his first action would be to request of you and others that such a search take place?

TM: May I finish?

PS: Of course, if you answer the question.

TM: I am trying to answer the question. I did tell him at the time that we intended to search the prison and I explained to him why that was, without going into explicit detail. We had intelligence and reasons for doing that, part of which I outlined to him and he agreed. You can say that I did tell him that we would search there.

PS: This document does not indicate that at all, does it?

TM: No, it does not.

PS: It gives a completely misleading impression as to the source of the request for that search action, does it not?

TM: It does not because the document was not intended for outside the search. The document was intended as an internal document for individuals who were already aware of what had been planned.

PS: Would Mr Bartlett have been appointed if he had said, "I don't want to search"?

TM: The situation never arose.

PS: Would a search have taken place if he had not formally requested that it take place?

TM: In my view, a search would have taken place because that decision had been made at a higher level. I could not envisage circumstances where a governor, confronted with the information provided as a basis for this, would have said, "We should not have a search."

PS: You would need prison specific information of very high quality to justify such a request to be made, would you not?

TM: Can you define what you mean by that?

PS: You have told us that the information you had was such, as I understand it, that you cannot conceive that an alternative decision would have been made.

TM: We had sufficient reasons for concern that warranted a search to be carried out.

PS: Of this particular prison?

TM: Yes.

PS: And without those specific reasons you would not recommend that such a search take place, would you?

TM: We would not have considered that.

PS: Can I take you to the last page of this document? You say here, "I have no information on the situation that currently exists at the other two main resettlement sites, Latchmere House and Kirklevington Grange, but the outcome of this operation must point to a need to subject both of those establishments to similar scrutiny."

TM: Yes.

PS: So, without any detailed information whatsoever in respect of those two establishments you say that they must need similar searches?

TM: No, that is not what I said. I was drawing attention to the fact that I had identified particular weaknesses in terms of the security of the establishment and that I was recommending and suggesting that the area managers of the other establishments should look closely at the procedures in operation.

PS: This is to the Director General?

TM: Yes.

PS: You confirm here that you have no information on the situation at Latchmere or Kirklevington.

TM: That is correct.

PS: Without that information, you nonetheless told him that the outcome of this particular operation must point to the need to subject both of those establishments to similar scrutiny?

TM: Yes, but scrutiny is not search. It is a close look at what is happening at those establishments, which actually did happen I believe.

PS: The suggestion that there is a necessity to subject both those establishments to similar scrutiny is irrespective of any understanding or evidence about either of those institutions or establishments? It is not conditional upon any information at all. You say you do not know any information about those establishments?

TM: That is correct. I make that clear.

PS: I am obliged. It is therefore not reliant upon any information about them or intelligence about those establishments whatsoever?

TM: That is correct.

PS: It is not reliant upon any information about the Governor?

TM: My statement that is here—

PS: Of either of those establishments?

TM: My statement that is here is stating that it might be appropriate in light of what we have found here to look at the procedures that are in existence in the other two resettlement establishments.

PS: For reasons completely unrelated to any intelligence about those establishments?

TM: I was not advocating any search of those establishments.

PS: I just wonder then, what is the similarity between those two establishments and this one? There is no intelligence about them that you had. The only thing that joins them is that they are both resettlement prisons, that is right, is it not?

TM: That is right.

PS: That is the only thing that joins them? Your evidence is that this search points to the necessity for all resettlement prisons to undergo similar scrutiny?

MN: Can I help?

PS: I am asking the author of this particular document who made the recommendation. It must follow, must it not, that you are advocating that all resettlement establishments be subject to similar scrutiny irrespective of any evidence or intelligence information about them?

TM: Regarding security procedures, yes, which is different from searching. That is not what I am advocating.

PS: The outcome upon which that conclusion is based is that which is set out here, the findings at Blantyre House following that particular search?

TM: Yes.

PS: The fact that, as you know, everybody passed the drug test, for example?

TM: Yes.

PS: That mandates, does it, a similar scrutiny of every other resettlement prison?

TM: No. What I was referring to was the security on the movement of prisoners, on the movement of items in and out of prison. That is specifically what I was referring to, not to do with drugs at all.

PS: Not to do with drugs?

TM: No, I was not specifically referring to drugs. I was referring to the lack of security on the perimeter and the ability of prisoners to move items in and out of prison that were unauthorised.

PS: That is very interesting because today we have heard that the officers conducting the search at your request were briefed that the prison was awash with drugs and yesterday you told us that your principal concern, as I recollect it, was with respect to the drug screening at Blantyre House.

TM: I did not say that the establishment was awash with drugs.

PS: No, I did not say that. I have said just now that today we have been told that the officers who undertook the search were briefed that the prison was awash with drugs and yesterday you told us of your specific concern about the drug screening at Blantyre House.

TM: With respect, that is not true. They were not briefed that the establishment was awash with drugs.

PS: You are not concerned with the prison being awash with drugs?

TM: I did not say that. What I said was the staff were not briefed about the prison being awash with drugs. I did indicate to you that there was intelligence, which I am sure we are quite happy to deal with in private session, which gave us cause for concern about the accuracy of the drug test results and that we took the opportunity to carry out the drug test during the search, bearing in mind that all prisoners in Blantyre have signed contracts agreeing to be voluntarily tested.

PS: When you took those drug tests everybody passed?

TM: Well, one prisoner refused to take the test and there was one diluted sample initially.

Gerald Howarth MP

GH: You know why the prisoner could not take the test, because he was incapable of passing urine.

TM: I am sorry, I do not know that.

GH: You ought to know that, Mr Murtagh.

Paul Stinchcombe MP

PS: Just to understand this. On the back of that search, you recommended to the Director General that every other resettlement prison undergo similar scrutiny. However, so far as drugs are concerned, on which you did have intelligence, the actual search showed you there was no use of drugs at all?

TM: That is correct.

PS: That would not justify, would it, similar scrutiny at other prisons?

TM: I was very pleased to see that. However, I was concerned that drugs were found. The issue I was referring to was the generality of security systems and the fact that staff are conditioned in these environments and we need to keep alert to that.

PS: It follows, does it not, that what you actually say in this report is that you do not need intelligence to justify such scrutiny of a resettlement prison? You do not need intelligence in respect of a governor. You do not need intelligence in respect of any drugs. You simply need the outcome of this particular search even though it shows there was not even drug use at this prison. That is what you are saying.

TM: No, I am saying in every prison—we are dealing with prisons here—prisons have basic security needs. They are defined in the search strategy agreed between the governor and the area manager of the respective establishments. What I am suggesting is that we need to ensure that in all the establishments these search procedures are being carried out and that the security procedures have been carried out because what we discovered at Blantyre was they were not being carried out.

PS: You see the concern that I have is a very simple one. It seems to me to be quite clear from this document that you do not support the ethos of resettlement prisons because you here request the Director General to search or to scrutinise similarly all resettlement prisons even without intelligence, and on the back of a previous search of one of these establishments which shows no drug abuse at all.

TM: I do support the whole concept of resettlement under the ethos of Blantyre. My correspondence with the Governor and the instructions I have given and the business plan of the establishment reflect what I believe. I am sure you have already had sight of the document that I issued to the Governor before there was any awareness of this going on at the moment. I fully support the resettlement concept. Where perhaps I might differ from some is that I believe there has to be a balance and that balance has to take into account of public protection in what we do. The risks are measured risks when we allow prisoners into the community and the circumstances in which we allow them into the community. I believe that I am right to do that. Can I finish, please, because I have not finished answering your question?

PS: Of course.

TM: Secondly, with regard to the broader issue of resettlement, I have already set up an additional resettlement unit at Rochester within my area and I am proposing the further development of another one at Stanford Hill. I became aware, as I have no doubt you have heard in evidence, that there was a lack of a clear policy in this area regarding resettlement. Two years ago, because I felt that through a lack of guidance and the fact that governors in these establishments were operating on their own initiative and sometimes on the parameters of what is acceptable in terms of public risk and taking initiatives themselves, I felt that there was a need to have clear guidance and clear policy on resettlement. Initially, I brought the governors of resettlement prisons together with a view to encouraging the service to develop such a policy which the Director General has picked up now and which others have. So two years ago, I was actually advocating a clear policy for the service on resettlement rather than seeing the situation develop where the whole concept of resettlement might be put in danger by mistakes being made. I am sorry, I do not agree with you.

PS: Can I just ask one final question? You have told us that the manager in charge of education must have been lying when she said that you told her that the inmates at this place were beyond redemption. Was the Governor also lying when he told us this morning that you called him and told him there were going to be shock/horror probe stories in the newspapers the next day and when he checked up there were no such stories and when he checked with you, you told him that you were winding him up?

TM: I have no knowledge of what he is talking about. I do not know what he is saying that I said was going to be in the papers the next day.

PS: You never made those calls?

TM: I do not recall ever making such calls.

David Winnick MP

DW: We have two witnesses who are lying to us.

TM: I am answering the questions that I have been asked.

DW: According to you, there have been two statements made to us which are lies?

TM: Mr Winnick, when I spoke to the education manager, I was in the presence of the prison Governor who I think is a third party who is aware of what was said. He can confirm that what I am saying is true.

Chairman

LC: Mr Narey?

MN: I thought it important as a recipient of that note to stress how I received it. I did not receive it as any suggestion that we needed to do the same things at Kirklevington or Latchmere but it would have been bizarre and, indeed, negligent of me not to learn from what we found at Blantyre and get the respective area managers to check the other resettlement prisons. Similarly, when we found out the drivers were driving uninsured the first thing I did was make sure that was not happening in other areas.

LC: I just want to get into the boardroom at Swaleside Prison at 6.30 on Friday May 5.

TM: Okay.

LC: Were you both there? Who actually gave the briefing?

John Podmore JP: I gave the briefing. At that particular meeting there were in the room what I would describe as the bronze commanders, those were the people with specific roles leading specific groups of people through the actual search.

LC: You explained the purpose of the search to them?

JP: Yes. I also at that point, as I did later on with the bulk of the staff, told them where exactly they were going because up to that point they did not know.

LC: Who briefed what we will call the Indians?

JP: I did.

LC: You did?

JP: Yes.

LC: Can you tell me the terms in which that briefing was given?

JP: Yes. I called all the staff together. First of all, I told them where they were going because at that point they did not know. I described to them the nature of Blantyre House because I could not assume people knew precisely how the prison worked. I would like to think that I have some understanding of how Blantyre House works in that I worked with Jim Semple in the early days in 1987 when he set Blantyre House up. I worked with Jim to arrange for the very first prisoners to go from Maidstone. Subsequent to that I have now been recruited by Sir David Ramsbotham as one of his team leaders.

LC: I just want to ask—

JP: No, what I am saying to you is I am heading up the resettlement thematic on behalf of Sir David. So what I am trying to say by way of preamble is that I understood fully the nature of the establishment and I tried to convey that to the staff that night because I felt it was important that I tried to share with them some understanding of what was a relatively unique establishment.

LC: Thank you for that. That is very helpful.

JP: Okay.

LC: What advice, if any, did you give them about degrees of aggressiveness that they were permitted to use against the background of your own knowledge of Blantyre House?

JP: It was my belief, and I shared it with the staff, that the prisoners would co-operate with the search. The likelihood of that co-operation would be enhanced by staff behaving and dealing with them in a reasonable manner.

LC: Yes

JP: One of my prime concerns that evening was the treatment and conditions of those prisoners at Blantyre House.

LC: Thank you. What comment, if any, did you make about the way in which the search was to be carried out in terms of where they should collect keys from, for example?

JP: There were relatively few keys for the establishment.

LC: You did not know that at the time, did you? I am talking now about 6.30, or did you know that?

JP: Yes, I have worked there. I was temporarily in charge for a period many years ago.

LC: When you say relatively few keys, what do you mean by that?

JP: Well, most establishments have what is known as class one, class two, class three. Class one and class two are the main security keys that you would find on the perimeter of the establishment or on the perimeter of buildings.

LC: Yes.

JP: The keys within Blantyre House are what are known as class three keys.

LC: You would know where they were kept?

JP: I took with me on the search as a matter of deliberate policy, a governor four who was working with me by the name of Alan Shipton. Alan had worked at Blantyre House, again with Jim, for a long period of time and I knew before we went, and it transpired that he had written the key systems for the establishment and that those key systems were theoretically still operating because the documents pertaining to the key systems of the establishment were still in his own hand.

LC: Right. When you arrived, did you check the key register? You will be aware that there is a key check carried out three times a day, the last one following the 8:30 roll call, so that would be about nine o'clock. Did you check that register?

JP: When we arrived, I would have assumed that a key check had taken place.

LC: I did not ask you that.

JP: Did I personally check them?

LC: Did anybody check the register?

JP: As far as I am aware, Alan Shipton did that as part of his attempt to get keys later on.

LC: Could you write to us and let us know whether he did, in fact, check that register?

JP: You are asking whether the key register was formally checked on entering the establishment?

LC: Yes.

JP: I can do that for you, yes.

LC: Can you then tell me, against your very detailed knowledge, as you explained, of Blantyre House, what grounds led you to equip some of the officers with sledgehammers and other instruments of that kind which would anticipate they were going to have trouble getting into at least some of the rooms?

JP: First of all, it has been said, and I accept that you refute the terminology, but we did not have sledgehammers. A key part of the search team was the National Dog Team, led by a very senior experienced member of the security group who I have worked with for many years, not least at Belmarsh where I worked also. Now they carry, and have developed over the years, significant expertise. They carry out lock down searches. They carry out wide ranging security operations, day in, and day out, across the Prison Service. They do some tremendous work. Now, they have developed, as part of their equipment, a whole array of things, and one of the many reasons for having them along is that they are prepared for every eventuality.

LC: Do not let us quibble about—

JP: They had equipment which was specifically designed to force entry into doors where entry by normal means was not possible.

LC: Are you aware of any requests being made by anybody concerned in that raid for keys and being told that they could not be found?

JP: Could you repeat that?

LC: Are you aware of any of the officers taking part in the raid requesting keys and being told they could not be found?

JP: Yes, every door that had to be forced, we looked as far as we could—

LC: You could not find the keys?

JP: We could not find the keys.

LC: This is why I asked you about the key register. So the inference then is that some officers had breached prison discipline by not returning keys to where they should be returned?

JP: I know of at least one admission of that case on one of the very first sets of keys we tried to find which was for the catering area.

LC: Are you aware whether that officer or any other officers have been charged with disciplinary offences in connection with not returning keys to where they should be returned?

JP: I have no knowledge.

LC: You have no knowledge. Would you accept from me that no such charges have been made? JP: I would accept that.

LC: Let us just stay with the briefing now. At any time, based upon your own personal live knowledge of Blantyre House, did you question what it was planned to do there? Did you say to Mr Murtagh "Look, are you sure that we should do this?".

JP: No.

LC: All right. Is that because you did not feel that you had the authority to question it and you were obeying instructions in that sense?

JP: I think it is well known my ability and willingness to question almost anything that I come across in the Prison Service.

LC: So you had no reason to doubt that this was a sensible thing to do?

JP: Reference has been made to the Chaucer Team. You may or may not be aware that I headed—well I did until I left to join the Inspectorate—up the Chaucer Team and I set up the model. In terms of the intelligence issues, I was well aware of those intelligence issues.

LC: Okay. Let me just get on to the actual search and then I will hand it over to my colleagues. There was a considerable amount of damage done around the prison, not just locks expertly opened, as it were, prised open, door frames smashed down, doors smashed off their hinges, is that right?

JP: I would refute anything other than the technique by which the National Dog Team—

LC: I am not asking about the technique. I am asking about the amount of damage. Is that a reasonable description of some of the damage done in the prison that night?

JP: I would not have used that terminology, no. There was forced entry to a number of doors.

LC: Door frames were smashed from the wall and doors smashed down. We have seen photographs of this, you have not?

JP: I was there.

LC: I know you were there. You did not see any of this?

JP: I saw doors damaged. I saw door frames damaged. When you are forcing entry into a locked door by means of which the dog handlers are well practised in doing, there will be damage that is inevitable.

LC: What was the point of breaking down both doors which led into the same medical room which also included dental and x-ray equipment? What was the point of that, given that prisoners are never ever allowed in there on their own?

JP: The strategy for the search which is a fairly routine strategy in lock down searches is that there will be a hand search by search teams. In this case, there were five teams of three searchers who were in direct contact with prisoners. There were 15 staff in contact with the prisoners in the prison area. The other element of the search is that the non prisoner areas would be entered and the ammunition and explosive dogs and the drug dogs would do a sweep of those areas. The object of the search was to carry out the A&E, the ammunition and explosive search, and the drug dog search in all those non prisoner areas.

Martin Linton MP

ML: Do I take it you were looking for firearms?

JP: We were looking for everything. One extreme would be firearms, ammunition and explosives and the other extreme the relatively routine contraband.

Chairman

LC: Are you aware that two hours before those doors were broken down, as a result of a prisoner being suspected of taking drugs and he said, "I am on medication which may give this result", keys were used to go into that centre to find the prisoner's records to confirm what he said was the case, then they were locked up again and then two hours later the doors were smashed down?

JP: I have no knowledge of this.

LC: You have no knowledge of it?

JP: No.

LC: You were in charge of this, were you?

JP: I was indeed.

LC: Were you in the training centre or in the prison?

JP: I was in the training centre which is the normal way in which something like this would be conducted. Towards the end of the evening I did go into the prison to see for myself how things were going, how the place was being left and to talk to the searchers and prisoners.

LC: As a result of you doing that that night, were you satisfied that there had been no excessive force used anywhere in the prison that you saw?

JP: Yes, I was.

David Winnick MP

DW: What was the estimated cost of the damage?

JP: The figures vary, so I am at a loss to put a precise figure on it.

MN: The cost to us was about £2,500, Mr Winnick. The commercial value had we had to buy materials which we manufacture ourselves, would have been about £6,000.

DW: Yes, that is the sum I heard. Mr Podmore, the door to the Chaplain's office was broken into, amongst all the other doors. It was felt that the prisoners had concealed things without the knowledge of the priest?

JP: With respect, I have described how a search of this nature is carried out and all non-prison areas—all non-prison areas—are swept for ammunition and explosives and for drugs, that is all the non-prison areas.

DW: On the basis that the key could not be found to the Chaplain's office?

JP: I would expect, and have experienced it myself, for my own office to be searched. It is not necessarily casting any doubt on the integrity of one individual, it is about the integrity of a particular type of search.

DW: Was any attempt made to find the Chaplain and ask him to open it?

JP: No.

Ian Cawsey MP

IC: On that point, I spoke to the Chaplain yesterday who said he was in that office that afternoon and had handed his keys in the normal way, so they were clearly there when he left the prison.

JP: I can only repeat, and this is clearly a slur on my own personal integrity, the assertion is that I went like some rambo raider beating my way around the establishment, smashing in doors for the fun of it—

IC: They are your words, not ours.

JP: The assertion that I would not attempt to gain proper entry into any room, the assertion that I would simply say "Okay, let us take the doors off, let us batter the doors down," I find quite disturbing.

David Winnick MP

DW: Mr Podmore, I do not think slurs on your integrity is the appropriate way to describe what we are trying to do. This inquiry is to try and find out, as far as we can, what happened during the night of 5/6. Therefore to start making remarks like you have made does not help us whatsoever. We are trying to find precisely, as far as possible, the truth and we will make a report accordingly.

JP: My apologies. You must understand that very much has been said about this search and this

is my first opportunity to personally put my side of the story.

IC: We are pleased to give it to you.

David Winnick MP

DW: What was found in the Chaplain's office?

JP: A sum of about £400.

DW: What happened to that money?

Humphrey Malins MP

HM: The total money recovered, which we were told was "large quantities of money", that is what the Committee was told, paragraph 12 on 16 May, "large quantities of money", turns out to be £370 of which £120 was the Chaplain's.

JP: I find that highly unusual. It was taken, its nature ascertained and it was returned.

David Mr Winnick MP

DW: There were no monies found which should not have been there?

JP: If I was the governor of an establishment I would strongly discourage, to put it mildly, the retention of such large amounts of cash in a non-secure part of the establishment.

Gerald Howarth MP

GH: Are you suggesting that the Chaplain was somehow irresponsible?

JP: I make no comment about how the money got there. I have not been party to any further investigations as to how it arrived there.

David Winnick MP

DW: It was not stolen money, unauthorised?

JP: I am afraid I have no idea.

MN: It was not but it should not have been held in his drawer in his office.

DW: We have got that cleared up. It was not unauthorised. It was not stolen money in any way.

HM: Chaplain to blame.

David Winnick MP

DW: The Chaplain, as my colleague is saying, was clearly to blame in your view?

MN: Not in the least. All that Mr Podmore is explaining is that it is unwise—and I have spoken to the Chaplain about this and I believe his account entirely—to have a sum of money of that magnitude. £100 may not be very much to us but it is a large sum of money in the context of a prison. It should have been securely locked in a safe in the administration.

DW: Can I just ask Mr Podmore about the board of visitors? Two were present, I understand, at the beginning of the search?

JP: That is correct.

DW: Up to what time?

JP: My recollection is 12.35.

DW: Were they under the impression that no further action was to be taken, hence they left the premises or not?

JP: No. They must speak for themselves but at 12.35, the search was barely half-way through. At 12.35 I think we had barely started: one of the key elements of my briefing which I did not get an opportunity to refer to was that the specific brief of the principal officer in charge of the search of the prisoner areas, who was responsible for the five teams of three searchers, was to spend as much time as was necessary walking around the areas, talking to prisoners, explaining to them what was happening and doing her best in what were clearly very difficult and unusual circumstances. She was to go as far as she possibly could to allay the fears of the prisoners. That took, I think, at least a couple of hours. My response when she contacted me and said she was worried about how long it was taking to start was "Take as long as we need to make sure that the prisoners fully understand and as far as possible we have their co-operation in the process".

DW: Would it not have been far better, if I may just put it to you, if the board of visitors had been encouraged, the two, to stay or their colleagues to come to the prison to watch what was being done to act as independent witnesses?

JP: I was astonished they left.

DW: Perhaps they left on the basis that they were not aware of what was going to happen?

JP: When I first learned they were leaving, I assumed that someone else was coming in their place. I was astonished that at that stage of the operation they would choose to leave. There was clearly an awful lot to do. My experience with boards of visitors at Swaleside and at Belmarsh—with whom I have liaised very closely and would like to think I had a very positive relationship over the years—was such that that was beyond my experience. I was astonished that they went.

DW: If you read the evidence of what was said to us yesterday, Mr Podmore, you might get a different impression.

Humphrey Malins MP

HM: One way I would like to describe this raid is a complete sledgehammer to crack a nut. Can I just say this: the inference we would draw from previous evidence to us would be there was a vast amount of items there which were illegal and dangerous, etc. Let me just analyse a couple of these for a moment. Firstly, Mr Murtagh's report talks about a prisoner having a lump hammer, a spirit level, very useful to prisoners to help them readily breach the perimeter fence. Further elsewhere, we are told about the spirit level being of some use for an escape attempt. Now let us get real. If this prisoner is working outside the prison and using a spirit level and a lump hammer in his job do you think it is going to be easier for him to escape from the prison simply by going to work one day and not coming back or putting a spirit level against the fence at midnight and hitting it with a lump hammer? Which do you think is easier?

MN: May I answer that, Mr Malins, because I heard some humour about this yesterday.

HM: It is not just humour, it is a real point.

MN: First of all, I will share with you, that I have known of a number of prisons where prisoners return from temporary release and then seek to escape. The point about the equipment which was found, which included an electric drill, was not that the particular prisoner who was using it outside might use it but another prisoner might use it. Can I just put it on the record because I have heard it a number of times, particularly in the press—and I have been frustrated myself and not been able to put on the record my side of the story, I do not want to prejudice my appearance here—that the suggestion that things found there were not of importance is quite untrue. There were three unauthorised mobile phones. One of them had a SIM card removed before we got to it but two of them had been used by prisoners at Blantyre House to speak to prominent criminals in the North West of England. There were credit cards which they should not have had, and a passport.

HM: Leaving aside for the moment those other matters, I have been addressing the issue of the so-called escape equipment and pointing out the silliness of the argument. Also 12 cameras were found. Now, were these not part of the camera club?

MN: Again, if I may, I think this is for me to answer. There were cameras, they should not have been in cells. The governor had no authority to let them be in cells. It is absolutely central to prison security and to prisoners that we do not allow cameras. One of the men who had a camera had taken photographs and had photographs in his possession of keys in the prison.

Chairman

LC: Sorry, let us just get this, you said "keys in the prison"?

MN: Yes.

LC: You used the plural. We were told yesterday it was a photograph of one key.

MN: Perhaps it was.

LC: No, no, you said the plural. Which is it?

MN: I do not know.

LC: You do not know? Mr Narey, shall I tell you then?

MN: Yes.

LC: It was a key to the prisoner's door of which he took a photograph.

MN: I would still not want any prisoner to take a photograph of a key to his own door—

LC: It was part of his project.

MN: I think that was unwise. May I put on record the list, Chairman, I think it is very important.

LC: Yes.

MN: Cameras, some cannabis, some ecstasy—

Gerald Howarth MP

GH: How much?

MN: A very small amount of cannabis.

GH: How small?

MN: I do not know.

GH: Well, it is time, Mr Narey—

MN: And a few ecstasy tablets.

GH: Do not please misrepresent to the public that somehow this raid divulged a substantial or significant quantity of drugs, it did not.

MN: I have not sought to do that, Mr Howarth. My submission to you makes it absolutely clear that it was a small amount. There were some ecstasy tablets, very few again, although I put it to you that if the prisoners were not using drugs, who were they for? I think that is a worry.

GH: They may have been for the dogs, to keep the sniffer dogs current with the sniffing out of cannabis.

MN: I am sorry, I do not understand, Mr Howarth.

GH: You understand more about the way sniffer dogs work.

MN: There are no dogs routinely at Blantyre House.

GH: No, they may not be routinely at Blantyre House but the suggestion was put to us that was what they may have been there for.

MN: If I could continue. I accept, and I am delighted that prisoners were not taking drugs at Blantyre, they are all drug free before they go there. We should still be worried about the presence of ecstasy tablets in their possession when prisoners are going out. There was a prisoner very recently working at a school in Kent. Tattoo equipment, car radios, presumably stolen, a Stanley knife and other knives, and extensive hardcore pornography. This is not stuff to lightly dismiss, Chairman.

David Winnick MP

DW: The executive report concludes by saying that the argument put forward was that "...nothing had been found to have gone wrong or no more than one might expect..." which does not hold water. It does not indicate, by any means, that some terrible revelations came to light.

MN: I agree with that. As I will be able to tell you in a closed session, it may have been that we could have found something considerably more serious but the suggestion that nothing was found would be quite misleading.

Gerald Howarth MP

GH: Chairman, can I go back to the actual raid itself because there have been complaints about the style of the raid? My colleague, Mr Malins, suggested a sledgehammer to crack a nut. Other people feel that it was a disproportionate response. In evidence to us, Michael Duff, one of the tutors at the prison, who ran the photography course—it was not a club. It was a course leading to qualifications, some of the inmates have gone out and pursued a career outside now equipped with photographic skills—wrote to us and said when he returned to his classroom on the Monday after the search: "... the sight that greeted me was one of complete devastation. The metal store cupboard where I keep students' work and camera equipment had been forced open and the contents were strewn about the floor.

On inspecting the damage, it seems that one of the students' work is missing. This student had produced a level three folder to a high standard. ... did a great deal of hard work and study to achieve this and he has been a very dedicated student. To have his work missing was bad enough but I cannot understand why it was necessary for the other student's work to be thrown on the floor and kicked around". You were the silver commander, presumably the gold commander was sitting next to you.

John Podmore: No, that is not correct.

GH: Who was the gold commander?

JP: The gold commander was Michael Spurr who was the area manager.

GH: You were the silver commander, you were in charge to the extent that you were there.

JP: Indeed.

GH: What was the justification for that? Did you know about this?

JP: No. I would like to answer the allegation you are putting before me. I have said already that as part of the team for the search I had someone by the name of Alan Shipton who used to work there. Also on the ground throughout a significant part of the night was the new Governor.

GH: He did not know the place, he was brand new.

JP: Also on the ground was Brian Pollet, who had been the Governor there for some considerable period of time. Also, I had with me the head of the National Dog Team, a man with, as I have said already, great experience and integrity. Now I needed and I wanted those senior people around, walking about, talking, supervising all the things which were going on. Towards the end of the evening, I went into the establishment myself. Throughout the key part of the evening, there were also members of the Board of Visitors. I am as saddened as anyone else that they did not choose to stay on. Now I did not see what you are describing to me. Neither was any such scene described to me by any of those key senior people that I had on the ground, precisely to supervise the activities which were carried out.

David Winnick MP

DW: You justify everything that happened? You have no regrets about any incident which occurred on the night of 5/6?

JP: I have not said that. I regret very much that it was necessary to force entry into certain rooms.

Gerald Howarth MP

GH: Was it necessary to damage prisoners' work? What sort of example does that send to the prisoner about respect for other people's property?

JP: Firstly, the initial reference you made to the prisoner's work was I believe a file of photographs that was part of the course work for that particular prisoner. That was removed and I believe—and I may stand corrected—it has been subsequently returned. The allegation that other work was damaged, destroyed and thrown around the place, I am afraid I have to refute.

Chairman

LC: Mr Podmore, you cannot simply refute it. Is he lying to us? Is that instructor lying to us? Why would he make that up?

JP: No. I am saying that when we left, I was adamant that we checked things, that we looked around, that we made sure that as far as possible—yes, okay, doors had been damaged—that sort of thing had not taken place and did not take place.

LC: Let us try this another way. If that is as it is alleged, would you still defend that?

JP: Of course not.

LC: Right.

JP: Of course not. If it did happen, and I cannot account for the action of every single member of staff who was under my command that night, if it did happen, and it was one of them, then I am responsible, I have no problem with that.

Ian Cawsey MP

IC: I am still trying to get to the end of my Chaplain's questions. We always seem to get off that subject. When I visited the Chaplain's office yesterday and spoke to the Chaplain, he told me about his key, as far as he was concerned, being readily available. He also wanted to show me, also, that the team broke down the door to gain entry but then left untouched a large locked cabinet. Now we have spoken about there being a clear strategy for this search. What strategy has the idea that you break down the door to gain access to an area and then leave a large cabinet locked and untouched?

JP: Can I help you by explaining to you the way in which A&E dogs and drug dogs work? They are able to detect the presence of whatever substance they are trained to detect in a cupboard. So breaking open a cupboard if it is not readily accessible is not necessary.

Paul Stinchcombe MP

PS: You were looking for money in the Chaplain's office amongst other things. You took 120 odd quid out. Why not open the cupboard as well?

JP: No. May I refer back to the overall strategy of the search which I alluded to earlier which was to check the non-prisoner areas via the use of A&E dogs and drug dogs for those substances? Now if they came across cash in that context then it was quite appropriate for them to remove that cash.

David Winnick MP

DW: The Chaplain was not hiding any drugs?

JP: As far as I am aware, there were no indications by the drug dogs—

DW: That surprises me a great deal, Mr Podmore!

Ian Cawsey MP

IC: Was this an intelligence driven, briefed search of Blantyre House or was it a fishing expedition?

JP: I would not describe it as a fishing expedition.

IC: You would not describe it as a fishing expedition. You have obviously done these sorts of searches before at institutions other than Blantyre House. If we go through what has been found, we have a small amount of cannabis, so small the Director General cannot quantify it. We have a small number of ecstasy tablets. We have what the Director General says is a considerable quantity of pornography, it was actually seven items, in a 120 man prison. Compared with other searches you have done, would you say this was a considerable amount of contraband and the

like, in your experience?

JP: I have recently visited Kirklevington as part of the Chief Inspector's recent inspection and I would have to say, having spent a week in Kirklevington walking around, talking to prisoners, talking to staff, that I would not have expected to find the same amount of material in Kirklevington Grange.

IC: I did not ask about Kirklevington Grange, I asked from your experience, which you have got in other prison institutions, would you say what you found in those searches would be higher or less?

JP: My main experience was searching in places like Belmarsh, which is a very high security prison. So it is not unreasonable to draw a comparison with other sorts of establishments. The comparison I would attempt to draw would be with a similar type of establishment.

IC: But in a high-security prison you might say that drugs would be even tighter to get through. If there was only a small amount of cannabis and a couple of ecstasy tablets, I am asking you whether that is a good catch from your perspective or whether it can be regarded as a very small amount compared with other prisons you have actually searched?

JP: It is a small amount of drugs, that is clearly obvious. As the Director General said, if the ecstasy tablets were not for use within the establishment where were they for use? I have to say, I do not know whether you have looked at the profile of the prisoners. It has been mentioned already that they were drug free when they got there so it seems unlikely that Blantyre was housing hard drug users in any event.

IC: Why the search then?

JP: The search was for a range of things, anything from drugs, ammunition and explosives, through to relatively mundane things like—

HM: Spirit levels.

Ian Cawsey MP

IC: Spirit levels and pornographic photographs.

JP: Can I address the point about the builder's tools? We seem to have lost sight of the fact that this prison houses I believe 20 lifers?

MN: 20 lifers, yes.

JP: One of whom is serving a long sentence, albeit a long time ago, for the murder of a police inspector.

Chairman

LC: Finishing a sentence.

JP: Indeed. There are still 20 lifers in that establishment.

Ian Cawsey MP

IC: Mr Podmore, you have just said that this search was for drugs, ammunition and explosives. So we know you have got virtually no drugs. What ammunition and explosives were there?

JP: I have said, the brief was to look for anything from the range at one extreme of drugs and ammunition and explosives across the spectrum. I did not know what we would find.

IC: It is a fishing expedition. Let me finish, Mr Podmore. At the end of the search, do you have a de-brief of your officers?

JP: Yes.

IC: Of the officers who took part in that, what were their comments about what they found?

JP: The main comment I got from the staff who I spoke to was the quantity of belongings in cells.

IC: Nothing to do with drugs or ammunition or explosives. They had a lot of personal gear, is that what you are saying?

JP: Yes. I am sharing with you what they were saying.

IC: That was what I asked you to do. I am grateful for that. Do you think there was a feeling of "what was all that about then"?

JP: You would have to ask them. I cannot speak for them. I am sharing with you the main bit of feedback that I got back from the staff that I spoke to.

IC: Mr Narey, related to this drug issue, since these changes have taken place at Blantyre House, which you have authorised, the drug situation at Blantyre House now is very much worse than it was before that raid.

MN: That is news to me, Mr Cawsey. Why is it very much worse?

IC: You are the Director General and I think six months down the line, you should know.

MN: Well, tell me your evidence to say that the drug situation is very much worse.

IC: Talking to prisoners and inmates at Blantyre House yesterday.

MN: Yes.

IC: Some of them were saying for the first time in their experience of Blantyre House that heroin was available for sale.

MN: I can promise you, Mr Cawsey, if heroin is available for sale in Blantyre House now, certainly it was more easily for sale before the events of 5 May. Certainly, although the prison is still relatively insecure, as far as secure prisons go, there is considerably more searching going on in that prison than previously. There has been the removal of certain prisoners who might have been involved in those activities.

Chairman

LC: No heroin was found prior to 5 May.

MN: No. I did not say that. Mr Cawsey said that heroin is now available in the prison.

LC: Yes?

MN: I am saying if that is true, and I am not sure if I believe it, I am saying if it is available now it would certainly have been more easily available on 5 May.

LC: On what do you base that?

MN: Because security has been improved since 5 May.

Ian Cawsey MP

IC: But it has not, has it? You have had more abscondence and escape. What sort of security are you talking about?

MN: I will tell you the sort of security, Mr Cawsey, the security which makes sure that we take away the nonsense of when I go to a prison, to Blantyre House, and hand my mobile phone in, yet prisoners do not, they take them straight into the prison. When prisoners go into a prison I expect them to be searched, they were not being searched.

Chairman

LC: Mr Narey, you know why that is. This gets to the nub of what this is about. You know the emphasis that was put on trust there.

MN: Yes.

LC: It may offend. Certainly it offended Mr Murtagh.

MN: It did not offend me.

LC: If you are going to run a regime which is based on trust, you are going to have different levels of security from your bog standard cat C prison.

MN: Indeed and trust is very important. I am fully committed to the belief that prisoners can change. I would not have spent all the years that I have in this service if I did not believe that. You have to pepper that with some realism about temptation.

LC: Yes.

MN: You must do that. A measure of trust in Blantyre House, if I may, Chairman, was that ten prisoners were so trustworthy they did not insure their cars; two others did not have MOTs. We would have had a very different view if a child had been killed in Tunbridge Wells.

Ian Cawsey MP

IC: Mr Narey, not for the first time today you are misrepresenting findings from Blantyre House, whether maliciously or just through lack of information, I have not quite decided. Is it not the case that with some of those people who did not have—and I accept did not have—valid insurance of their cars that was because the brokers had said it was valid but it was actually a disagreement between the broker and the insurance companies which neither the prisoners nor indeed the staff at Blantyre House could possibly have known?

MN: A rather larger number than ten had not identified to their insurer they were serving prisoners. My information, and I can check it, is that ten, in the event of an accident, would not have been insured.

Chairman

LC: I am sorry, that is not the evidence we have had. We have had evidence given to us that some of those who for example simply gave their address as "Blantyre House", when the insurance companies were phoned up they said "We know from the postcode it is a prison". Some insurance companies take it and some do not. Please do not just telescope all these things together. It does make a difference.

MN: My belief, my information—I will check it—is that ten of the prisoners were not insured. I heard Mr McLennan-Murray express considerable regret about that this morning and he was quite right to do so.

Ian Cawsey MP

IC: All I am saying is I think you are misrepresenting the degree to which the prisoners were misleading or abusing the trust. You were using that as an example of abuse of trust.

MN: I am trying to demonstrate, Mr Cawsey, that if you run a regime such as Blantyre House—and Blantyre House is very different from Kirklevington and Latchmere House, it is much higher risk, there are more serious prisoners/criminals there, serving longer sentences—it is a high-risk operation, risk management is central, you have got to be realistic about that.

IC: I accept that entirely but can you explain to me, if your changes are to improve security, why have there been the abscondence and escapes since these changes were made?

MN: My understanding—again I will have to look at this[3]—is that we have had one escape since May 5. A few weeks before May 5, there was an attempt to escape, a serious attempt to escape, by three prisoners and those prisoners were apprehended and transferred to other prisons. I draw no conclusions but in fact, there were three serious attempts before May 5 and one escape subsequent to May 5.

IC: There have been some absconders as well?

MN: There have been absconders before as well.

IC: Not in the same quantity. It has declined considerably in the six months since you made the changes.

MN: In the six months since May, I understand there were five absconders, about the same number as previously. I do not measure the effectiveness of prisons on their popularity. If prisoners choose to abscond, I do not think "Well we must be doing something wrong".

IC: No, no. It is interesting that before May an attempted escape failed but with your improved security the one after May succeeded.

MN: I am afraid the reality of Blantyre House, as the previous Governor made clear this morning, is such that there is a risk involved in that. It means the balance of security must be right. I am not wanting to turn it into a Cat C prison. I just want proper measures to be taken so the prisoners are supervised when they are at work and they are searched when they come into establishments, and things like that.

IC: Yesterday we had evidence from a prisoner at Blantyre House, who had a placement out in the community, due for parole in about six weeks' time, and he had a paid job, about £480 a month, with a guarantee of a job the day he walks out of the prison at £22,000 a year plus a car plus expenses. He has clearly done extremely well and you have stopped that placement and jeopardised that relationship. What is the gain in the resettlement policy that leads to that?

MN: I know nothing of that case.

IC: Well, take it from me, that is true.

MN: Let me answer your question, Mr Cawsey. Since May 5, we have had two job placements stopped. One of them may be the one you referred to, I do not know. The other one has been restored. Two more have been found and we are on the verge of introducing perhaps as many as ten additional work places. I am committed to the ethos of Blantyre House. I am committed that prisoners will be given every opportunity to demonstrate their fitness for release. I will look into the case you mentioned. I do not know about it.

IC: I am pleased you are going to look into that. Finally, because I do not want to take any more of your time, other colleagues want to come in. Can I say this: what do you think the result of your decisions has been on the performance of Blantyre House and the morale of the staff and the local authority workers and the volunteers who were involved in this? How do you think they feel about Blantyre House now?

MN: I know from my own visit to the establishment a few weeks ago when I spoke to all the staff and my numerous discussions with members of the Board of Visitors, that morale has been knocked and it is very important that we pick it up. I put it to you, Mr Cawsey, the changes that have been made at this prison where morale is supposed to have been destroyed are that the senior management team has been changed, four prisoners have been removed and not returned. You have the same staff, the same prisoners and there is no reason at all why all that was good about Blantyre House cannot continue. There is a greater consideration and acceptance of the need to protect the public. Some of the things which were happening I believe were unacceptable. I am prepared to mention some of those now but there is a great deal more to mention in closed session.

IC: Just to finish then—this is not really a question, it is a comment for your ears as the Director General—you can take it from me then, and I am sure colleagues had the same experience, that yesterday we could not find anybody who could have a single good thing to say about the post 5 May regime.

Janet Dean MP

JD: What made you think that over 80 prison officers involved in this search would be necessary? Why 80? Why 84? Why that number?

JP: Would you like me to run through the breakdown of how that 80 odd was made up?

JD: Yes.

JP: Clearly, there was myself and other senior managers that I have referred to. There was the need to run a command suite in the education area. There was the dog team, which routinely consists of ten dog handlers and 20 dogs, they have two dogs each with different specialisms. The bulk of the staff—I will not go into the full detail, the information is available to you—consisted of the search teams. I have made reference already to the fact the search teams were five teams of three, 15 staff. I know it has been described that we descended on the place like Rambo raiders descending from helicopters, body armour, goodness knows what, that is complete and utter nonsense. The searchers were in civilian clothing. They entered the building and they liaised with the prisoners. They ascertained the cooperation of the prisoners. It was 15 prisoners (sic) in the house block who were doing most of the routine searches. They were later augmented because of the time it was taking, because of the amount of equipment available, by others. The other main group of staff were two teams of what is termed C&R units, control and restraint teams, and two teams of 14. They were there as a precautionary measure should there be any problems with the prisoners.

Chairman

LC: Were they in uniform?

JP: They were in uniform. They were not in riot gear. They did not have body armour, as has been alleged continuously by the press, and I think by my own Association. That would not be the normal way in which they were deployed. The only time at which any member of staff donned any sort of protective gear was initially. If you are familiar with the place you will know there is a closed courtyard, overlooked by the cells. At the start of the search it is routine to have someone outside the cell windows to observe whether any kind of contraband would be thrown out. It is reasonable for anyone in that kind of situation who is overlooked by prisoners in their cells to wear some form of protective clothing. All the other talk of body armour and helicopters and SAS style raids is complete and utter nonsense.

Janet Dean MP

JD: Who was responsible for breaking doors down? Which of these groups?

JP: That would have been at the hands of the dog teams because they had charge of the equipment to do it.

JD: Are you aware that we have been told that Mr Shipton appeared once the medical room had been broken down, certainly two hours after it had been opened by a team, saying "Why did you not wait until we had a key"?

JP: I am not aware of that.

JD: You are not aware of that. Did you say at the briefing that the prisoners were in control of the prison?

JP: That is nonsense.

JD: Either figuratively or not?

JP: Complete nonsense.

JD: It was not said at all?

JP: No.

Martin Linton

ML: I am looking forward to getting on to broader subjects, such as trust and the resettlement ethos. I just want to try to explain to Mr Podmore what our difficulty is about the nature of this search. I think everybody completely understands that some things were found as a result of this search which were very serious, including the fact that several people had failed to declare that they were prisoners on their insurance and also the charity funds not being accounted for. I understand that it is now being investigated and as far as I understand, it is a question of dishonesty.

For a lockdown search, and I am not subscribing to any of these wild exaggerations that have been made about it, even without all of those exaggerations, there are half a dozen things about it that seem unusual to us. Number one, the fact that force had to be used and the keys were not found, although admittedly keys had been left, which one must admit is strange. Second, I would maintain that there were not very significant findings as a result of it, certainly no positive tests on the drugs which is almost unheard of in any category of prison. Third, it was carried out at night and I do not understand why that was necessary. Fourth, and perhaps most importantly of all, most mystifying to us is that the governing Governor was not informed about this in advance, which I think is very unusual. Fifth, it was felt necessary for it to be carried out by an outside team You have given very full replies to most of these points and maybe we should not keep the subject going forever but the problem for us is there are only two possible explanations for all of this. Either the intelligence that you had was very poor and misleading, or it was a disproportionate reaction. Mr Narey said in his report that he did not feel that it was a disproportionate reaction. We are left in a position where we cannot make all of the facts fit together. The suspicion that we have, and I am really asking you to put it at rest, is having instituted a search on intelligence which then turned out to be that you got much less than you expected for it, there would be a natural human tendency to want to look for something to justify the scale of the search. I found in the report on the management of Blantyre House some evidence that maybe this is what is going on. I will just quote to you from this report. This is not one of the bits that is in any way confidential. It points out that "the argument often put forward because nothing has been found to have gone wrong, or no more than one might expect, does not hold water. There have been serious difficulties at Blantyre House in the past six years." This is the bit that worries me enormously: "We are sure that it is likely that there have been ones of which we are not aware", almost as though there was an attempt to find problems even though you actually returned from the search with very little to show for it. We just want to be assured either in the private session or in some other way that there really was justification for a search. We know there were some things found but a search on this scale at night, with 84 people, not informing the Governor and with the use of outside forces, in the history of lock up searches, as far as we understand it, this was quite an exceptional search.

MN: I think I should answer that, if I may, Mr Linton. You are quite right, although I have identified the things that were found here were still serious, we did not find what we might have thought was there. I need to explain in a closed session the full concerns and the intelligence which led me to make a decision on this. I do not think a decision to make a search can be justified retrospectively on what you find. I have just had at Full Sutton Prison, Wakefield Prison and Long Lartin Prison, lockdown searches for, in each case, more than 24 hours each where we have conducted extensive searches and in none of those situations found what we thought might be there. We do very many more searches than those that are justified by what we find. The decision has to be made, and I made the decision, to conduct this search on the basis of what was known to me at that time, as I will be able to tell the Committee in closed session. Because I was aware that you might be sceptical about that intelligence I have gone back to those sources and asked them and they agreed to give me much greater and specific details, which I think you will find convincing.

ML: I look forward to it.

Humphrey Malins MP

HM: I will just tell you what really worries me about this, Mr Narey, is when the Committee was spoken to on 16 May, being told respectively by the Minister and yourself that there was "a quite frightening amount of contraband material" and "large quantities of money". That is the sort of phrase which, in effect, makes us think that there is a gold mine of stuff that should not be there. When we see an internal document confirming that cash was only £370, of which £120 was the Chaplain's, nine mobile phones, bank cards, cameras, building tools, a spirit level, and hard pornography, we turn over to find where the real stuff is and none is there. It is difficult to avoid the conclusion that on 16 May, we were not given the correct picture.

MN: I am sorry if you think that was the case, Mr Malins. I do think those things that we found were very serious. I have explained that already and I have tried to tell you why. There were things there which prisoners could escape with, for example the possession of a passport, and the Prison Service would have been held up to ridicule. I accept and volunteer that we did not find everything that we might have found relative to the intelligence which was in my possession.

Paul Stinchcombe MP

PS: Can I just ask a few further questions, Mr Podmore, about the search and what the briefing was and what the mechanism was? You have said that you never used the words in the briefing that the prison was "under the control of the prisoners"?

JP: That is correct.

PS: Did you ever use the words "the prison was awash with drugs"?

JP: I never used that phrase, refute it totally and absolutely.

PS: Did anybody use those words?

JP: Not to my knowledge.

PS: Have you heard those words used at all?

JP: In relation to Blantyre House?

PS: In relation to Blantyre House?

JP: No.

PS: Why is it that when we went round the prison yesterday, so many of the officers to whom we talked had been told by colleagues who undertook the search that they were briefed that the prison was awash with drugs and under the control of the prisoners?

JP: I cannot comment.

PS: Why did the Prison Officers' Association have the same words in front of them this afternoon?

JP: I can only tell you the briefing I gave to staff. I am either a liar or I am not.

PS: I am not suggesting that at all. I am just trying to understand how it is that we have been led to believe that many of the people undertaking that search were briefed in those terms.

JP: Can I perhaps give you a rationale for why I would not have said that why is it highly unlikely that I would have said that? I was Governor of Swaleside for some four years and at Swaleside I had a number of projects, offending behaviour projects. I also ran the largest drug treatment community in the Prison Service, that was a 120 bed specific drug treatment unit. That was providing drug treatment with the assistance of Addaction, who you may be aware of, and my officers working in conjunction with them. I dealt with and we treated and provided aftercare for a significant number of difficult, damaged prisoners who had a range of drug problems. I have to say to you that in the four years that I was Governor of Swaleside, not one of those prisoners ever managed to get to Blantyre House. My perception of the profile of the prisoners that were getting to Blantyre House were the sort who were not the difficult and damaged prisoners that I was dealing with in my drug treatment programmes but had other backgrounds which would probably not lead to them being widespread drug users. The figures are available and you may find that a more significant number are there for trafficking and importation rather than use thereof.

PS: How did so many people get the impression that the prison was awash with drugs and under the control of the prisoners?

JP: No doubt to discredit the search and discredit me, I must imagine.

TM: Can I be of help because I was present when the briefing took place? I can also confirm that those words were never used in the briefing.

PS: The search was nonetheless to look, we have just been told, for guns, arms, explosives, drugs and anything down the range of contraband.

JP: That is correct.

PS: And we know that you found no drugs and no arms and no explosives and we know the extent to which you found drugs.

JP: Yes.

PS: The dogs that you referred to, presumably they were used principally to search for explosives and for drugs. Would they have been used to search for anything else?

JP: It is possible to use them in what is known as a sweep across open areas to detect, shall we say, unusual items. If you had a football field, say, you could deploy them as a kind of zig-zag sweep and they would find something out of the ordinary.

PS: There is a football field at Blantyre. Were they deployed for that purpose?

JP: No. The grounds of Blantyre House, as you will be aware if you have been there, are quite extensive. The technique of letting dogs loose in that kind of operation was not something that I wanted to do, given that it was at night. Okay, there was some lighting but it was relatively limited. If there are dogs loose when a number of people are around, that is not good practice. Can I finish? They were used to search certain areas on what is called a long leash which would allow them to partially carry out that manoeuvre but they would still be under the control of a handler and not a danger to anyone else who might be around the buildings.

PS: The fact is, is it not, that because you chose to search at night you could not search the bottom of the compound and some of the other ground areas at all?

JP: That is correct. I would have to say that in any search, you have to draw certain limitations as to the extent of that search.

PS: But you had intelligence here that led you to go in heavy-handed, mob handed.

JP: No, I am sorry—

PS: Can I at least put the question to you? You may answer it in whichever way you wish.

JP: Okay.

PS: You had intelligence which justified, so we are told, going in with 86 or whatever it was officers in order to search for arms, explosives and drugs and yet by going in at night it was impossible, was it not, to search the bottom compound, other ground areas and the Portakabin used as a recording studio? You could not search anywhere in those areas for that contraband, drugs or explosives.

JP: First of all, you have made yet another pejorative reference to the nature of the search. I have tried as best I can to address that. You are saying that, no, I did not search every square inch. As ever in these situations I have to make certain decisions as to how much I can search and where I can search. I decided not to and I take responsibility for that.

PS: So you did not search the bottom compound, the other ground areas and the Portakabin used as a recording studio?

JP: We searched some ground areas but I am pretty sure we did not search the bottom of the football field.

PS: Let me take you back into the Chaplain's office, where you broke the door down, even though the Chaplain told us he left his key at the gatehouse. Just there we are told that you did not search the locked cupboard either.

JP: I have attempted to explain that.

PS: It would have been impossible, would it not, to have found whether there were mobile phones, cash, bank cards, passports, forged driving licences, cameras, building tools, pornography, tattoo equipment, screwdrivers or car radios in that cupboard or any other cupboard without opening it?

JP: Again, I refer back to the strategy of the search, which I think I have explained about three times now, which was that the hand searching, looking for the whole range of items, was done in the prisoner areas. The communal areas were only being searched for ammunition, explosives and drugs. So, yes, you are absolutely right, that cupboard could have been awash with mobile phones but I was not looking for mobile phones or cash cards in those communal areas. It is about drawing certain limitations and parameters on the search to make the exercise practical.

PS: We know you found no explosives, we know you found very little drugs and we are now aware that it is thought that what was found was so significant that this particular raid was nonetheless justified. That is the list that I have just described to you, and yet you made no effort at all to look for any of those things in the locked cupboard in the very office that you broke into.

JP: As I say, I have explained the strategy of the search and I think that answers your question.

PS: I am trying to understand whether there is any rationale for the strategy of the search. You did consider it sufficiently important to look for money in the Chaplain's office to take the money from his desk. Why was it not sufficiently important to look for these other items in the cupboard?

JP: As far as I am aware, the cash was discovered. There was not a specific, deliberate attempt to search for anything other than ammunition, explosives and drugs. I do not know, I can make some enquiries and write to you, but it may well be that the dog had indicated, and it is possible for dogs to indicate for a whole variety of reasons. For an A&E dog, it is possible to indicate the presence of the chemicals found in ammunition and explosives which are fairly innocuous things, it may well be there was a minor indication of some sort in a drawer. If there had been an indication by the drug dog or the A&E dog to the cupboard then the cupboard would have been emptied by some means.

PS: The office in the gym, was that also searched?

JP: As far as I am aware, yes.

PS: Was the door also broken in there?

JP: I cannot recall.

PS: We were told yesterday that the door was broken in even though, again, the key had been left at the gatehouse.

JP: Yet again, I have addressed the issue of the keys. If I was aware that the keys were available and the keys were available then the doors would not have been broken down.

PS: What instructions did you give to those undertaking the search as to whether to look for keys before breaking down a door?

JP: I spoke with Alan Shipton, who was the guy who wrote the key systems. On one occasion, there was a particular set of keys that initially we could not find but we were able to obtain them by examining the systems. He was key to my information and my decision to force doors on the advice that as someone who was familiar with the place, familiar with the situation, he was not able to obtain the keys.

PS: Were medical records checked in the health area before the doors were kicked in?

JP: I have no knowledge of that information.

PS: No knowledge as to whether that door was opened by a key before it was thereafter broken down?

JP: I am not aware of that. I would be surprised if that was the case.

PS: Were you aware of the graffiti left by some of those officers on the blackboard in the gym?

JP: I am aware that it is alleged that the words "We woz 'ere"—excuse my grammar—were chalked on a blackboard.

PS: Are you impressed by that?

JP: Of course not.

PS: Is that provocative?

JP: It is totally inappropriate behaviour.

PS: Is it provocative?

JP: It probably is, yes.

PS: Do you think knocking down the doors when keys might have been found is provocative?

JP: You are saying that I knock down doors regardless of—

PS: I am just asking whether you consider it to be provocative to break down doors if keys are available?

JP: As far as I was concerned, the keys were not available.

David Winnick MP

DW: Mr Narey, is it not unfortunate that we are discussing what happened at an institution of which you yourself in June 1998, when you were Director of Regimes, said "If any establishment is delivering the Government's manifesto commitment on constructive regimes, it is Blantyre House. Its offending behaviour programme, education and general atmosphere are all impressive, including the staff and prisoner relationships, and are likely to make a real difference." Do you remember?

MN: Very well, Mr Winnick, yes.

DW: So when you wrote those comments you had visited the prison, seen around the establishment, am I correct?

MN: Yes. That was at the time of my first visit to Blantyre House. I have visited probably half a dozen times since.

DW: And on the later occasions?

MN: My view of Blantyre House, as I made plain to the Committee when we first discussed this, is that it has a great deal to commend it. I think the word I used to describe it the last time we spoke was "precious". There is something very, very special about Blantyre. There are exceptionally good staff-prisoner relationships. At the same time as I have written very complimentary things in the visitors' book I have also expressed some concern to the Governor about certain matters relating to security. When I went, for example, in June 1999, I said there was much there that I admired but I expressed frustration at the failure to properly supervise temporary releases and I am still anxious about those. I expressed considerable anger at finding in the education block only three prisoners there and made the observation that I believed prisoners were pleasing themselves whether they went to education or not. I may say I was delighted three weeks ago to see the education block for the first time in my experience teeming with prisoners, including so many in a literacy class that they were overflowing into the chapel.

DW: Your predecessor as Director General of the Prison Service, Sir Richard Tilt, visited and he said that he was "delighted to see such a constructive atmosphere in a small establishment. The Governor and the staff", that is the Governor who has been removed, "are to be congratulated for what they are doing".

MN: I can only repeat, Mr Winnick, that there is much about Blantyre House that I admire but there are certain things more recently which I do not admire. I do not find it acceptable, for example, without making any indication of how it came to happen, that £2,000 from a prison charity account held by the prison, apparently donated by a broker in the City, denied by that broker, was paid in cash—

Chairman

LC: Mr Narey, it is entirely up to you what you talk about but we were advised that you did not want this discussed in public.

MN: I am being very careful, Chairman. I am not making any comment at all on how it happened or who was culpable for it. The fact is I was seized with information before the search that charitable funds were not being properly managed and subsequently I discovered that £2,000 in cash was placed in the hands of a serving prisoner serving a very, very long sentence. I do not think that is acceptable and I think that damages the prison.

LC: I must stop you because you do not know whether that is acceptable or not because that issue has not been resolved as far as I am aware. You are quite right to raise the concerns.

David Winnick MP

DW: I get the impression, perhaps my colleagues are coming to a different conclusion, that every effort is being made to try to find fault with what happened in that regime under the previous Governor. Everything is being brought up which is totally at variance with what was said previously by you and by Sir Richard Tilt. If we can bring ourselves a little nearer to March of this year, the Chief Inspector of Prisons—I do not want to get him into trouble—said "I conclude by praising the consistent and courageous approach of the Governor and Staff at Blantyre House for their very difficult and challenging task on behalf of the public". Presumably, Sir David has pretty good knowledge of what is going on in prisons.

MN: He has a very good knowledge, Mr Winnick. He also said in the same report, "We were concerned that much of the routine of the prison and its discipline depended on the prisoners behaving and policing themselves." I think that is an example which David acknowledges of the balance not being right. When staff informed me that a released prisoner on temporary release appeared on *Stars in their Eyes* on a Saturday evening, apparently drinking in a pub with people, that does not suggest that I am serving the public very well and I could be gravely embarrassed by that. All I am trying to do, and all I did in making the decision to move the Governor and to effect this search, is to try to ensure that all that is good about Blantyre is protected, because I know if there was a major controversy surrounding Blantyre House its future would be in considerable doubt, as it has been in the past.

DW: Mr Narey, if you were in our place and you were taking evidence like we did yesterday, I wonder how far you would have been surprised to find that no one, in fact, was defending the change of regime and no one was defending the search on 5/6 May. The prisoners perhaps are biased so you can say that they do not count. The prison officers were highly critical and the Board of Visitors. In fact, as I say, no one was defending what occurred. Would that not have surprised you if you had been in our position?

MN: I would not say for a moment that the prisoners do not count. I never go to a prison without spending a great deal of time talking to prisoners, and I do at Blantyre. I would, however, have been somewhat sceptical of the criminal background of those you formally interviewed yesterday, five of the six of whom had convictions for very serious drug offences. I would certainly have taken that into account in what they were saying about the availability of heroin. I am well aware that the staff, the Board and the prisoners have been dismayed by the occurrences of this search.

DW: Why should prison officers be so critical?

MN: Because the prison officers have seen it as an implicit criticism of their work at the prison, and to some extent it is. I do not think they have been carrying out and taking to work a proper security consciousness. When I met the POA, this was just a few weeks ago, the POA Committee expressed surprise at my suggestion that visitors to prisons should be (a) supervised and (b) a number of them should be randomly searched. They did not seem to think that was necessary. I find that extraordinary.

DW: So for the prisoners, you have a reason to give us as to why they are critical: because they are not having such a nice time. The prison officers are critical because it seems, according to you, they are being criticised for the way in which they have acted. What is your explanation for the Board of Visitors? They are naive perhaps?

MN: No. I take the worries of the Board of Visitors very seriously and I have gone to considerable lengths, both before 5 May and since then, to spend time with them and convince them of my anxieties. I attended a board meeting in June 1999. The Board Chair and the Vice Chair visited my home and I have given them a reasonably thorough briefing on the intelligence behind this. I saw the Board Chairman last Friday. I take their concerns very seriously. I will offer the view that I do think certain members of the Board have allowed themselves to get rather too close to prisoners and have ceased to be as dispassionate and objective as they might.

DW: Do you know that the Chief Inspector of Prisons, giving evidence this morning, in reply to a question from my colleague, Mr Malins, described the search as "ghastly"?

Humphrey Malins MP

HM: "A terrible and ghastly mistake".

MN: I was pretty surprised at that because I spoke to Sir David about this just the other day in the knowledge that John Podmore had managed the search. I asked David for his view as to whether or not it was conceivable that John would have allowed wanton destruction to take place and Sir David was unequivocal in ensuring me that he did not believe that. I want it put on record that I accept entirely, for example, the Chaplain's views that his keys were there, but I also consider it inconceivable that Mr Podmore would have proceeded without genuinely trying to find them. I find that inconceivable. I trust John Podmore. I do not think he tried to do anything that was unnecessary during that search.

David Winnick MP

DW: You should be very, very concerned indeed at the situation at that prison now, the low morale, the lack of confidence in the new regime. These are matters that I would have thought are of the gravest concern in an institution that has been so widely praised and which undoubtedly has played a very important role in trying to reform criminals.

MN: I am extremely concerned about it, Mr Winnick. I did not join the Prison Service 18 years ago with any other intent, perhaps somewhat idealistic at the time, than to help criminals reform themselves. I am entirely committed to it. I might say as Director General, I have made some pretty impressive moves during that time. I have made huge inroads into literacy and numeracy never done before in the service, 32,000 qualifications last year, and drug abuse has plummeted right around the prison estate. I have doubled the number of offending behaviour programmes, which have now proven to reduce offending. I pay acknowledgment to Eoin McLennan-Murray who played a pioneering role in the development of those programmes some years ago. I am entirely committed to the things that it is clear the Committee are concerned about as well.

DW: I do not question that, Mr Narey.

MN: If I may finish. I am desperately realistic about the way that security problems can blow the service off course. In 1990 following the Woolf Report this service saw a considerable emphasis on resettlement and rehabilitation. In 1995, when the service had lost its grip on security and we had five Category A escapes and about 250 other escapes, we had security, security, security as the mantra and everything stopped. I have been a very fortunate Director General, I have received an unheralded investment from this Government in constructive regimes to the tune of about half a billion pounds. There is not a choice between resettlement and security, you can have both. I am very proud of the fact that in simultaneously making the sorts of improvements right around the estate that I have, in the first half of this year we have had eight escapes compared within 1993, for example, in the same period 116. That is how you retain public and parliamentary confidence.

DW: You have just spoken about your commitment to education and how you have seen it improve in Blantyre House since the new Governor has been in post and since 5 May.

MN: I did not say since the new Governor, I said since my last visit. I acknowledge entirely that some of the improvements in education have been delivered by the previous Governor.

DW: Let me just read to you a very small extract, the final paragraph in fact, from the recent submission to us by Blantyre House Education Manager and Curriculum Leader, a joint submission: "There is less of a Governor presence in the prison; previously, Governors visited the Education Department daily, speaking to tutors and students alike. This no longer happens. Staff feel less supported and their work is devalued. Students feel isolated, mistrusted and disheartened and feel their achievements are not actively recognised. The strong leadership coming from the Governors is no longer visible. It is becoming increasingly difficult to perpetuate the previous climate of trust, loyalty and working together to maintain all that Blantyre House stands for." That comes from people who are delivering your education service in your establishment, so how does that lead to the standards you wish?

MN: It comes from an Education Manager brand new to—

DW: Not just the Education Manager.

MN: The Education Manager is brand new to the Prison Service, whose experience of prisons and prisoners goes all the way back to last November.

DW: She has done six months of the old regime and six months of the new regime.

MN: I acknowledge the improvements made by the previous Governor but I can tell you for the first time a few weeks ago, during this apparent regime where the Governor does not visit, I saw more evidence of genuine learning in the education centre than I had seen before. Blantyre was not alone. I inherited a situation where education was altogether too recreational. We have turned that about and Blantyre, like other places now, has many prisoners who are doing things which will make them employable.

DW: Are these two more liars to add to our list?

MN: They are not liars at all, it is an opinion and I do not share that opinion. The evidence that I have seen from the Education Department very recently is that it has been much improved although nowhere near as much as it should. I do not accept that I am getting value for money for ministers with an average class size of six, which is what I have at Blantyre even now, considerably more than it was.

DW: Why did you close the photography class down?

MN: For the reasons I mentioned, because I do not think cameras should be in prisons. As a matter of fact, I do not think photography should be—

Gerald Howarth MP

GH: You have a competition amongst prisons, the best photographic work by a prisoner.

MN: Prisoners do not have cameras in their cells.

Ian Cawsey MP

IC: That is a different issue.

MN: It is not a different issue, Mr Cawsey.

IC: Of course it is.

MN: The cameras were all in prisoners' cells and they should not have been there.

IC: You can deal with that issue without closing the photography class down.

MN: I do not think that against a statistic where two-thirds of my population of 66,000 men have levels of literacy so low and levels of numeracy so low that they are ineligible for 96 per cent of jobs. That is not my statistic, it is the Basic Skills Agency's statistic. My belief is the priority is literacy and numeracy and not recreational courses.

Chairman: The time is getting on and I am very conscious, Mr Boateng, that you have been very patient.

Ian Cawsey MP

IC: We have never known you so quiet.

PB: It has taken some self-control.

DW: He wishes he was not here.

Janet Dean MP

JD: We visited the joinery shop while we were there with good examples of creativity but also work that could actually lead on, as photography can, to work when they are in the outside world. We heard there are less students in the joinery shop than there were before 5 May.

We are deeply concerned about the photography, especially since other prisons are doing it. Surely it must be possible to ensure that cameras are not in people's cells and that course continues. We appreciate all that you are doing in literacy and numeracy, that is great, but are you saying that all other things go out of the window?

MN: No, not at all. What I am saying is that the priority has been on literacy and numeracy. As a matter of fact, I spend about 40 per cent of our total education budget on literacy and numeracy and we have a full range of other courses, Open University courses and so forth. I am not saying that there is not in any circumstances room for photography and I am not saying I would prevent the Governor from reintroducing some element of photography there, so long as it did not result in prisoners having possession of cameras in their cells, that is the issue. I do not think it is a high priority. I am fascinated to hear evidence of a prisoner who has left for a photographic career, that is the first I have heard of it but I will certainly check up on it.

Chairman

LC: Thank you. Mr Boateng, as I say you have been very patient. Could we just go back to when Mr Narey came to you and said, "I have got this intelligence which in my view, justifies this kind of search at Blantyre House", whenever that was? Do you have the power to advise him that it is not a very sensible thing to do or it is a bit over the top or "take your time, do it during the daylight"? Where is the line between your responsibilities and the Prison Service?

PB: Chairman, my responsibility is for policy, the Director General's responsibility is for the day-to-day administration of the service and for operations and it is a very onerous responsibility which he discharges with enormous distinction. My primary concern has to be, first and foremost, the protection of the public and the prevention of crime. That is the bottom line for me as a Prisons Minister. I believe the public is best protected and crime prevented by ensuring that we hold prisoners in safe and decent conditions and that we address effectively the causes of their offending. That is why resettlement is enormously important to me and this Government and, I know, to the Committee. Indeed, it was partly as a result of my understanding of what Blantyre House was achieving, my knowledge of the Committee's view of Blantyre House and its achievements, that caused me to express the view that any change in the status of Blantyre House as anything other than a resettlement prison would be undesirable. That is a view that I share with the Director General. That is a view that I believe reflects my responsibility for broad overall policy and resources.

The management, however, of resettlement prisons is a matter that I believe falls squarely within the operational responsibility of the Director General. I would not expect him, nor did he, to seek authorisation for a lockdown and search of this nature. He has not in other cases where there has been a lockdown and search and I would not have expected him to have done this. However, he is aware of my interest in Blantyre House and resettlement. He was obviously aware of the sensitivities around Blantyre House and on 4 May, my private office and myself were informed that it was his intention that there should be a lockdown and search of the premises and we were informed that there was intelligence, the nature of which we will be disclosing to you in more detail in the private session, that would warrant such an action. That, so far as I was concerned, was the end of the matter because if the Director General, in whom I have trust, comes to me and says "Well, there is an issue, criminal intelligence backing it up, around Blantyre House. I believe I have got to have a lockdown and search", then I am glad he has informed me of that but it is an operational matter for him and I would not dream of interfering.

LC: Did he tell you at the same time of the planned career move for Mr McLennan-Murray? PB: I would not know and I would not—

LC: Did he tell you about the change of Governor?

PB: I would not expect him to seek approval from me for changes in terms of the structure of staffing. He may have felt it necessary to do so and if he would seek to inform me through my private secretary or directly of the fact that at the same time, he intended to do x, y and z, that would be a matter for him, but it would not be for me to say "should we not be using him over there" or "should we not be appointing x, y and z", that really is not a matter for me.

Gerald Howarth MP

GH: Chairman, rather than go back over some of the nitty gritty that we have discussed before, I think this really comes to the nub of the issue. I do not think anybody on this Committee would expect you to have complete details of every single governor and where they are moving, that is a matter for the Director General, but given your recognition of the sensitivity of Blantyre House and the uniqueness of the regime that was being operated there, you must have been aware that this kind of search that was planned could have very serious repercussions on the way in which Blantyre House was going to continue to operate?

PB: Mr Howarth, my first concern has to be the protection of the public and the prevention of crime. As an integral part of resettlement, and you will appreciate this I know, there is a need to get the balance right between security and a sufficient degree of freedom to enable that resettlement to be effectively brought about. It does require a degree of trust undoubtedly, and that trust is important. I have listened to the proceedings so far and I have visited Blantyre House on two occasions now since the action that the Committee is investigating and there is no doubt that trust has been shattered. There is no doubt that it is going to be a long, hard job to restore it. I want it to be restored and the Director General wants it to be restored, but it has to be restored on the basis that we have got the balance right between the requirements of security and the requirements for—

GH: Yes.

PB: If I can just continue because I have been very quiet.

GH: Yes, you have, I will acknowledge that.

PB: And unusually so, as you well know, Mr Howarth. That does mean that we do have to get the balance right between security on the one hand and effective resettlement on the other. If we do not and there was an incident involving serious crime or a threat or a danger to the public as a result of something that was going on at Blantyre House, it would discredit not only Blantyre House but resettlement generally and the work that we are seeking actively to promote, not only in the three institutions where it is currently taking place but across the whole piece, and I cannot afford for that to happen and neither, I believe, would this Committee wish it to happen. I back the Director General 100 per cent in ensuring that we do now what is necessary to get the balance right, to restore trust, so we can get on with the business of actually evaluating and spreading what works in Blantyre House because I believe it to be of value in the important job we are doing, which is turning lives which in the case of the inmates of Blantyre House have been lives of deep criminality. Let us be very clear, we are dealing in Blantyre House with people who have criminal records of a grave and serious nature. If we can turn their lives around, as I believe it is possible to do because I do believe it is possible to change lives, then we will do the public a great service. We do have to make sure that we actually do it well and do the right thing and do it in a way that can command public confidence.

GH: Minister, I do not think there was one word of that with which any of us would disagree. We understand this question of getting the balance right but on the evidence we have seen it has been suggested to us, and I think we are minded to accept, that the regime that did operate was a better balance than that which has been introduced. We have to accept, and you know me, I do not have a reputation for being a softy, that these are people, however grave the crimes they have committed, however despicable those crimes, who are going to be released into society. The issue is surely this, is it not, that Blantyre House gives the Prison Service an opportunity with a very different regime to prepare men for release into society, the result of which is that society will be less at risk from those men than they would have been had that resettlement facility at Blantyre House not been made available to them. The evidence is there in the recidivism rates: eight per cent for Blantyre House, and roughly 50 per cent for the general body of the prison population.

I think what has really upset us is whereas morale was high and enthusiasm was great, that morale has been profoundly damaged. You have said you are committed to the concept of Blantyre House but I do not think you are committed to the concept that previously ran. Can I just draw to your attention what Sir David said in his report: "It is an intrinsic part of the regime being offered that risks must be taken with those prisoners being released on temporary licence to do work in the community... Far better for society that such risks are taken within the more controlled environment of a prison sentence than after a prisoner has been released." Surely that is the point, that what haunts all of us—you, Mr Narey, Mr Murtagh, Mr Podmore, us—is some headline like "Multiple murderer having a whale of time out of Blantyre House" when he should have been inside breaking up stones or something. It is that fear of those tabloid headlines, is it not, which is driving us to a more controlled regime which is reducing the trust between staff and prisoners and therefore making them more likely to be ill-prepared for the outside world than they would otherwise have been?

PB: My concern is not headlines, tabloids or broadsheets. I do not make the distinction that you do in that respect. My concern has to be, and I have to repeat myself because I cannot stress this sufficiently, how do I best protect the public? How do I ensure that prisoners are held securely, safely and decently and that they address the causes of their offending in a way that commands public credibility? That has to be my primary concern. I must not allow headlines, tabloids or broadsheets to deflect me from that. I hope you will feel, as a Committee, that I have not in terms of the issue of public protection, allowed headlines, tabloids or broadsheets to deflect me from my primary task.

My concern has to be in relation to Blantyre House or in relation to any other prison getting that balance right. I accept that they were aspects of the previous Governor's stewardship of Blantyre House which were wholly commendable, wholly commendable. I am also bound, Mr Howarth, to take the professional advice of those who work for the Prison Service on other aspects of the regime at Blantyre House that did give cause for concern. When you have heard, as you shortly will, the evidence given in closed session, you will understand the grave nature of that concern which I could not, and I do not believe this Committee will possibly be able to, ignore. That does not mean that we do not want, and are not determined to achieve once again, in Blantyre House something that can be held up as an example of the best that the Prison Service can do. I believe we can achieve that without prejudicing security but I am not prepared to prejudice security because my first duty has to be to protect the public.

GH: But you are prepared to prejudice security in so far as you let these people out of jail.

PB: I do not let them out of jail. The law takes its course and in due course, they are released. What I have to do is to—

GH: I mean while they are at Blantyre House on work placements. So far as there is a facility for work placements you are taking the risk.

PB: That is precisely why, Mr Howarth, we do have to have a concern, for instance, as to where they go and work. If somebody goes and works some distance away in circumstances which do give cause for concern as to the bona fides of the employment, if somebody goes to work in circumstances where there is reason to believe that contact of a criminal nature has been made, then I would expect my Director General and my Area Manager to be concerned about that. They were, and as a result of their concerns they took certain actions.

Paul Stinchcombe MP

PS: Would you expect them to tell the Governor?

PB: I would expect them to take such steps as they felt necessary in order to protect the public and to prevent crime. That would normally include informing the Governor of their concerns. There might well be exceptional circumstances when it was not possible to do that for one reason or another. Yes, that would normally include informing the Governor.

Gerald Howarth MP

GH: Minister, we are looking forward to the compelling evidence which we are disappointed has to be heard in private.

PB: When you hear the nature of it, Mr Howarth, knowing your concerns, as I do, you will well understand.

GH: Fair enough, we will accept that, but please understand where we are coming from. We are coming from a position where we do not have, I think it is fair to say, the same confidence in the Prison Service that you as the Minister do. We have noted Sir David Ramsbotham's remarks today that he has a very high regard for Mr Narey but, having said that, when you came here, both of you, on 16 May, which was ten days after the search, we were told that there was this frightening amount of contraband, money and all the rest of it and in answer to my concerns about damage done, Mr Narey said: "The total amount of damage, I might say, is in the region of £400; and that meant we could be absolutely sure that every area of that prison had been searched." It was not £400, it was £6,000, although £2,500 actual cost to the Prison Service.

MN: And I did correct that afterwards. I did correct that and wrote to the Committee immediately afterwards.

GH: We know that every area was not searched. We know that the total cost was actually £26,700 because that is Mr Murtagh's calculation of the time of the staff, etc. We were told that you did not have access to the keys but we were told that Mr Shipton actually had the keys to the health centre and as the men were beating down the door he came in jangling the keys and said "here they are" and they apparently laughed and said "it is too late". This is why we find we have some difficulty, Minister.

PB: Mr Howarth, I well understand and I do not want you to believe for one moment that the concerns you have about the conduct of the action are not concerns that I take seriously. I do take them very seriously. I do take very seriously the nature of the damage and the mystery that still does surround the issue of the keys. I take that very seriously and I will want to ensure that the findings of your Committee in that respect inform the future conduct of such actions. I am not, however, so naive and so unused as a criminal lawyer of many years' standing, a real hack in terms of the criminal courts—

Humphrey Malins MP

HM: Never a hack.

PB: --who, like Mr Malins, has heard many, many accounts of searches in similar circumstances, although not in my case of prisons but certainly other premises, to believe that in the course of those searches there is not sometimes done unwarranted damage and, indeed, remarks and graffiti of the sort you have heard described and, quite rightly, deprecated by the silver commander. I am not so naive as to believe those things do not happen and where they do, they are reprehensible and we need to make it absolutely clear to all concerned in such actions that it simply will not be tolerated. I do take that very seriously indeed.

HM: Minister, very briefly, like you I have been around a long time in the criminal justice system. This has been a very tough two or three years. Let me say, and I am sure I speak for all of us, I happen to regard you—I hope this does not sound odd—and Mr Narey as men of great ability, men of great integrity, great knowledge, sensitivity and enlightenment. That is me saying to you that I admire you both.

MN: Thank you very much.

HM: There has got to be a reason why people like Sir David Ramsbotham and me and others on this Committee feel very unhappy. There has got to be a reason for Sir David saying that the nature of the raid was a terrible, ghastly mistake.

PB: He did also make that remark with the caveat that there may well be information of which he was not aware. There is information of which he is not aware and he is not aware of that information for very good reason.

HM: You have got to understand that good, reasonable, sensible people, as you are, share a real concern about this. I am looking for some acknowledgement at some stage today that if you went through it all again, you might do it differently. That is all.

PB: First of all, if I can ask the Director General to deal with his part of it and then I will deal with mine.

MN: Mr Malins, if I have given the impression this afternoon that I do not regret any part of this, then that is quite untrue. There is a lot of learning in this for me. Although no member of the Board of Visitors was sent home, and no Governor has the power to do that, you can be quite sure that if anything like this was happening again, I would ensure that whoever was in charge would make it absolutely clear to the Board of Visitors how important it was for them to stay. I think much of the controversy over the conduct of this search would have been much clearer to us if they had stayed and been witness to it. I regret very much that they went and were not called back. I think they might have been called back. I also understand that difficult decisions were being made late in the night by people and I do, as I stress, trust Mr Podmore. There are a number of other learning points in this about the way we gather police intelligence. This is not just a matter of the extent to which it is shared with the Governor, and I will assist you about that later on, it is also a matter about collating police intelligence from different police forces and, indeed, from other agencies.

I have spoken to David Phillips from Kent Constabulary just this lunchtime and he and I, along with a police commander from the Metropolitan Police who is my police adviser, are going to be meeting shortly after this to try to get a better grip on this. To some extent, what was happening at Blantyre, as I will explain later, was complicated by the fact that different agencies had an interest in it simultaneously and there was not anybody holding the reins and seeing all that was going on at once. I will make sure that not just at Blantyre House but every other place we will do a much better job of that.

PB: I think my concern is very much along the lines of that of the Director General, save that I would add that I believe it was unfortunate that as to the extent of the matters, which will be disclosed to you in the private session, because these matters are of a very highly sensitive nature, that we were not in a position to have made them known to you earlier. Had that been done I think some of your concerns would have been allayed. Nevertheless, I think there is also a job of work to be done around ensuring that the Board of Visitors not only had the opportunity to be present throughout the whole incident, and I think it is very, very unfortunate that they were not and I am still not clear in my mind why they were not, and I do not lay the blame at their door for one moment. I also think that we do need to look very carefully at the issue of communication in this, communication between ourselves and the Prison Service and BOVs, communication between management and staff, and to recognise that perhaps when we look back at this incident communication has not been as good as it might have been. I think there are lessons to be learned from that.

David Winnick MP

DW: I think the Minister and Mr Narey , in the last few moments in reply to the question put by my colleague have made some progress. We have not had "it has all been right and necessary and that is the situation", I think we have moved the situation forward. My question to you, Minister, is will there now be an input from you and the Director of the Prison Service into the future of Blantyre House?

PB: The answer to that is unequivocally yes. I took the opportunity when I last appeared before the Committee to make it absolutely clear then that the future of Blantyre House was as a resettlement prison. I certainly believe that it is right in terms of policy for us to make sure that we learn what works and what has worked in Blantyre House, that we restore it, and across the Prison Service, we look at ways of ensuring that we spread the good practice and get that balance right in terms of security on the one hand and the proper element of trust on the other because there are lessons to be learned there too. I am quite sure we can get it right. I also think we need to look at the basis, and it touches on something Mr Podmore raised earlier on, upon which prisoners get into places like Blantyre House because I think the regime there is one which other prisoners could benefit from. I know the Director General has had concerns about the selection criteria because I think the public is well served if more prisoners, and appropriate prisoners, gain the benefit of what resettlement can offer.

DW: There is a tremendous amount of mending to be done. I hope that both of you will be doing your best to start that mending as quickly as possible.

PB: Mending and healing.

Martin Linton MP

ML: I do not think I want to disagree with you that public safety must be the first concern if you are going to put concerns into order of priority. It must be public safety not only during the sentence of prisoners but after their release as well. The fact that Blantyre House has achieved such a low reoffending rate is in itself an enormously important reassurance to the public, certainly in the area. I have never known an institution of that kind being so well regarded and welcomed in an area. I know the emphasis of penal policy under this Government has been what works but surely Blantyre works, that is the truth. I think everybody in this room hopes that it will continue to work. I think we are 99 per cent in the world of unintended consequences here. There is a very real danger that the unintended consequences taken in the name of security will, if not destroy, at least inhibit that very fragile plant of a public institution that really serves its purpose and has the confidence of the public. I very much hope that the actions that the Director General and you, Minister, will take will enable that plant to thrive again.

PB: I have been struck by the level of community support and I think we have to build on that. We also have to ask ourselves some questions as to how it is that it has been possible to grow that level of support in that community and we have not always been able to do so with such a great degree of success elsewhere.

Ian Cawsey MP

IC: I want to ask the Minister to play the evangelical role that he does so well in terms of how people feel at Blantyre House. I thought it was tremendously encouraging actually in some of the recent answers that Mr Narey spoke about morale being low and he acknowledged that. People will welcome that because it is the first stepping stone, is it not, to acknowledge. You spoke about your own visits where you said that trust was shattered and I think we were very struck by that yesterday. Before we went and visited the prison yesterday and met the prison staff, we started off with a session with the Governor and then Mr Murtagh and I asked, as I asked doggedly of everybody we spoke to, "How do you feel about staff morale and the way people feel about it?" The answer we got at that level, and these people were day-to-day management, was that we may find a small percentage who are resistant to change. You know from your own comments, and I know, that is not in the real world what is happening at Blantyre House. I am really looking for some reassurance that you will ensure that the message gets out and will be acted on accordingly.

PB: On all occasions, I visit prisons, and on both occasions at some length at Blantyre House, I have met with all levels of staff, not just POA, and with the BOV. I am under no illusions as to the journey we have got to travel. I have a very clear idea of what it is that we have to do. We are determined to do it and to learn the lessons and your inquiry will help us in that.

Chairman

LC: Thank you, Mr Boating. Mr Narey, I have got one final question before we move into the private session. There is a reference in the executive summary to the report on the investigation mounted at Blantyre House to a further investigation requested by the Deputy Director General which is the subject of a separate report. Can you tell us what that report is about?

MN: I believe you have a copy of that, Chairman. That was the report by someone entirely unconnected with Blantyre House or Kent prisons into the conduct of the search.

LC: A final question to you, Minister, if I may. We put the point to Sir David Ramsbotham this morning. In the aftermath of the search of the prison, did you consider asking Sir David, as he has the powers to request it, to carry out an independent investigation into the events of 5/6 May? The situation where we now are, and I think this is the fact of the matter, is that it is the Prison Service investigating itself.

PB: No, it did not occur to me.

LC: It has been done in the past.

PB: It did not occur to me to do that because I am aware of a number of tasks that we are working on with Sir David. It did not occur to me to ask him to carry out an investigation. I am also aware of the work that is being done generally on resettlement by Sir David and his team, ably assisted by Mr Podmore, who has had a long-standing record of commitment to resettlement. I am looking forward very much to the product of that work. No, it did not occur to me to ask Sir David to carry out—

David Winnick MP

DW: Will you consider it?

PB: I do not believe it would serve any useful purpose now because of your own investigation and that has been carried out. We will certainly be looking to the Inspectorate, the theme on resettlement having been completed, to return to Blantyre House in due course in order to assess progress.

Chairman: Thank you, Minister. We are now going to move into a private session and I am going to ask you to leave, please. Thank you very much for your attendance and for your patience.

Chapter 21

As we retraced our journey home we spoke about how we thought the day had gone. We all agreed that the HASC seemed to be supporting me and Blantyre but in the back of our minds was this sinister information which could only be shared in camera. Could this change everything? What could it be? I simply had no idea but it was eating away at me. I actually felt quite exhausted and emotionally drained, although relieved that the evidence giving had come to an end. It was just a matter of time now before the HASC would publish their report and I knew that my professional future would be determined by that outcome.

That night, the TV news channels covered the day's events and it felt a bit surreal to see and hear myself giving evidence. Narey was interviewed on the BBC news and challenged over some of the criticisms levelled at him by the HASC.

BBC Reporter: *"Thank you for talking to us. Surely this is very embarrassing, very costly and personally damaging for you to be described by a select committee chairman as totally unconvincing?"*

Narey tried to deflect this criticism and minimise its significance. He then went on to make an allegation, which was part of the disciplinary charge brought against me by Spurr in late September, that had not yet been considered and to which I had not had an opportunity to respond.

BBC Reporter: *"But it does look as if there is nothing seriously wrong at Blantyre. This was two cultures clashing in the Prison Service very embarrassingly and very expensively."*

Martin Narey: *"Well, well it depends, it depends, it depends whether you think that there is nothing wrong with a serving prisoner being given £2000 in cash from a Prison Service account. I think that is unacceptable to the public. It is certainly, certainly unacceptable to me."*

To me, this was another example of Narey lashing out when he felt under some pressure and having a total disregard for the rules of natural justice.

Over the next few days, I received a transcript of the evidence I gave and was asked to check it for accuracy. Everyone who gave evidence has the opportunity to do this. There were no errors in my transcript and I returned it quickly along with a short note enquiring about when the final report would be published. Andrew Kennon, the chief clerk to the HASC, came back to me quite quickly and said that Lord Corbett was looking at a late November date. Not such a long wait, I thought.

Although I had been doing some work with the Education Services based in Croydon I had been interviewed and selected to take up a post within the Adult Basic Skills Strategy Unit (ABSSU). This was a new unit set up in the Department for Education and Skills. Essentially, its role was to improve the levels of literacy and numeracy within the adult working population. However, it was decided that my appointment would not be confirmed until the HASC report had been published. If the report was critical of me then there would be no job. I continued with my life in limbo.

On 16 November, the HASC published their report. To my relief it was incredibly critical of the Prison Service and concluded that the committee were unconvinced that the raid was necessary based on the reasons given both in public and in private by the Prison Service. It also recommended that there should be a review of the Chaucer team and how its intelligence is gathered and assessed. It described the raid as, "a self-inflicted wound."

At one level it felt that I had been totally vindicated. However, I did not feel like celebrating. I was drained of feeling and emotion, exhausted by the process and battered by the system. If this was a victory, then it was a pyrrhic victory. I knew the story had not finished yet, and there would be repercussions for Tom Murtagh and no doubt for me. I was expecting to become involved as a witness in a disciplinary investigation into the very public allegations made by the BOV about Murtagh bullying me. I believed he would not survive such a process professionally and would retire from the service. How wrong I was about that. I still find it hard to understand how such high-profile allegations can be made in public and yet the service does not even deem it necessary to investigate them.

I started my new job at ABSSU and it was a totally alien environment to that which I had been used to. That's not to say that I did not enjoy the experience. The work was fascinating and I was lucky to have some very able and talented civil servants in my team. Although I liked my new job, I was still annoyed that the service had not initiated any investigation into the bullying allegations and so I decided to force the issue by lodging a formal complaint about being bullied by Tom Murtagh. Furthermore, I raised this complaint with the Permanent Secretary of the Home Office, then Sir David Omand, and requested that the investigation should be independent of the Prison Service as the HASC had already expressed concerns over this issue in their report.

A disciplinary investigation was commissioned but it would not be independent. It would be conducted by a prison board member, Clare Pelham, who was line-managed by Martin Narey. To counter the non-independence argument, a senior manager from the Home Office, Deborah Louden, was also a co-investigator. She was also a colleague of Martin Narey. As I feared the outcome was disgraceful and my view was that the whole investigation process was severely flawed.

The disciplinary charges against me and Margaret Andrews were due to be heard in January 2001 by Michael Spurr. These charges had been recommended by Adrian Smith following his investigation into the management of Blantyre House. They were serious charges but I could not find any evidence which supported them. I had co-operated with the investigation and told them the truth. Despite me knowing that Margaret and I were innocent I believed we would be found guilty and I had already mapped out my grounds of appeal.

The hearing date was set for 25 January and I was being supported by David Rodden from the PGA. The process for hearings is highly regulated. Everything is recorded and verbatim transcripts are produced. The case against me was presented by the Head of Finance and Internal Audit, then Joyce Drummond-Hill. She presented the evidence that supported the various charges I was facing and in turn, I and the hearing officer, Michael Spurr, could question it. I could also counter her evidence with my own and I could really interrogate the evidence she produced. Spurr could also question me if he felt that Drummond-Hill had not explored some element of the charge well enough.

Using a mix of facts taken from Smith's investigation report, the finance manual, several letters from recipients of some of the charity funds as well as newspaper coverage, I was able to clearly demonstrate that the charges against me were groundless. At times, the exchanges between myself and Drummond-Hill were tense and bad tempered but at the end of the day, I felt I had made my case well. Spurr adjourned to consider his verdict and I had an agonising wait until I was told that he was ready to reconvene. Usually, the process is that the hearing officer will simply say that having considered all the evidence, I find the case proved or not proved.

However, Spurr did not do this but instead gave a rather confusing monologue which totally baffled me. When he stopped I asked him:

"Have I been found guilty of this charge or have I been acquitted of it?"

His reply was vague, he said:

"Right, I think in terms of looking at what a disciplinary process is about it's about actually taking the issue as a whole, and I don't think guilt and innocence in this instance is, is appropriate. I am, my view is and it is an objective and an honest view that actually all of the procedures that should have been in place to protect you as governor and others at Blantyre House to ensure that funds, special funds were used properly, were not there as thoroughly as they should have been." He added, "The last point of me saying I think there is substance to the, to the issue about not supporting donations, but that does not merit in my view a disciplinary charge. I am not saying there is guilt, I am saying there are issues which should have been better handled and better managed, but it doesn't merit a disciplinary penalty."

My PGA rep whispered in my ear: "Well, that's a not guilty then," and then he said to Spurr:

"We would want to say, er, to those that enquire that Mr McLennan-Murray has not been found guilty of any charge which warrants a disciplinary award."

Spurr replied: "That would be a factual case."

A few days later I received his note which included the following bullet points:

- The level of documentation to support receipts/payments from special funds was not sufficient and adequate in all cases.

- The lack of documentation could have presented a risk of fraud, misappropriation or potential embarrassment to the Service.

However, having regard to the full circumstances surrounding the case, I concluded that the award of a disciplinary penalty was not appropriate on this occasion. This was because:-

- I was satisfied that work had been undertaken to address the action plan requirements following the previous internal audit, most of which had been rectified.

- Although documentation was not adequate in all cases within the accounts there was no evidence of impropriety or misuse of funds. Issues raised within the investigation report were addressed within the hearing and confirmation was provided from recipients to satisfy me that monies had been allocated appropriately within the scope of the funds.

- I was satisfied that there was no potential loss of £240 to the Prison Service as had been indicated in the investigation report.

- The payments of £2000 to Mr T Burns from the MENCAP fund were made specifically to provide a funfair at the 'Stir Crazy' MENCAP day in August 1999. This was within the

scope of the fund, although documentation to support the transaction was not sufficiently adequate.

A couple of weeks later, I bumped into Michael Spurr in the staff canteen at headquarters. He told me that he was quite disturbed about the hearing and he went to see Martin Narey to say that he felt every Governor in the Country would probably have similar lapses in their financial, paperwork. His point being that to charge me under the serious code of discipline for such minor matters was not appropriate.

I had thought that I would be found guilty as I had no faith in the Service. I had first-hand experience of their so called independent investigations and I doubted that anyone subordinate to Narey would have the balls to do what was right as opposed to what was wanted. Michael Spurr helped restore my faith, he maintained his integrity and I never would forget that when I had future dealings with him.

Chapter 22

I was relieved that my disciplinary charge had now been dealt with and I was exonerated. I felt as if a page had been turned. However, the disciplinary investigation into Tom Murtagh was about to begin and I had no idea what a drawn out saga it would become. I was summoned to appear before the investigation team so that I could present the evidence that supported the four allegations I had made. Three of these were allegations of bullying and one was about a failure by the Service of their duty of care to me.

On 9 February, Clare Pelham wrote to Gareth Hadley:

"As you know, I have not had any formal training in conducting investigations. I have discussed this briefly with John Marsh and he has agreed to arrange for training for myself, Deborah Loudon and Charlotte Miller (my staff officer, who will be assisting us with this investigation). We will not start the investigation until we have received this training, and John Marsh is kindly expediting this. You asked me to provide my report on the investigation by 28 February. I must say this will not be possible. We believe it would be more reasonable, particularly taking into account the need for us to receive training, for us to aim to provide the report to you by the end of March".

The investigators decided that the interviews would not be recorded, this was contrary to best practice as set out in the Prison Service policy and must bring into question the thoroughness of their training. I and my PGA rep were not happy about the interviews not being recorded. A junior governor grade had been co-opted onto the investigation team and one of her tasks was to take notes of the interviews.

My first interview was on 29 March 2001 and my second interview was on 4 May 2001. On 27 November 2001, I received a copy of the note taken at each interview, six and eight months respectively after the event. The notes of the interviews were inaccurate. On 13 December, I wrote back to say that there were eight substantive errors in the notes of the interviews with me. Of course, had the investigation team recorded the interviews then everything would have been voice recorded and there would be no inaccuracies.

Tom Murtagh had indicated he would be available for an interview in May. However, he kept declining interview dates that were offered and things got to such a point that the investigation team wrote a note to their file dated 13 September 2001:

"I would like to record for the file that in spite of repeated efforts in trying to confirm interview dates with Tom Murtagh since the beginning of May, and notwithstanding both his and Bob Mullins (his representative) absences on annual or sick leave, it has not been possible to confirm a date for the first interview until 23 October 2001. The second interview will follow on 8 November 2001".

I had indicated that I had seven witnesses who I believed should be interviewed. All of these witnesses were interviewed on 30 November. I wrote to Gareth Hadley on several occasions enquiring as to when the investigation into my complaints would be completed. I had a series of responses giving a variety of platitudes as to why there was further delay. Eventually, early in the New Year the investigation report was completed and I was given a copy.

Despite this being a disciplinary investigation, the purpose of which is to determine whether there is sufficient evidence to support formal charges being laid against Tom Murtagh, the investigation team took it upon themselves to find Murtagh guilty of just one allegation of bullying and not guilty of the other three charges. I was so angry that they had not followed due process and simply dismissed witness testimony and other evidence that I decided to apply to the High Court for a Judicial Review. There are three basic grounds on which the High Court will consider whether a JR is justified.

- Illegality
- Irrationality
- Procedural impropriety/unfairness

Illegality

A decision of a public body may be illegal if the decision maker:

- Acts outside or beyond its powers, also known as 'ultra vires'
- Misdirects itself in law - for example the decision maker does not understand and apply the law correctly
- Exercises a power wrongly or for an improper purpose – a decision must be reached on the basis of the facts of the matter in question

I thought it was arguable that the last bullet point was relevant in as much as the investigation team had exercised their power wrongly and not followed the correct procedures as per Prison Service policy.

Irrationality

A decision may be irrational if;

- It is so unreasonable that no reasonable decision maker could have come to the same decision, also known as 'Wednesbury unreasonableness' (although a less strict test applies if human rights are at stake)
- The decision-maker takes into account irrelevant matters or fails to consider relevant matters
- If the decision maker acts in bad faith or dishonestly

I believed that the first 2 bullet points here were applicable. The investigation team ignored hard evidence and then took account of information provided by Tom Murtagh which had never been presented to me for challenge.

Unfairness/Procedural impropriety

A decision may be unfair if the body:

- Does not properly observe and comply with its procedural duties– a decision maker must always act fairly

- Fails to consult or give reasons for its decision
- Shows bias

The first bullet point here is key. The investigation team did not observe and comply with its procedural duties. They failed to follow the Prison Service Order 1300 on the conduct of a disciplinary investigation. I instructed a solicitor who in turn instructed a QC.

Murtagh was due to retire in May 2002 and my secondment to the ABSSU was planned to end in March 2002. I had been in regular touch with Prison Service Personnel Director, Gareth Hadley about where I would work when I returned to operational duties. My wish was to take up an in-charge position within Kent since this is where I lived and where my children went to school. I did not want to uproot the family and relocate to another area in the Country. Even through the difficult times I had with Tom Murtagh, I still wanted to stay in Kent. My priority was to allow the children to finish their secondary education within the Kent schools. My career choices would reflect that and were more important to me than a difficult working relationship with Murtagh.

There were three in-charge positions coming up in Kent and I discussed these with Hadley. However, the Service had not forgotten the events of the last two years and were reluctant to give me anything that I wanted. I was clearly told that I would not be considered for any of the available in-charge posts in Kent. However, I was offered the in-charge position at HMP North Sea Camp, an open prison close to Boston, Lincolnshire.

Bearing in mind, that Hadley knew of my desire to stay in Kent for family reasons this offer was totally disingenuous. It would be too far to commute. If I accepted the post, I would have to live away from home. Also, I was aware that the author Jeffrey Archer, convicted of perjury and sentenced to four years, had been moved to North Sea Camp and the last thing I needed was to be running a prison with such a high profile prisoner in it. His notoriety and my recent history could be a magnet for potential media interest. I declined the posting and the only option left for me was to accept a deputy governor position in Kent.

Tom Murtagh was still the area manager for Kent and by accepting a posting to HMP Swaleside, I would be in post for just a few weeks before his retirement. The Governor of Swaleside was Mike Conway. He had been supportive of me during all the Blantyre drama and totally believed that the raid on Blantyre was unwarranted. On a personal level, I knew we would work well together and prior to me accepting the posting, we had a meeting at the Hilton Hotel in Maidstone. Swaleside had its problems, there were regular incidents of violence and a poor prisoner subculture existed which impeded good staff-prisoner relationships that are the bedrock on which safe prison regimes are built. Our meeting was constructive and it also confirmed to both of us that we would work well together. The following day, I confirmed with Hadley that I would accept a posting to Swaleside as deputy governor and ironically, my start date would be 1 April.

Tom Murtagh was winding down to retirement now and he was visiting each of the Kent prisons on a farewell tour. I agreed with Mike that I would be away from the prison on the day of his visit since I had no real desire to spend any time with him. However, fate was to bring us in close proximity to each other. Mike was away on annual leave and I was acting up as governor during the week that a retirement bash had been organised for Murtagh. Adrian Smith, who was Murtagh's successor, told me that I had to attend the event as all Kent governors were expected to attend. I left the celebrations as early as I could and did not speak with Murtagh. He formally retired from the service the following week.

The wheels of justice turn slowly and it took over two years and three separate High Court appearances before I got to the end of this judicial process. The High Court rejected my case and this was confirmed by the Appeal Court in May 2003. My solicitor issued the following Press Release dated 20 December 2002 after the initial Court judgement:

Mr McLennan-Murray's application for judicial review to quash the findings of a Prison Service investigation, into complaints he made in respect of the circumstances of his removal as governor from HMP Blantyre House came before the High Court, yesterday and today.

Mr Justice Stanley Burnton, giving judgement today stated that the contents of the investigation report "go beyond the unimpressive". He went on to say, "that the investigation in respect of the failure of the Prison Service to fulfil its duty of care to Mr McLennan-Murray appears at least as far as the contents of the report are concerned to be superficial".

He also described some of the findings of the investigation as being "irrational" and being "sympathetic" to Mr McLennan-Murray's cause.

However, he declined to exercise his discretion to grant permission, in essence, because a fresh investigation would be futile having regard to the passage of time and the fact that Mr Murtagh, the area manager subject of many of the complaints of Mr McLennan-Murray, has now retired from the Service.

Mr McLennan-Murray, although encouraged by some of the judge's remarks is very disappointed that the court will not go on to consider the merits of his complaints.

The Prison Service were not awarded any costs of the proceedings as "there were valid grounds of complaint to the investigation report."

This was a moral victory in as much as the Courts had agreed with my criticisms of the investigation into Tom Murtagh. But it was also another pyrrhic victory as, in financial terms, it cost me thousands of pounds. I was never after financial compensation, I simply wanted the Prison Service to follow its own policy and procedure with respect to a disciplinary investigation. If that had been done Tom Murtagh would indeed have faced a disciplinary hearing.

Chapter 23

My work at Swaleside as deputy governor was busy. Most of the day to day running of the prison was my responsibility and my style of management of getting out of the office and onto the landings where staff and prisoners interacted was something different to what had gone before.

I was on duty when we had our first area manager visit from Adrian Smith. I had already had some limited dealings with him but on this occasion it was to be a more in depth meeting.

During our meeting, he said that he would not hold Blantyre House against me, he would judge me on my performance at Swaleside. I simply could not contain myself. Here was the guy who had recommended that I should be charged under the serious code of discipline, something that could have had a dramatic effect on my career prospects. A charge to which, not only was I found not guilty of, but the hearing officer concluded that it was not even a disciplinary matter. Politely, but firmly, I reminded Smith of this fact and asked him where his integrity had gone since I had said nothing at my disciplinary hearing that I had not said to him and his Chaucer investigators in the hours of questioning I was subjected to. He maintained that it was his opinion at the time and he stood by it. Our meeting finished on that note and during the next several months, both of us tried to rebuild a cordial and professional relationship. It is odd that my future career prospects were in his hands but with all that had gone on he had to be careful how he handled me. In fairness to him, he played with a straight bat and I began to trust him again, albeit with some caution.

Mike and I were a good team at Swaleside and slowly but surely the levels of violence within the prison reduced and there was a better staff and prisoner culture. We did so well that the BOV at Swaleside even referred to Mike and I as 'the dream team'.

After a few months a governing governor post became available at Dover and I decided to apply for it. Dover would be accommodating foreign nationals who on completion of their sentence would be subject to deportation. I did not really want the position and a good colleague of mine was also applying for it. She actually lived in an old quarter close to the prison so domestically, it would suit her down to the ground. By contrast, it would be a ghastly daily journey for me from Tonbridge but I wanted to throw my hat in the ring just to demonstrate that I still wanted to govern again.

I was selected for an interview and it went very well. Although not selected, my interview feedback was very good and I was delighted that my colleague was appointed as the governor. Within a few more months, three further prisons came up for grabs: HMPs Coldingley, Highdown and Lewes. Candidates could not apply for a specific prison. If selected, they would be posted to one of the three prisons. I applied and was interviewed along with a number of other candidates. My preference was Highdown as this was the closest prison to Tonbridge. Sian West, another candidate who applied wanted Lewes.

Sian and I were successful but I was posted to Lewes and she to Highdown. Both were local prisons, that is they take prisoners directly from the courts they serve. I was never privy to the reasoning behind the posting decision but in the back of my mind, I wondered whether it was still payback. I was given a start date at Lewes of early November 2003 which suited me as I would have a chance to tie up all my loose ends of work and give a good handover to my successor. However, on the morning of 8 October, I woke up to the news on Radio 4 that there had been a serious disturbance at Lewes the previous evening. I turned to my wife and said

"Well, they will want me to go there now." Within half an hour of that I took a call from Adrian Smith, the area manager who told me that I had to start at the prison the following day. So much for my plans for an orderly exit from Swaleside.

Lewes was an old Victorian prison built by Napoleonic prisoners of war and completed in 1853. Like all other local prisons in the Country it was overcrowded and in need of serious renovation. It was also a Grade 2 listed building and mainly constructed of flint. My first job was to get the prison back to a normal routine following the disturbance and thereafter address some of the managerial issues which had adversely impacted the prison. By and large, the staff were good and loyal and the vast majority of prisoners were from the local Sussex area and thus were able to maintain good links with family and friends.

There was an incredibly top-heavy management structure which I dismantled and replaced with a more balanced team that facilitated appropriate delegation of work. I felt that good progress was being made and I was keen to introduce ROTL for certain prisoners. Until my arrival, there had been no ROTL at Lewes and thus its introduction had to be managed carefully. After a couple of years, I was informed that an in principle decision had been made to invest in the prison and renovate most of the existing buildings as well as constructing two new house blocks. This would raise the Certified Normal Accommodation (CNA) from 535 to over 800. The service was facing a rising prison population and thus required new accommodation. The scheme was costed at £38 million. As governor, I would play a pivotal role in the redevelopment of Lewes and although I had been in post for nearly three years, I wanted to remain at Lewes and see this project through.

My daughter and eldest son were both due to graduate from Portsmouth and Aberdeen Universities respectively in July and so my wife, Dorit and I had arranged to take leave so that we could attend the ceremonies. We flew up to Aberdeen to attend the Graduation and returned on an early morning flight so that we could get to work on Friday, 14 July. The following day we were heading up to Nottingham to visit my Brother-in law and celebrate his wife's 50th birthday.

On that Friday evening, I returned home from work and when Dorit arrived, she was complaining of an ache in her jaw. Earlier in the week, she had some aches in her joints which we put down to a cold and we thought the jaw ache was just another symptom of that. We decided to order a takeaway and Dorit would then have an early night. Throughout the evening, I checked on Dorit and got some pain relief for her. It was at 10.30 pm that I found her unconscious and almost lifeless. I tried to resuscitate her and when the paramedics arrived, they spent 45 minutes trying to do the same thing, but she had died in my arms.

I cannot describe how I felt. I was just in a total state of shock and disbelief. She was young, slim, fit and did not have any serious medical issues. I just felt that my life had come to an end, I could not imagine continuing without her. On the morning of Saturday 15 July, I was surrounded by family but still in a state of shock and disbelief. I could not eat and I could not tell friends and distant family of this tragic event. That difficult task fell to my daughter, Natalie. My son, Edward took a call from the prison. They urgently wanted to speak with me and refused to tell my son what it was about. Reluctantly he passed the phone to me and I was told that there was a passive demonstration on the exercise yard and the duty governor had opened the Command Suite and I was required to come in and run the incident. I could barely get the words out that my wife had just died and on hearing this, the caller said he was so sorry and would contact the area manager.

My area manager then was Colin McConnell and he and the Prison Service gave me all the time I needed to grieve and come to terms with the loss of my wife. It was not until late September that I made a phased return to work and was back on a full-time basis in October.

The passive demonstration by prisoners on 15 July was brought to a successful conclusion and the governor of HMP Ford, Fiona Radcliffe was brought in to command the incident.

Over the following three years, I was heavily involved in the design, refurbishment and construction of the existing prison and the two new residential wings. It was a fantastic experience and I was delighted with the outcome. Throwing myself into this work helped me rebuild my life that had been shattered when Dorit died. It helped to restore my self-confidence and with the support of my daughter, I realised that I just had to get on with life.

My staff and I achieved a lot at Lewes and I was proud of the progress we had made over the previous six years. In the summer of 2009, I was informed that Claudia Sturt would be the new area manager and even before she had taken up post, she decided to visit the prison. Unfortunately, I was on leave when she visited and thus did not meet her until she took up a post in July and visited the prison again.

Although I had heard of Claudia, I did not know her and so this was to be our first meeting. Following the customary walk round, we returned to my office and I was not surprised when she began to say that I had been at the prison for a long time and I half expected our conversation to end with a suggestion that I think about a new posting within the next month or so. However, I was amazed when she announced that she wanted me to undertake some project work at the area office in Woking and I should leave the prison later that month. The date she said I had to go by would only have given me 3 working days in the prison. Not surprisingly, I challenged her on the proposed speed of my departure and told her it was totally ridiculous. I even said that I thought it would constitute an unlawful order. There was a tense silence which I broke by asking who she intended to replace me with.

"Robin Eldridge," she replied.

I subsequently learnt that she and him were good friends.

After she left the prison, I contacted an employment lawyer and explained the situation to him. His advice was clear, if she tried to impose such a short notice move for me then it would be akin to constructive dismissal. A little later on, I received a call from Claudia's boss, Roger Hill. He said he wanted to see me the next day. I said I'd only be available during the lunch break as I was hearing a disciplinary charge on a member of staff. He agreed to see me during the lunch break.

When we met, he told me that the project work at area office was really important. "You are just the right person for this important job, you have all the skills we are looking for," he said.

I knew that I could not refuse the move as contractually I had no choice. However, I was not prepared to leave Lewes so soon and told Roger that the date Claudia had given me to leave was totally unreasonable. He just told me to sort it out with her. Later that day she contacted me and said she had reflected on our earlier conversation and agreed that I could stay longer at Lewes to wind up my affairs in an orderly way. I was content with that outcome and began to prepare for my move and handover to Robin.

As part of the handover, I was preparing a file on areas of work that were still ongoing. I thought it would be useful to see if Claudia had identified any issues on her recent visit which should be included in the handover notes. Accordingly, I contacted her and asked for a copy of the report which all area managers write following visits to their prisons.

"I did not write a report, I did scribble a few pencil notes so there is nothing to send you" she said.

This was very unusual and I did share it with my SMT. I suspect that this got back to some of the staff who worked at area office in Woking because two days later I received a copy of her report visit. Someone at the area had accessed the central filing system and retrieved a report which, according to Claudia, was never written.

I suppose it was possible that she changed her mind about writing a report so I thought I would check. I asked Stella, my P.A. to phone Claudia's and request a copy of the report. She spoke with the P.A. who, having just checked with Claudia, confirmed that there was no written report.

I asked Stella to make a note of this so that there would be a written record. I read the now found Claudia's report carefully and there was nothing in it of a critical nature and also nothing worthy of being included in the handover file for Robin.

I had no idea why Claudia would not have revealed that she had written a report. It was such a relatively trivial matter. She had taken a very unreasonable stance with me right from our first meeting and it was only when I came to write this book that I discovered Claudia had been tasked to contribute to a strategy that Martin Narey could use when he appeared before the HASC all those years earlier. I can only surmise that she had formed a view of me then which was evidently not favourable and allowed that to dictate how she was going to treat me, albeit some nine years later. Her final parting gift was to instruct me not to give the new governor a handover. I simply had no idea what was going through her mind but this was hardly going to pave the way for a constructive working relationship at Woking.

I left Lewes at the end of July and embarked on my project work at Woking which would take six months to complete. I and a small team of colleagues were tasked to develop a Reducing Reoffending Strategy for the South East Region. I did not have to work hard and six months was an over generous amount of time to undertake this project.

While working at Woking, I was approached by the General Secretary of the PGA, Paddy Scriven. She told me that the NEC had met recently to discuss succession planning for President of the PGA and there was unanimous agreement that it should be me. The current holder was due to stand down later in the year. I was incredibly flattered to be asked but felt that I had to decline due to my history with the Prison Service over Blantyre House. I felt this would be an obstacle to me being able to negotiate with senior officials as they could always accuse me of trying to settle old scores. Paddy seemed disappointed at my response but appeared to accept my reasoning.

Having finished my project, I was then tasked by Claudia to make an assessment of Portsmouth prison to determine whether it should be closed or re-rolled. In my eyes, this was a proper project, it would use my operational skill set and be an interesting piece of work. She told me that I could have two months to complete the work but I knew it would not take so long and suggested two weeks would be adequate. I enjoyed this project and produced a report which impressed Claudia. I concluded that Portsmouth prison should be re-rolled.

I had now been at Woking for over six months and was eager to return to operational work. I was due to meet with Claudia to discuss the next steps and was somewhat surprised when she told me that she wanted me to govern HMP Reading. This was one of the prisons in her area and if I accepted, then I would be working for her. I thanked her for the offer and said I would think about it overnight.

In truth, I had already made up my mind not to accept. I could not forget how unreasonable she had been towards me and I felt there was no trust between us. I very much wanted to govern a prison again but not if that meant being under her managerial control. The following day I told her that I had thought about it but for personal and domestic reasons, I could not accept her kind offer. She seemed surprised but accepted my decision.

I knew that my decision would not go down well with Roger Hill. He had obviously been consulted about the offer and sanctioned it. I knew I had to get out of Woking but there was no quick fix. Whether news of my situation had reached the ears of Paddy Scriven I don't know, but I received another call from her. She said she had discussed my reasons for declining to stand as President of the PGA with the NEC and collectively their view was that my past problems with the service would not be an obstacle. Again, Paddy urged me to accept the nomination to stand for President. I said I would think about it carefully and get back to her. The next day, with a little trepidation I contacted Paddy and said I would accept a nomination to stand for election as President of the PGA and was elected in the Spring of 2010.

Chapter 24

Michael Spurr was the head of the service by then and when I met with him as President of the PGA we agreed that I would undertake this role on a full time basis. Ken Clarke MP was the Secretary of State for Justice and Crispin Blunt MP was prison's minister.

One of my first challenges was to represent a governor grade colleague who had been charged under the code of discipline. It was a difficult case and evidentially I was convinced that there could be no finding of guilt. However, a guilty verdict was arrived at and even upheld on appeal. This case gave me a good insight into how there could be collusion between senior managers and how the disciplinary system could be used to settle old scores. It certainly was not justice and unfortunately, throughout my tenure as President, I saw other examples. On a number of occasions I was able to ensure that justice was done but I'd learned the hard way that speaking truth to power does not make you very popular.

My dealings with the Prison's Minister were constructive and we both agreed that the Indeterminate Sentence for Public Protection (ISPP) was a disaster. At my first PGA annual conference, I moved a motion urging the government to scrap this appalling sentence which I described as a "stain on our criminal justice system". It was heavily supported by governor colleagues.

I was really pleased when Ken Clarke and Crispin Blunt announced that the ISPP would be abolished but disappointed that they did not make it retrospective. There were thousands of prisoners still serving an ISPP when it was abolished in 2012. Even today there are hundreds still in custody who have served more than their tariff, which was the length of sentence deemed necessary to punish their offence.

Another policy area that I and the PGA campaigned on was the so called, 'War on Drugs'.

The conference overwhelmingly voted for a root and branch review of the existing policy and strongly advocated that there should be decriminalisation and that organised crime should be excluded from the production, distribution and sale of drugs. Currently this multi-billion pound industry is totally unregulated and run entirely by criminals who use violence and coercion as the only regulatory means of control. Surely we should have learnt our lesson about prohibition not working from the American experience with alcohol and it was from this that organised crime originated. Sadly, little progress has been made on this important policy issue and drugs continue to disrupt prison regimes and drive extreme violence both in prison and in the community, where rival gangs often use knives to control their criminal trade.

Some months after my election to President of the PGA I received an invite from the secretary to the All Party Parliamentary Penal Affairs Group (APPPAG). I was pleasantly surprised to see that Lord Corbett was chairman of this Group and so I had no hesitation in accepting the invitation to speak about 'PERSPECTIVES ON BREAKING THE CYCLE'. Lord Corbett welcomed me in his typically comical manner, noted by the verbatim stenographer:

Lord Corbett welcomed everyone to the meeting, especially the three speakers. He noted that the last time he had met Eoin McLennan Murray, President of the Prison Governors Association (PGA), he had just been fired as Governor of Blantyre House, as a result of a 'coup' by the Regional Manager. This had led to an Inquiry by the Home Affairs Select Committee, of which Lord Corbett was then Chair.

The talk went well and after the session, Lord Corbett invited me to have a drink with him in one of the many bars within the House of Lords. As we chatted, I said to him: "It's been more than 10 years now since the raid on Blantyre and I was wondering whether you could share with me what the damning intelligence Narey and co gave you in your closed session".

He gave me a broad smile and said. "Well, they all trooped in and gave us this intelligence report and then they all trooped out. I turned to my colleagues and said, well I don't know about you but I think that is a load of old bollocks."

"Yes" I said. "But what was it they said?"

"Oh, something about the prisoners buying you a Microlight aircraft in exchange for you turning a blind eye to their criminal activities".

I sipped on my drink while processing this piece of information. When intelligence is received by HMPS it is always assessed in terms of who the source was and their reliability and the significance of the intel. A scoring system is used and if the intel is from a very reliable source and is very significant then it would be graded as A1. The Prison Service must have assessed this intel and graded it highly as they made so much about it when they gave their evidence to the HASC.

To recap:

Gerald Howarth MP

"Minister, we are looking forward to the compelling evidence which we are disappointed has to be heard in private".

Paul Boateng: "When you hear the nature of it, Mr. Howarth, knowing your concerns, as I do, you will well understand".

What I could not understand is that owning an aircraft is like owning a car. It has to be registered. Cars are registered with the DVLA and aircraft are registered with the Civil Aviation Authority (CAA). Anyone can go on to the CAA website and find out who owns what aircraft and when it was purchased and sold. If this simple check had been made it would have revealed that I purchased the aircraft three years before I became Governor of Blantyre House. It is inconceivable that the Prison Service and or police did not perform this simple task in order to assess the reliability of the intel.

So, either the Prison Service/police are totally incompetent when it comes to assessing intel, which I know is not the case, or they knowingly misled the HASC with intel that they knew to be totally untrue.

We finished our drinks and said our farewells but on the way home I had to pinch myself to make sure I was awake and that this had not been some bizarre dream. Historically, the POA had always been antagonistic towards the PGA. The origins of this antagonism stemmed from when the PGA was formed. Prison governors, being civil servants, were able to join the main civil service union but there was a general view that we were not being properly represented. So, in 1987, a group of senior governors decided that they would set up a new union exclusively for prison governors. The main civil service union opposed us breaking away and, with the assistance of the POA blocked our application to be affiliated to the TUC. This did not prevent the PGA from being recognised as an independent trade union. However, ever since then, the POA would not attend official meetings if the PGA were on the invite list.

Colin Moses was then the long standing chairman of the POA but a surprise election result saw him replaced by a very different individual, PJ Mcparlin. In comparison to Colin Moses, PJ Mcparlin had a reputation of being moderate and I thought it would be a good opportunity to make contact with him to see if there was scope for our respective unions to work together. Luckily, one of my colleagues on the PGA committee knew PJ and agreed to ask him if he would take a call from me. PJ was agreeable and we arranged a secret meeting between him and his general secretary, Steve Gillan, and me with my general secretary, Paddy Scriven. The meeting was very cordial and we agreed to share information and where possible act in tandem. We also agreed that our meetings would have to be secret for the time being as there would be many within our respective unions who would be unhappy about our arrangement of mutual cooperation.

After several weeks we decided it was right to be open about our meetings and PJ and I were invited to make a joint presentation to the APPPAG. Our presentation was well received and it was certainly a public display of our closer working relationship.

Ken Clarke and Crispin Blunt were replaced by Chris Grayling MP and Jeremy Wright MP. This marked a dramatic change in the Prison Service and with the policies of austerity, life in prison became very problematic.

Staggering cuts in prison budgets ensued which resulted in the loss of 7000 prison staff, many of whom were very experienced. Alongside this was a freeze on recruitment and over the next two years I witnessed irreparable damage being done to the service as prison regimes crumbled, drug related violence soared and staff morale slumped. At the Conference, I spoke about "a perfect storm" and predicted that worse was to come unless the recruitment ban was lifted. It would be more than a year after these warnings that the service and ministers decided to take action.

However, it was too little too late and many prisons still remain in a precarious state today. The progress made following the Woolf Report of 1991 had been squandered by policies that Chris Grayling introduced while he was the Secretary of State for Justice, and at best, it will take a generation to undo the damage he inflicted on the prison and probation service.

Following a legal battle, the PCS union won a case against the government and in retaliation the then Minister for the Cabinet Office, Francis Maude insisted that facility time for trade union officials should be reduced. Facility time allows trade unions to have a certain number of full-time officials who are paid from the public purse and undertake trade union activities. Big unions such as the PCS or POA, who have thousands of members can afford to fund their own officials. Small unions like the PGA cannot and Maude's actions threatened to destroy them.

Fortunately, I was able to speak with the then prisons minister, Jeremy Wright and he understood my concern and suggested I put forward a proposal to the Prison Service. He indicated that he would look at any reasonable proposal sympathetically.

A further restriction imposed by Maude was that there could be no full-time officials funded by the public purse, only part time officials. This meant that a facility time post holder would be able to spend 50% of their time on trade union activity and 50% on their departmental job.

Since I was full time it would mean that I would have to take a 50% part time job at HQ. As part of my negotiation with the service, I said I would return to a prison as governor and take no facility time. The facility time given to the PGA was 3 X 50% posts, i.e. 3 people working on trade union activity for 50% while working the other 50% in prison.

In the Spring of 2013, I took up my new post as Governor of HMP Coldingley while still being the President of the PGA. This meant that I had to undertake some of my trade union activities within my own time and most weekends were spent dealing with various aspects of trade union work. I was fortunate to have an excellent deputy governor, Jo Sims and she provided cover for me whenever I had to attend meetings or deal with the media.

While I was at Coldingley, the service probably reached its lowest point. Most prisons were struggling to run a normal regime and there were acute staff shortages in virtually every prison in the South East of England. There were other parts of the Country too that were badly affected and this resulted in tens of thousands of prisoners being locked up for many hours during the working day. Prison regimes across the Country had been decimated, assaults on staff reached record highs, self-inflicted deaths had increased and organised crime syndicates were flooding prisons with drugs, especially a synthetic cannabinoid drug generically termed as New Psychoactive Substances (NPS) but better known to the general public as 'legal highs' or 'Spice'. Prisons were in crisis although Chris Grayling denied this.

I have to pay tribute to all staff who were working in prisons during this time and it is a miracle that there were no major incidents which resulted in the loss of entire prisons. I decided to speak very honestly and freely to the media about the state of our prisons. I did this because I represented the governors who were struggling to manage their prisons and they provided me with the information. They wanted the truth to come out and were frustrated with the political rhetoric that attempted to underplay the crisis that was unfolding. On a number of occasions, I was warned by senior officials not to say so much because it was not in line with the Ministerial view. I was clear where my loyalty lay, it was to represent my members and ensure that the public understood the daily challenges they faced.

The role of President is time bound to three years and I had been re-elected in 2011 for a further three-year term which would expire in 2014. I decided that I would not seek re-election as I wanted to retire in November 2015. After 37 years of public service I formally retired on 30 November 2015 and moved to Spain on 1 December. I walked away from the service I served loyally for nearly four decades with my head held high, knowing I did my best to promote rehabilitative initiatives which in the main changed the lives of prisoners for the better and consequently made our society safer. I have no regrets.

Blantyre House

Scene of one of the greatest outrages in modern Prison Service history.

www.ingramcontent.com/pod-product-compliance
Lightning Source LLC
Chambersburg PA
CBHW041304240426
43661CB00011B/1015